THIRSTY

THIRSTY

Confessions
of a Fame Whore

JOEL CREASEY

WITH JANELLE KOENIG

**SIMON &
SCHUSTER**

London · New York · Sydney · Toronto · New Delhi

A CBS COMPANY

THIRSTY: CONFESSIONS OF A FAME WHORE
First published in Australia in 2017 by
Simon & Schuster (Australia) Pty Limited
Suite 19A, Level 1, Building C, 450 Miller Street, Cammeray, NSW 2062

10 9 8 7 6 5 4 3 2 1

A CBS Company
Sydney New York London Toronto New Delhi
Visit our website at www.simonandschuster.com.au

National Library of Australia Cataloguing-in-Publication entry
Creator: Creasy, Joel, author.
Title: Thirsty: Confessions of a fame whore/Joel Creasy
ISBN: 9781925310771 (paperback)
          9781925310788 (ebook)
Subjects: Creasey, Joel.
          Comedians—Australia—Biography.
          Entertainers—Australia—Anecdotes.

Cover design: Christabella Designs
Cover photograph: Mark Lobo Photography
Typeset by Midland Typesetters, Australia
Printed and bound in Australia by Griffin Press

FSC
www.fsc.org
MIX
Paper from
responsible sources
FSC® C009448

The paper this book is printed on is certified
against the Forest Stewardship Council®
Standards. Griffin Press holds FSC chain
of custody certification SGS-COC-005088.
FSC promotes environmentally responsible,
socially beneficial and economically viable
management of the world's forests.

For Joan Rivers,
the greatest of all time

THIRSTY

CONTENTS

FOREWORD

BY CHRISSIE SWAN

Let me tell you about my friend, international restaurant guide and muse, Joel Creasey. Around 2012 I'd started to hear whispers of this new 'It' boy. Just like frozen yoghurt bars, suddenly he seemed to be everywhere all at once. In fact, the first time I uttered his name he was the punchline in an ongoing joke I had with my colleagues at the radio station I was working at.

Radio jobs are notoriously impermanent. And by that I mean you can get the arse with no warning, no reason and no chance to ask why. What a way to keep you on your toes! Around the time Joel was starting to make his mark and being Mr Everywhere, I'd done three years straight on a breakfast show, which in radio meant I was up for long service leave. Me and my on-air partner knew our time was almost up whenever we made a mistake, missed the mark or spoke over each other. We'd laugh and say, 'Look out, it'll be the Joel Creasey and Ricki-Lee Coulter show starting tomorrow, I'll just clear out my things.' Little did I know that Joel had grander plans . . . you know . . . like world domination. Or at least his own fragrance.

The first time I met Joel was a few years later at a studio in Port Melbourne where we were filming a TV gameshow pilot that never saw the light of day. On a producer's request for a segment, he was dressed as Cindy Brady and he was, of course, magnificent. He was obviously a very young person, but what struck me first about him was that he possessed the maturity, work ethic and comic timing of someone much, much older – but with the skin and glow of someone who had recently signed a skin care endorsement deal. I instantly adored him. Pretty soon after that we were thrown into the jungle together for the inaugural season of *I'm a Celebrity, Get me Out of Here!*, which he writes about in this book. Ironically, with another Brady sister – Marcia. I can't read that particular chapter myself because I'm still in shock from the whole experience and I don't want to trigger memories of face-crawling Wolf spiders and weeks of my hair smelling like decomposing offal. What I'm happy to remember, though, is that without Joel in there with me I would have gone totally mad.

The first day was possibly the most brutal. We'd been flown into the jungle in chopper formation, thrown into an African river teeming with crocodiles and hiked sockless up a vertiginous mountain. At one stage I tripped and slid down a muddy rock face on my boobs while Joel clutched his stomach in hysterics, which depleted any remaining energy we had left. By the time we'd reached the perimeter of the camp, we'd been on the go for more than twelve hours and we were exhausted, mainly because we are both the sort of people who get upset if we have to get out of the car at the drive-through when there's a problem with our lattes.

Even so, on the edge of death and with bleeding feet and armpits reeking of souvlaki, we managed to make each other laugh with over the top impersonations of how we imagined Rhonda Burchmore might react to a Tucker Trial. Or which Real Housewife we'd most like to see parachuted into camp.

I didn't love much about my time on that show, but the fact that Joel and I became soulmates means I would do it all again tomorrow. He knows how much it means for me to say that!

Sometimes I feel as if I'm Joel's secret bit on the side. He leads an outrageously busy and glamorous life. If you imagine that he lives in a neat, inner-city high-rise apartment with a life-sized cut-out of himself and little more than a bottle of Bollinger and one solitary gyoza in the fridge, you'd be right. If you imagine that he parks his designer suitcase by the door and has to consult his iPhone to see not only if he is available on any given day, but if he'll even be in the country, you'd also be right. He has a luxury car that he freely admits he can't really drive, he slays red carpets like Valyrian steel, is never too busy to take a selfie with a fan (he has to hold the camera and choose the filter, though) and he has a rather embarrassing allergy to mangoes.

But there is whole other side to Joel that I like to think is just for me. He is the friend who lets my kids empty an entire sticker book onto his face. He is the guy who drops over when he's in my neighbourhood, toting a strong flat white without me even asking. He is the mother I never had, the sister everybody would want. He is the friend that everybody deserves. I don't know a better person.

Okay, okay, full disclosure – that last bit was Oprah talking about her best friend Gayle, but the bit about the stickers and coffee was all me and you knew what I meant.

I'm sure Joel won't mind me telling you that he is incredibly intelligent. In fact, he kind of told me to tell you that. But the truth is, he really is. You don't get to where he is today on the world stage, while barely out of the womb, by being a vapid bystander. He's a switched on human being, and he is also a wonderful friend and an exceptional son. He could probably be a better brother if he tried a bit harder, but we all have our works in progress. And now he is a writer. There aren't too many people Joel's age who could fill a book, but he has. And what's more, just like last night's Mystery Box challenge on *Masterchef*, this one is interesting, juicy and at times raw. Enjoy the world according to Joel. I know I certainly have.

Chrissie Swan

1

BJC (BEFORE JOEL CREASEY)

U m, hi!

So you're reading my memoir ... That's pretty terrifying, right? For me, I mean. Not for you, I hope.

But first, let's clear this up right away – you might think it's weird for a 27-year-old to write a memoir. 'A memoir? At your age? Really?' you might be asking.

But yes, that's right. I have written a memoir. I'm basically Michelle Obama.

'What could you possibly have to tell me after 27 years on this earth?' I hear you ask. Well, I do have some pretty good stories to tell, you know. I've performed stand-up on Broadway, eaten elephant shit in Africa, hosted a TV show in Ukraine and hit on Neil Patrick Harris in Montreal. Yep, you read that here first. I've also made frequent love, fallen in love, had that same heart broken ... and also been covered head-to-toe in cow semen in a rural town in Australia. I bet you've never read those four things in a sentence before. Or maybe you have. What you get up to in your private time is completely up to you. No judgement here.

Look, I guess it's already pretty clear what kind of book you're going to read. There's lots of swearing, sex stories, celebrity scandal and far too frequent mentions of me drinking myself to oblivion (I'm guessing Michelle Obama's book doesn't open like this). So if that's not for you, maybe it's best you put this down . . . but for everyone else, pour yourself a wine, kick back and strap on . . . I mean . . . in!

My parents, Terry and Jenny Creasey, are pretty fucking amazing. Inheritance = confirmed! My mum, Jennifer, is the daughter of Elsie and Jim Beamish and was born and grew up in Gloucester, England. Gloucester is kind of like the Adelaide of the United Kingdom: a little rough around the edges, famous for churches and murderers, but every now and then a Sia will come from there. In this analogy my mum is Sia. Except I know what her face looks like.

Mum grew up just down the road from Gloucester Cathedral, which was used for part of the Hogwarts exterior shots in the Harry Potter movies. And as for the 'murderer' part? *Well!* Jenny was living in Gloucester while Fred and Rose West were busy murdering people in their house only a few blocks from her family home. Fred and Rose West were a sexually deranged couple who would lure young female victims to their home and perform monstrous acts on them, then kill them before burying them in the backyard.

At fourteen – a common age for the Wests' victims – my mum would jog past the house every day. Lucky she was a fast runner and never piqued the interest of the Wests. Fred West did once try to lure my Aunt Sally into a van. Terrifying. Also, not sure why I've brought this up. Especially not in the first few pages of my book. What a ride it's gonna be, eh?

Times were tough on my mother's side of the family. Mum's father – my grandfather – was orphaned at thirteen when he lost both his parents to tuberculosis. Both my maternal grandparents were working by the time they were fourteen. My grandmother Elsie started work in an American uniform factory. How very Fantine in *Les Misérables*, except for the eventual prostitution, of course (Fantine's, not Elsie's, although there's not much Elsie wouldn't do for a cream bun and a cup of tea by all reports). In this metaphor I'm obviously Cosette. And yes, the tigers do come at night, thankyouverymuch.

My grandfather Jimbo contracted tuberculosis when he was twenty-six, resulting in a year in a sanitarium. (This is an old-fashioned word for a medical facility for those with a long-term illness. Which makes me wonder why people named their cracker and cereal product company after one. Long-term illness? Mmm, that makes me feel peckish!) Once a week, in any weather, my grandmother would cycle to visit him, a two-hour journey. My grandfather was also the local driving instructor (though he clearly never taught his wife – why the fuck was she on the pushie?), which is why my mum claims to be such a good driver. She is usually saying this on the phone as she speeds through a red light applying lippy, by the way. I, on the other hand, am a terrible driver. I don't really understand what any of the knobs in my car mean, don't know how to put air in a tyre and refuse to reverse park. One of my earliest pieces of stand-up was about my seriously questionable road skills and how I like to take street signs more as just a friendly suggestion than a rule. Give way? Nah, I'm very busy. But I might give way twice next time.

Jenny was a champion athlete – running, long jump and hurdles – and represented her school at the All England Athletics Championships. Even writing this is putting me to shame – I was kicked off my Grade 3 egg-and-spoon race team. Neither me nor my sisters picked up our mother's abilities in the track and field department. Although cross either of my sisters on a netball court and they will cut a bitch. (Side note – netball . . . what a silly sport. I've got the fucking ball, just let me run with it.)

Mum also has an amazing soprano singing voice and performed in many of the Gloucester Operatic & Dramatic Society shows. After school, she attended the Rose Bruford College of Speech & Drama in Sidcup, Kent, for three years. And yes, saying the word Kent out loud is a great way to practise your New Zealand accent.

After studying and performing in various shows, my mother joined CTC Cruises, a Russian cruise line, performing on board the MS *Shota Rustaveli* as a singer and ballroom dance instructor. She did two world cruises, and even visited Scandinavia and Russia. I used to love hearing stories of my mother's time working on the ship – cruise ship life seemed like such a far-off, glamorous world. And her stories gave me an early thirst for the showbiz life. Essentially, Mum was Judy Garland to my Liza.

Terry Creasey was a little less academic than Jenny. Naturally blessed with good looks and a shock of blond hair, Dad was more interested in surfing, ladies and getting into trouble. Although also born in England, he had moved to Merrylands in Sydney when he was four. Not on his own, obviously, that would be grossly irresponsible. My paternal grandfather was in the merchant navy and after falling in love with the Blue Mountains, he decided to relocate to Australia. Dad was an only child so, with my grandfather Ernie and grandmother Muriel, he jumped on a ship and headed to Sydney.

Once again, in complete contrast to me, my father was a sports fanatic and played A-grade rugby league all through his high school years. After a broken jaw and fractured cheekbone, Dad decided to give up football, as his looks were far too precious (in this respect I am most certainly my father's son). Dad had started modelling from an early age and couldn't insure his body JLo style, so the football had to go.

My parents met on the cruise ship. Mum was working on board when Dad and a mate were on what I can only imagine was a 'lads' trip' (*shudder*). Dad always tells the story that he walked into the ship's theatre while my mum was on stage singing 'Don't Cry For Me Argentina' as they crossed the Argentinian border. That was simultaneously the moment he first laid eyes on her and the moment he fell in love.

In contrast, my ex and I met at the Mardi Gras after-party at 3 am. I'd drunk my body weight in vodka and we shared our first kiss as Samantha Jade sang 'Firestarter' and a drag queen overdosed on ketamine beside us. I drunkenly bring this story up with Samantha Jade every time I see her and I think she's getting a little bit over it, to be honest.

Mum and Dad had a torrid affair aboard the ship. Mum was seeing another man at the time, who proposed to her when she returned to England. She said yes and then immediately called it off the same weekend. *Scandal*! Plus I think having relations with a passenger was against the rules. What a rebel.

Given they were both pursuing jobs in the arts, it was an easy decision for Dad to move back to the United Kingdom. They eventually moved in together in a tiny flat in London, living for a time above IRA members involved in the Canvey Island bombings. Mum likes to tell the story about how small the flat was: 'I could stir a pot on the stove while leaning against the wall behind me.' I also get my pot-stirring skills from my mother, socially and gastronomically. She normally reminds me of this when I complain about my spare bathroom taps leaking or something very #firstworldproblem. Note to self: Put advertisement on Airtasker tomorrow for someone to fix said taps.

Mum and Dad went after many jobs. Mum appeared in several West End shows, including understudying Fiona Fullerton in *Barnardo*. She also had a starring role as the receptionist in the film *Silver Dream Racer*. Terry continued modelling as well as being the long-shot Flash Gordon in the sci-fi hit *Flash Gordon*. If you ever watch that film, if it's not a close-up – that's my dad! Oh, and be warned: if Terry ever invites you back to our place for drinks, you'll be forced to sit through it. Jesus, the more I write, the more I realise I am my father.

Although not their most prestigious or most artistic, arguably my parents' most famous work (apart from the night they had sex to make me) was as extras in *The Empire Strikes Back*. They were members of the Rebel Alliance working to fight the Emperor on Echo Base on the planet Hoth. That's the one with all the snow – think Thredbo but with more Wookiees and less Gucci. My mum only flashes by in the background of one scene but my dad is quite clearly featured in the historic scene where Princess Leia briefs the snow-speeder pilots, ultimately sending them to their death. Dad is the guy rocking the orange speeder suit and matching orange moustache. So I guess when I say they were rebels for hooking up on the cruise ship, well, they really were.

I was naturally a massive Star Wars fan growing up and used to think it was the coolest thing ever that my parents – *my parents* – were in Star Wars. I used to love Dad recounting the story of his snowspeeder to me. Apparently they had to stop filming several times as its roof kept malfunctioning and hitting him on the head. Eventually George Lucas himself came over to apologise. I still often suggest he should sue George Lucas for delayed-onset brain damage – we'd be minted!

I think if I were to exist in the world of Star Wars, I'd probably be a commander on a Star Destroyer – ie, a bad guy. I just can't go past their shiny polished ship floors, our shared love of the colour (sorry, *shade*) grey and their immaculately tailored uniforms. The Rebels were always messy, lacked organisation . . . and I just don't think I'd look good in an X-wing. Plus those Star Destroyers were just heaving with male crew. Imagine the staff bar. Heaven!

In 1981, Mum and Dad made the move back to Australia but after two years, Mum's visa expired and she returned to England. There was a tense period of limbo when they were separated – until my mum called and proposed to my dad. Such a modern woman! And it wasn't even a leap year! Terry claims he was going to call her and propose the following day but she beat him to it. Lucky, otherwise I would've been born a Brit. Anyway, in 1983 Terence Creasey and Jennifer Beamish got married in Gloucester before moving back to Australia.

Dad continued working in the media a little in Australia. He was also notably the Solo Man in the famed seventies and eighties television commercials. That was a big deal, as he was the soft-drink answer to the Nutri-Grain Ironman – or the *Cleo* Bachelor of the Year. The ad he appeared in is quite homoerotic. It involves my dad and several other ripped men performing different 'manly' tasks: battling river rapids in a canoe; rock climbing; running up the side of a mountain. My dad was the mountain runner in the 1983 ad (you can find it on YouTube, just ask Terry). He races up the mountain in short shorts and a yellow singlet with a blue heeler in tow. I mean the dog breed blue heeler – I don't mean, like, Lisa McCune. It'd be weird if she were chasing him up the mountain. When Dad and the dog get to the top of the mountain, Dad cracks open a Solo to quench his thirst. Because that's exactly what I feel like drinking when I'm dehydrated: lemon-flavoured sugar syrup.

Anyway, the ad was quite a hit and whenever it comes up in conversation, Dad pretends to be embarrassed for all of three seconds and then delights in the recognition.

But the one thing I've always known about my parents, the thing I've never questioned, is how in love they are. Whatever my family has been through, Mum and Dad's love has never wavered. And I truly do hope to be just like them one day. Anyone who knows them will tell you they are kind, inspiring and loving people who only want the best for anyone around them. They truly are good guys, just like the Rebels they played in Star Wars. How they managed to give birth to me, I have no idea. I've got more of an Anakin Skywalker vibe going on.

My older sister Holly was born in 1986. She was obviously a practice baby. When Jenny gave birth to a little girl who looked like someone who might grow up to be a successful, gorgeous, independent marketing executive, Mum and Dad must've said, 'Damn! We were hoping for a campy, nasal-voiced comedian,' and tried again.

I was born in Baulkham Hills on the 11th of August, 1990. Mum was out at a dinner party celebrating my grandma's birthday. Muriel decided that I simply must share her day of birth so I arrived at 11.55 pm, fashionably late for the party, of course. Nan and I have celebrated our birthday every year together and I've loved that we get to share the day each year. It normally involves us getting drunk at a restaurant, much to the horror of the other paying customers.

Apparently I was a great baby – loved sleeping and eating and looked super cute rocking a powder blue jumpsuit. 'Not much has changed,' you might say . . . Oh, stop it, you!

My feisty younger sister Alice arrived four years later and rounded out the Creasey clan – five blondes living in a brick two-storey house in a cul-de-sac. My parents built the house and, from memory, it was pretty fancy for the early 90s. But I think it may have been a case of the fanciest house on the worst street. Which is probably a pretty good metaphor for my career.

I don't remember a lot about Sydney because we moved to Perth when I was five. Plus I was drinking and drugging pretty heavily in those first few years (mostly formula and Nurofen for Kids) so it was mostly a blur. I do remember having a best friend called Jamie, a yellow-walled bedroom (and unless you're Michelle Williams' dress at the 2006 Oscars, yellow is *never* necessary) and one birthday, Mum made me the train cake from the *Women's Weekly Children's Birthday Cake Book*, AKA the most difficult birthday cake of all!

I don't think I particularly cared about moving to Perth. I probably subconsciously knew Sydney was the boss level for showbiz and I needed to hone my skills in a quieter part of the world. Off-Broadway, you might say.

Terry was working for the Swan Brewery and he'd been promoted to sales director over in Western Australia. I'm not sure what that kind of important role in a brewing company entails ... 'Man in charge of getting others drunk'? If so, I've had that role on every date I've ever been on. I'm not sure if my dad ever finished a day stumbling down Swanston Street yelling, 'Why won't you love meeeee?' after a potential client, though. Which I have done, by the way: I was leaving a party after ingesting a few too many Negronis and asked a complete stranger that exact same question. I also once told a guy on a first date, 'I feel like I've known you forever.' *Cringe.*

So in 1995 our little blonde posse swanned our way to Perth. Gonna have to be honest, not a *lot* happening in 1995 Perth. Thank God I was five and hadn't quite yet acquired a fake ID. I imagine the nightlife of Perth at the time wasn't 'hopping' as the kids (never) say. But I've no doubt some of the crusty old gays who've grabbed my arse over the years at Connections Nightclub (Perth's gay club and a favourite spot of mine) would've been there even back then: in their same seats, sipping on a whiskey soda and fiercely discussing whether Kylie has or hasn't had work. (I don't think she has, by the way.)

I actually had a Kylie moment a few years back. I was sitting in an airport lounge in Hong Kong Airport late one night awaiting a connection to London (other than the Spice Girls). The airport was dead quiet and the only other person in the lounge was the one and only Ms Minogue. Travelling solo, might I add – no bodyguards. Very brave. She was very lucky (lucky, lucky, lucky) I didn't lunge for her. I have a few friends who would've crash-tackled her to the floor as she had a second helping of brie. (Hi Kylie, if you ever read this, yes, I saw you go up to that buffet table several times and, look, no judgement here. All power to you, sister. I was going to go for my third pass but was trying to impress you.) We were in the lounge for a couple of hours together. We never spoke but exchanged knowing 'Oh, you're an Australian entertainer too' nods. I try to play it cool around other celebrities, I want to act like we're 'industry peers'. Yes, I did just call Kylie Minogue my peer.

Ever since the Creaseys moved to Perth we have always lived in Applecross, a beautiful suburb just south of the river. I've always loved Applecross. It's quite an affluent suburb with a cute coffee strip called the Applecross Village, where you can buy a burnt, over-priced coffee and watch women in Lululemon workout gear try to force some expression into their freshly botoxed faces. Helen and Nyssa will share a $72 bowl of ancient grain salad opposite their friend Tania, who peers over her dinner-plate-sized Gucci sunnies while recounting her recent trip to Bordeaux. She apparently had a fabulous time, sampling wines and olives while simultaneously pretending to still be in love with her banker husband, Craig. She doesn't even *mind* that he's having a secret affair with his personal trainer, Nadine. Tania's just waiting for him to die so she can sell their holiday house on the coast and move to the Maldives.

For about six months we rented in the dodgy end of Applecross. We're talking Audis, not BMWs, up that end – can you imagine? From memory, the house was pretty crappy and always damp. Terry and Jenny then bought a house up the better end (thank *God*). This time it was a case of the worst house in the best street. It was an old one-storey house on the corner about a block away from my primary school. It had stained-glass windows, wooden floorboards and a garage that had definitely seen some illegal shit.

Terry and Jenny are the type of people who are never content: they will renovate, clean, tweak and plump all day long if they can (their homes and themselves). Over the twelve or so years we lived in that house it took on many different looks. They added a pool, bedrooms, a movie room, an outdoor kitchen. No matter the day or time of year there was always a tradesman somewhere in the house adding or refining something. I swear I've even seen an electrician installing downlights on Christmas Day as the

13

rest of us ate lunch and pulled our crackers. Mum and Dad always had, and still have, their finger on the pulse of fashion. And living in Applecross, you can't fall behind or you just know Helen and Nyssa will be talking about you over their next soy chai latte. It was never gaudy though – Terry and Jenny have great taste.

This isn't going to be one of these books where I lie and say home life was terrible, or we had to scrape money together for dinner. We didn't have cabbage soup every night, excepting those on-purpose times when we were all doing the Atkins Diet before bikini season. All four of my grandparents weren't sleeping in the same bed à la *Charlie and the Chocolate Factory.* I was very lucky to grow up with a great home life. I can confidently say for all us kids, that none of us ever grew up feeling unloved or unsupported. And never once did our parents dissuade us from pursuing our dreams.

So they are to blame for this strange career I've carved out for myself in the Australian entertainment industry. And they are probably to blame for the fucked-up stories you are about to read.

Because, trust me, it ain't all Solo Man commercials, glamorous intergalactic wars and romantic proposals!

2

SCOOTERS, WITCHES AND AIR HUMPING . . . OH MY!

My sisters and I all attended primary school at Applecross Primary School. It was a relatively small school with quaint, old-fashioned classrooms – so quaint, in fact, they often used them to film the 90s kids' TV show *Ship to Shore*. I'm such a star-fucker that even back then I demanded the primary school I attended was famous!

The school was a block away from our house, so of course we were in the catchment area. It's a weird term, 'catchment area', isn't it? Sounds like a sustainable seafood reference. Well, fish *are* in school, I suppose. (Boom! I'm here all week!)

From about Grade 5, I was allowed to scoot down to school with my best friend Ashleigh Bell. Remember when scooters were a thing in the mid-90s? I don't mean motorised scooters – although they were doing a roaring trade in the over-eighties demographic too – I mean scooters you'd kick along yourself, Flintstone-style. Everybody had one. On the news they showed even businessmen in cities like Sydney scooting to work and folding them up and storing them under their desks. I vividly remember thinking at the time: *Well, that's a bit sad, get a car.*

The best birthday present I ever got was a Lazer scooter on my tenth birthday. It's still the best birthday present I've ever been given. Last year I got a slow cooker. What am I? Ninety? It had pink wheels (the scooter, not the slow cooker) that I would insist were burgundy . . . Even back then I was all about the alcohol references. I used to say, 'The wheels are definitely burgundy. They probably *look* pink because I've been scooting so much. I scoot really fast, actually.' I've always been able to talk myself out of pretty much any situation, even in primary school. But I mean, the wheels were definitely pink. I actually loved, and still love, the colour pink. But as all the dead-shit guys in my year would repeatedly tell me, 'Pink is gay!' I was like 'Um, no she's not . . . She's just made some dodgy hair choices!'

One of the most exciting days of the entire year was actually two days before school would commence. That's the day all the classrooms would post their class lists for the year on the door and you'd find out which teacher you'd have. I would get extreme anxiety in the weeks leading up to this day because naturally I had already decided which teacher I wanted months in advance. Always female. And always fabulous. I didn't care about their academic abilities as a teacher, I just wanted them to wear a lot of chunky jewellery and have fun hair.

It was also very important for me to have my best friend Ashleigh in my class. Ashleigh and I met in primary school. I can't remember how or why we became best friends but it was destined to be. She was always a great athlete, a total tomboy and a complete hard-arse. In fact, she is one of those annoying people who is good at everything. Even more annoying is that she doesn't even brag about it. I knew I could always count on Ashleigh for anything, and still do. Ashleigh also happened to be my neighbour, which made the friendship extremely easy. A few years ago, Ashleigh worked for me as my tour manager on one of my stand-up tours and we laughed about how convenient it was that I started hiring staff at such a young age.

In Grades 2 and 3, I had Mrs Wills. Great teacher. Ashleigh and I were in the same class and it was awesome. I can't remember why. Perhaps because we just sat around and ate Clag glue all day. Oh my God, I ate so much Clag in primary school, just to make people laugh. What a prop comic! It came in an opaque tomato-sauce-looking bottle and I worked out pretty early on it was just flour and water (fuck, at least I hope so . . . although if it wasn't, it would explain a lot) and I knew I could make people laugh by eating it. We honestly never used it. I don't think we ever used anything on our stationery list outside of pens and pencils. Has anybody? I'm not sure where or when you went to school, but in Perth in the 90s, your stationery list *always* included coloured moulding clay. Which we never used. Ever. Every student in the class would get their own 'big drawer' up the back of the room and the coloured moulding clay would just sit there doing nothing. Much like the basketball I got for my 11th birthday. About halfway through the year I couldn't resist any more and I'd have to put finger marks in every piece of clay in the class. I should have tried eating it for my end-of-year performance.

I was always a good speller in primary school. I wish *The Great Australian Spelling Bee* had been around back then, I could have embarked upon my quest for fame much earlier. In fact – and I hate to boast as you know – but I *was* in the advanced spelling group in Grade 3. Yes, you'd better believe it. The first word we learned in the elite spelling team was 'chlorine'. Silent 'h' . . . tricky. (Remember that 90s band Steps with the singer called H? I wish he'd stayed fucking silent.) Once the spelling of chlorine had been imparted to me I felt ready to run the country, or at the very least the local swimming pool. I mean, what else was there for me to learn? Ten bucks says Trump can't spell 'chlorine'. Although I get the feeling he's ingested a fair bit.

By the end of Grade 3 I was starting to worry. Grade 4 was proper school. You had to learn stuff in Grade 4. You couldn't just eat Clag and stress over the untouched moulding clay all day. Not only that, there were two teachers up for grabs in Grade 4. One was a fairly normal, female teacher. I think. I can't remember, to be honest. Could've been male. I wasn't paying attention. Because I was terrified.

Scooters, Witches and Air Humping . . . Oh My!

The *other* teacher on the menu in Grade 4 was Mrs Smirke. Yes. That Mrs Smirke. Have you ever met someone whose very name defines the attitude you expect them to have? (I hope I don't ever meet Mr and Mrs Kuntz.) Mrs Smirke, the older kids told me, was a witch. *Checks out*, I thought, *she does have long white hair, pale skin and wears a lot of black.* This was pre-Harry Potter, before witches received their long overdue renaissance. Witches are cool now. They also live in a fabulous house in New Orleans and Jessica Lange is in charge, if *American Horror Story* is to be believed.

This was the Mrs Smirke who apparently tortured students in her class. The Mrs Smirke who apparently lived under the stage of the primary school auditorium. To be honest, I always found that last one a bit weird. Why was she living under the stage? Couldn't she afford a house? If she was a witch, couldn't she just magic herself a house? Perhaps she just loved theatre? If I saw an apartment up for rent underneath a theatre I'd live there in a heartbeat. But it would depend on what show the theatre had on. I don't think I could deal with *Jersey Boys* every night – no sassy female lead or big belting torch song. No. Thank you. Not. Interested.

So two days before Grade 4 in 1998, Mum and I went to the school to see if I had 'the witch'. We headed over to Mrs Smirke's classroom to look for my name. Mrs Smirke's classroom wasn't even part of the main building, it was its own demountable building on the other side of the school. Ah, of course! Witches love demountable classrooms.

Frog spawn, eye of newt and asbestos are key ingredients in most witch recipes! What more proof did I need?

Ashleigh was already there. When I saw her face I knew we were in trouble.

'We're in Mrs Smirke's class, Joel. You know she's meant to be a witch.'

'Yes, thank you, Ashleigh. I am aware. I just wrote an entire paragraph about it. Ugh. Read my book in twenty years' time, won't you?'

I was terrified. I was admittedly always a little obsessed with witches growing up. I watched *The Wizard of Oz* and *The Witches* on high rotation. My grandma and I used to always play 'witches' in her caravan/coven in the backyard. But I was always shit-scared of them too. They were fine to watch from the safety of the couch, but in real life? Absolutely not. A witch teaching me maths? Nah, I'm good. A witch teaching me English? Well, that should be all right. I could spell 'chlorine' so she couldn't catch me out there.

I'm an incredibly judgemental person. Disgustingly so. If I pass you on the street, I've judged you. Within two seconds I'll have convinced myself I know exactly who you are, what you're about and where you're going. And I *definitely* don't think those shoes go with that skirt. But on many (read: *most*) occasions, I've been wrong. And Grade 4 was the first time I really learned that time-honoured lesson: 'Don't judge a book by its cover'. Or, as my friends call it, 'Don't be an arsehole, Joel.'

I fell in love with Mrs Smirke. So in love. Turned out everybody loved Mrs Smirke. She was sweet, caring and found me really funny. I can definitely credit her as being one of the people who planted the seed in my mind that I might be a funny person.

Mrs Smirke was the teacher who introduced us to the concept of the oral presentation. (I know you're expecting a cheap gag here but I am far too mature and classy and will save that kind of smut for later in the book.) Whenever we had to give oral presentations to the class she would clap and praise us from the back of the room. I gave a present-ation on Africa one day which possibly (definitely!) involved me wearing a loincloth fashioned from one of Nan's old faux-fur stoles and singing 'Circle of Life' from Disney's *The Lion King*. I received my first standing ovation that day. It was from a beaming Mrs Smirke at the back of the room who yelled, 'Bravo! Encore!'

At the end of the year we did Secret Santa and I rigged it so she would receive my present. I just wanted to buy her gifts and let her know how much I loved her. It was all terrible jewellery but she happily wore it like it was the Hope Diamond. I cried when Grade 4 ended.

Grade 5 was an important year for me. It was a coming of age of sorts, in that I heard my first serious swear word. Why does my first swear word 'experience' even require a mention in my book, you might ask? Because I'm a stand-up comedian. This is a big moment! If I were a pilot, this would be the story about my first experience on a plane. Or if I were a hooker it would be my first blow job in a carpark . . . that I got paid for, obvs.

I love swearing. *Love it.* I think it's funny, fun and fucking highbrow. I feel liberated when I swear and some-times nothing but a perfectly placed 'fuck this', 'fuck that', 'fuck you' or 'fucking fuckedy fuck' will do.

But, surprisingly, it wasn't me who said that beautiful, handy, versatile word first. It was Ashleigh. And she didn't waste the occasion.

It happened one lunchtime.

In primary school, our lunchtime activity changed from week to week. And being the social butterfly/desperate-to-be-universally-loved person that I am, I always had a packed schedule. One week it might have been *Animorphs*, the next week it might have been Pokémon cards, the next week soccer. Ugh, I hated it whenever the activity involved sport. I hated the school oval because I don't like grass. Actually, I'm allergic to grass. I remember having desen-sitisation treatment in primary school for my grass and dust allergies. We went through a big *Xena: Warrior Princess* phase at lunch time. For a few weeks a bunch of us would re-enact scenes from *Xena* in the playground. Naturally I'd always be Xena and the less gender-secure eight-year-old boys would be Hercules. Ashleigh would often be Gabrielle as it gave her an excuse to go around whacking people with a big stick. This isn't the first time Xena will be discussed in the book, just so you know.

We would also play tennis on the quadrangle. We had no net, we'd just smack the ball back and forth in a bit of a round-robin scenario. Tennis was super popular so there was always a queue of kids waiting to play. On this particular day I was standing in line. Ashleigh was standing behind me, waiting eagerly. She was one of those people without grass allergies who could play every sport. She was a champion cross-country runner too, and I always loved watching her beat the boys in our year. Standing behind Ashleigh was our friend Daniel. Daniel was one of my best friends in primary school. We were so close before we ended up going to separate high schools and I haven't really seen him much since, even though he still doesn't live far from my parents. I think.

Daniel used to come over to my house every day after school to play dress-ups. My mum always had a very well-stocked wardrobe (or the dressing-up box, as I called it) and performing was always encouraged. I had a vast variety of characters. I was like Meryl Streep in that way. Who knew which character I'd become after school? Daniel really only had one. Every afternoon without fail he'd go rifling through the dress-up box and pull out one of my mum's old, black, fitted cocktail dresses. And while most boys would put the dress on and muck around saying, 'Oooh, look at me! I'm a girl,' Daniel would just put it on and get on with his afternoon. Like throwing on a pair of track pants, Daniel would

23

pop on the dress and go about eating his afternoon tea or playing Lego. He was extremely fabulous and, according to Facebook, has grown up to be rather handsome. Haven't seen any recent pics of him in a cocktail frock, though.

Admittedly, he could also be quite hyperactive (that's adult talk for 'annoying'). So this one lunch time in Grade 5 we were standing in line to play tennis and Daniel was behind Ashleigh and he kept bopping her on the head over and over with his tennis racquet. Ashleigh kept politely saying, 'Daniel, stop that. Daniel, please stop that. Daniel, can you stop?' Daniel ignored her and kept going and giggling like a maniac while Ashleigh continued patiently asking him to 'Please stop, Daniel, it's annoying!'

It went on for about two minutes before Ashleigh lost it. Completely and utterly lost it.

'Daniel, stop that . . . Daniel, please stop . . . Daniel, stop it . . .' And then at the top of her lungs, ten-year-old Ashleigh snapped. 'DANIEL! WOULD YOU JUST FUCK OFF?'

I was stepping up to play but I stopped immediately. I couldn't believe it. Ashleigh had just said *that* word. Everybody stopped, in fact. The whole school stopped. The tennis ball stopped mid-air. Kids playing on the playground stopped. People running on the oval stopped. Teachers in the staff room stopped drinking their Nescafé Blend 43 and wallowing in their self-loathing.

It felt like an eternity passed. All eyes went from Ashleigh to Daniel, where those words had definitely had their desired effect. Daniel had stopped hitting her and stood, mouth open, staring at her. And I will never forget his response. It was perfect. It was equal parts the campest, lamest and freakin' coolest thing I have ever seen. He timed it to perfection.

It was as if a spotlight appeared on Daniel from nowhere. He was centre stage. He shut his mouth slowly and composed himself, a glimmer appearing in his eye. Then he said, 'Okay Ashleigh, I *will* fuck off then,' and proceeded to air-hump his way the entire four hundred metres to the canteen, buy himself a Calippo and lie in the sun for the rest of lunch time.

Incidentally, I was given a Calippo on a domestic flight recently. I don't think Calippo-licking techniques are something you want to experience from a group of strangers in a confined space. However, that said, to the gentleman in 23C – impressive work.

That day, Ashleigh taught me the world-stopping power of a well-chosen swear word. But more importantly, Daniel taught me that no matter the situation, no matter the time of day, no matter who was around, and no matter how old you are, there is always an opportunity to steal the spotlight. And if worst comes to worst and a joke doesn't land, a bout of air-humping will always get a laugh.

So that's what I'm doing right now with this book, Daniel. Stealing the spotlight back all these years later. This is my story now!

3

NOT YOUR TYPICAL BOY

Holly, Alice and I were kept extremely busy with co-curricular activities when we were younger. The money and time my parents invested in us is astounding when I think about it. That said, I think they're getting a bit of return-on-investment now that I'm writing a book about it.

Holly was a state-level swimmer, training every morning as part of the Belmont Aquajets swimming club. This would involve my mum driving Holly to training at 6 am, waiting there and bringing her home before she had time to even think about things like lunches, Alice and me, Dad, the rest of the day or, y'know . . . herself. And remember – this was waaay before smartphones. What did she do all that time? She would have had to actually watch her child! How boring!

Alice was more arts-based and was a ballerina and ballroom and Irish dancer. Mum spent hours on the sewing machine creating elaborate beaded costumes or putting

Alice's hair up in various Irish-dance-appropriate hairstyles. (The Irish, like Emma Bunton, love a crimper.) We weren't even Irish, but Alice learnt Irish dancing because she used to involuntarily do it before she was even properly taught. Like Irish dancing Tourettes. Every Christmas Eve we'd have our family friends the Mellors around for drinks and we'd all put on a talent show, parents and children alike. Mr Mellor would usually be Santa Claus, Terry Creasey would tell a politically incorrect joke or do his famous Kermit the Frog impression and Alice would dance. I remember she was probably about only four or five when she had found a tartan flat cap in a dress-up box somewhere and decided to do Irish dancing for her talent. Her commitment to her act was so cute that Mum signed her up for lessons soon after.

Both the girls were also Girl Guides. Or Brownies. I never know the difference. All I know is one sounds incredibly stuffy and boring and like a compass would be involved . . . and the other goes great with ice cream. My mum enrolled me in Joeys for a short period but I didn't last long. Joeys is the junior version of Scouts. Or is that Cubs? I can't be quite sure. All I know is that in the gay world, a 'cub' is something very different.

I've never been good at anything too male-dominated, unless it's an orgy with a couple of my mates. Then I'm right at home.

Even though I didn't ever quite hit it off with the lads at Joeys, I was quite lucky to discover who I was in my early teens and become supremely confident in my own skin – prior to this discovery I was always very insecure. I knew I wasn't like the other boys and I knew I wasn't stereotypically 'masculine'. Being in situations like Joeys or sports clubs never sat well with me because they only highlighted what I perceived to be my inadequacies. Also, who needs to learn to cook damper in a camp oven? I grew up in the age of the Thermomix – throw it all in, hit go, and a couple of hours later you're Bush Tucker Man without having to deal with the whole 'bush' part.

Like Holly, I was into swimming from a young age and was naturally pretty good, one of the few sports I had any success in. Unfortunately, I was lazy when it came to training. The early morning starts didn't go well with my sleep schedule and beauty regime so Mum would take me for training after school, which meant another trip to the aquatic centre for poor Jenny Creasey. If you didn't know she had kids you'd think she was having an affair with the swim coach.

Till the age of about twelve I swam with a swim club and in the odd competitive event, being pretty good at back-stroke. I was also the Applecross Primary School champion each year. That was until Grade 7, when Patrick Henning arrived at the school and beat me. I gave up swimming pretty much instantly. Also all the boys' bodies were starting to develop and since I was particularly skinny, I didn't feel comfortable being shirtless around them any more. (Also, I didn't grow any armpit hair till about Grade 10. Up till that point I was giving off serious greyhound vibes.)

Not only was Patrick Henning a great swimmer, it turned out he was good at everything else too. And was very good looking. I was furious, but of course I fell madly in love with him at the same time. I think I still am in love with him. What better way for him to find out, eh? Hi Patrick!

Like Joeys, another activity that really didn't click for me at all was football. No surprises there. I was ten when my parents signed me up to play for the local football team, the Applecross Hawks. They trained on Wednesdays around the corner from our house at Gairloch Oval, which is where everything in the local area takes place: football, soccer, dog walking, drug deals, wristies behind the footy club. It's an extremely versatile patch of grass. I'm not sure why I was signed up to play – the rest of my family have always been mad AFL fans but I've never particularly gotten into it. They are all huge Fremantle Dockers fans. And I mean tears-when-they-don't-win fans. I guess you can't blame my parents for at least *seeing* if I was interested or hoping that I might be unexpectedly good.

Turns out I was neither. I went to three training sessions or, as I kept calling them, 'rehearsals'. I have very little co-ordination and as I've always been tall and lanky, I couldn't quite get the ball to connect with my foot. As my parents love telling people, they'd come to watch me play and I'd spend most of the time up the back of the field, hand on hip, gossiping with Daniel, who also wasn't particularly interested in the game either. Meanwhile Ashleigh was probably down the other end of the field kicking goals and running rings around the boys.

I do remember at the end of one of the training sessions (rehearsals), the coach (director) was giving us our uniforms (costumes). All the boys were standing there beside their fathers as it's a bit of a ceremony when you receive your first football guernsey. I knew full well I wouldn't be playing in the actual game on the coming Saturday. I knew I would be on the bench (oh my God – understudy!) and, frankly, by this point I was over football altogether.

The uniform for the local team was the traditional Hawthorn Football Club colours – we were called the Applecross Hawks after all – a chocolate brown and mustard yellow stripe. Although I'm not sure if many Hawthorn fans go into the detail of the shade of brown. But it's chocolate if we're getting specific. Well, a coffee kinda chocolate. Tiramisu-esque you could say.

As the coach handed me my costume I stared at it, mortified. Brown and yellow? Were they kidding?

Without even thinking, a few seconds after staring at my chocolate-and-mustard atrocity with disgust, I turned to my dad and said loudly in front of everyone, 'Oh, Dad. I don't think I can play football any more. There is no way I can wear this. I will look like a giant diarrhoea.'

And my dad, to his credit, turned to me and said, in front of all the other dads (many of whom were his mates), 'That's fine. Those colours don't go with your eyes anyway.'

Not Your Typical Boy

Ever the metrosexual, Terry Creasey.

When I was twenty I had a run-in with a football team. And 'run-in' isn't code. I'm not talking a St Kilda football club–style, banged-the-whole-team scandal. I am open to the idea, though. The run-in was with the Sydney Swans, a team name I've always thought was better suited to a ballet troupe.

It took place one Saturday morning at the Qantas Club at Melbourne Airport. It turns out, the Sydney Swans had won their game the night before and they were flying home to Sydney.

I was on the same flight and feeling cocky because the night before I had made one of my first ever TV appearances on a *20 to 1* – one of those countdown, clip-recap TV shows. It was on late at night and I was only on for two seconds but I was walking around the lounge assuming everybody was staring at me thinking, *That's that guy on the TV! He's even more handsome in real life!*

For my first few years on television I was completely like that – I loved it. All I wanted was for somebody to recognise me from TV so I could talk about it. I truly thought nothing was cooler. So many celebrities play this down. They pretend that getting recognised is such a pain in the arse. But they only do that because that's apparently how we're 'meant' to act. We're supposed to act all cool and nonchalant and 'Yep, I'll take this photo with you but please leave me alone the split second it's been taken'.

Get fucked.

For someone like Taylor Swift or Beyoncé, okay, sure. It must get exhausting. But Australian celebrities have nothing to complain about. No Australian celebrity gets bothered relentlessly and therefore they have no excuse to act like an arsehole. They should be thrilled. Sadly I've seen so many Australian celebrities (sometimes friends of mine even) be rude to fans and it blows my mind.

I'm also always shocked when someone stops me on the street and says, 'Sorry for bothering you but I think you're great,' or 'Sorry for bothering you but can I get a photo?' It makes me wonder who they've stopped in the past who's been rude to them. Or not given them the time of day.

I always like to remind people that it doesn't bother me. At all. The twenty-year-old strutting around the Qantas Club after his first appearance on *20 to 1* is fucking stoked to get a photo with you. If I've got the time, I'm more than happy to stop and chat. These people are stopping me to talk about *me*. To compliment *me*. I am my specialty topic. You wanna talk about how hilarious you think I am? Sure! Sit down, I'll buy you a coffee!

In Australia, another good measure is that if a celebrity is whingeing on Twitter or Instagram about being harassed or recognised everywhere, it's because they aren't being harassed or recognised. And they usually spawn from shows that don't require any talent like *Big Brother* and *The Bachelor*.

Anyway, it was 6 am Saturday morning and I was swanning (ironic) around the Qantas Club hoping somebody –

anybody – might recognise me and validate my existence. All I needed was for one person to stop for a photo so I could announce loudly: 'OH, WHAT'S THAT? YOU WANT A PHOTO WITH ME BECAUSE YOU SAW ME ON THE TELEVISION?'

Look it wasn't going well, so I ended up getting in line for a coffee, behind what seemed about half the Sydney Swans football team. Obviously I had no idea who these players were – I read the team name on the back of their tracksuit jackets. As if I know who plays for the Sydney Swans. For all I knew these guys could've been Wayne Carey, Gary Ablett and Warwick Capper . . . I've got no idea . . . Also, I totally just googled 'famous AFL players' to get that reference.

As I joined the back of the queue, though, the footballer standing immediately in front of me turned around and very dismissively said, 'Nah, mate, no thanks . . . We aren't signing autographs this morning.' Like a slap to the face.

How dare he! Did he not realise that for at least fifteen seconds last night I was the star of *20 to 1*?

I knew I had to respond so I channelled my bitchiest David Jones make-up department counter assistant voice and said, 'Um . . . I'm just waiting for a double-shot flat white, mate. Not after an autograph.'

He wasn't expecting that and turned back around quite abruptly. He was shocked, like I'd thrown glitter in his face Spiderman style, and his football mates in the queue sniggered at him. I was pretty happy with myself.

And it got better.

I truly could not have timed this better if I had tried.

I hadn't noticed earlier, but as well as the Sydney Swans, a bunch of Sydney Swans fans who must fly around the country each weekend to watch their team play was also sitting in the lounge. Not my thing personally, but all power to ya, girlfriend. One of them was a young guy about twenty years old, decked out in full Sydney Swans gear: jacket, beanie and scarf. About thirty seconds after I'd shut my football player mate down, the football fan approached me from where he'd been sitting, tapped me on the shoulder and in front of the entire queue – still silent from my deadly zinger moments prior – asked, 'Excuse me, are you Joel Creasey? I saw you on *20 to 1* last night and I think you're really funny.'

I can't be sure, but I think I may have open-mouthed kissed this man before running a victory lap of the lounge and thanking the Academy.

This was six years ago now, so I assume most of the players have moved on, swapped teams, gone on to nuclear science . . . whatever it is they do in the AFL. But I did get to see the Sydney Swans again recently when I was honoured with the privilege of MCing the first ever Pride Round of AFL at Etihad Stadium – Sydney Swans versus St Kilda Football Club.

It's no secret that homophobia is rife in the AFL among both players and fans. I live near Etihad Stadium and have on many occasions heard the word 'faggot' being sniggered as a group of footy fans walk past me. I often think, *I wish these guys would come to my show, what an easy crowd. All I've got to do is stand there and breathe.*

I know there's been a push for years for an AFL player to come out of the closet, too. A dear friend and ex-flame of mine, in fact, is the (what league does he play for again?) footballer Jason Ball who has very much led the push for equality in footy. Jason, like me, would agree that a player coming out would certainly help counter the stigma, but I don't think anyone should be forced into it.

I'll never forget having a conversation with football legend Barry Hall a few years back when we were both contestants on *I'm a Celebrity . . . Get Me Out Of Here!* He had the balls to say on national television that he believes homophobia in the league is disgusting and he won't stand for it. Gosh, I love that man.

It always makes me laugh when conservatives say, 'There aren't any gay players in the AFL.' As I mentioned, I live near Etihad Stadium. I can assure you there are – I slept with one. I'm not in the business of outing people, though. That was very much Barbara Walters' domain in the 90s (remember when she outed Ricky Martin?). And we only slept together a couple of times. But I always did love the juxtaposition of him coming over after a game to me lying on the couch watching *The Devil Wears Prada*. He had a great sense of humour and would understand the ridiculousness of the situation too. And he'd always laugh when

I asked him, 'How did your football concert go tonight? Did you get an audience?'

The one sport that did work out for me, though, was tennis. Obviously it didn't work out in the sense that I won Wimbledon. At least, I don't think I did. I'm terribly forgetful so I could be wrong. But it worked out in the sense that I certainly played tennis longer than I did Joeys or football. Or Taekwondo. I did *that* for a year and threw in the towel when I realised black belt wasn't the belt immediately following white. I just couldn't cope with a yellow belt. It's an aesthetic thing. Also, was it a coincidence I signed up to Taekwondo the same year *Charlie's Angels* with Cameron, Drew and Lucy came out? I think not.

I played tennis till I was about sixteen. I started around age nine. I trained twice a week after school at the tennis club down on the Applecross foreshore with my coaches Diego and Adriano. I know, right? They sound like characters in a Dreamworks film. I loved tennis, as opposed to other sports, because it was a performance. When I think about it, I've never been great at team sports. I guess it's weird to admit, but I'm not a team player. I'm stubborn, I like to call the shots and, to be completely honest, I get jealous very easily. (I guess there's a reason I'm a solo stand-up comic and not a member of a sketch group.) Tennis suited me perfectly. I also wasn't half bad at mixed doubles because my mixed doubles partner, Holly Brindle, had something in her arsenal that I never quite mastered – an ace-delivering serve. In tennis it's usually more common for the male to serve first. The roles were very much reversed between Holly Brindle and me.

I also love how tennis is about the fashions. I always enjoy seeing what Serena or Venus wear to a tournament; I recently saw Venus wearing more jewellery than the trophy she was competing to win. I was completely obsessed with Serena's black Puma catsuit in 2002 and regularly imagined myself in it whenever reaching for a tough forehand. And I even remember adoring Jennifer Capriati's American flag dress when she won the US Open in 2000 and totally credit the dress for helping her win. I think there's a place for fashion in every aspect of life, but tennis is one of the few sports that seems to have incorporated it well. Take note, Applecross Hawks.

During my early teens, on top of my twice weekly after-school training, I'd also play Junior Club on Saturday mornings, which is basically social tennis for juniors. It would involve me going down to the tennis club, playing a few games and asking everybody to compliment me on my new tennis shoes. I also once rocked up in head-to-toe New Balance gear and convinced everybody that New Balance were now sponsoring me and I was the new face of their brand. I was eleven. Oh, and Dad knew someone who worked in the marketing department at New Balance.

Then on Sundays I would play pennants. I was in a team with three other boys – the Applecross team. We'd play against other suburbs and it was quite competitive. Not just between the boys on the court but also between the mums. Because, let's be honest, posh parents make their kids play tennis. The mums would rock up in their BMW X5s and set up their Louis Vuitton folding chairs courtside to watch their sons play tennis in the scorching summer heat, attempting to cheer the teams on without blowing their botox or spilling their travel coffee mugs full of vodka.

True to form, Jenny Creasey would be there every Sunday morning, cheering me on. In fact, she used to drive our entire team to most games. She wouldn't get too involved or be too overbearing and would normally just shoot the other mums an icy glance when they were getting too over the top.

Mum always made me feel good, regardless of the result. However, I do remember having a particularly bad match one day and seeing her whisper under her breath, 'Oh, for fuck's sake.'

The other boys on my team were Richard, who would screech like Sharapova and had a very aggressive forehand; Christian, who was the best player of the four of us but who would lose his temper on the court; and another boy whose name I can't remember. What's weird is I've met this other boy since. A few years ago I was home in Perth and kissed a guy on the dance floor of Connections Nightclub. We pulled away for a few seconds and I said, 'Don't I know you?'

And he said, 'Yeah, we used to play tennis together.'

I said, 'Oh. Cool,' kissed him again and left. Admittedly I'd had eighty-three shots of Jäger so this could all have been in my head and I was in fact kissing a drag queen. Or a wall. But if it is true and you're reading this, sorry I forgot your name. Again. Are you still playing tennis? Do you tell people you've kissed a D-list celebrity?

I wasn't a naturally gifted tennis player like I was a swimmer, but I loved it. In my spare time I'd find any wall I could hit a tennis ball against and at night I'd sit in bed flicking through tennis books, looking up player statistics, or fashioning that Jennifer Capriati dress out of my doona.

One of my biggest heroes was the Belgian tennis player Kim Clijsters. When I was eleven years old, my parents took me to see Belgium versus Italy in the Hopman Cup – the Hopman Cup is the Perth tennis tournament and it's a big deal . . . tens of people go. The day we went also happened to be one of Kim Clijsters' first tournaments. She was ranked about 150 in the world. I remember saying to Dad, 'She is going to be a star one day.' Who did I think I was? Simon Cowell? Anyway, turns out I was right and only a couple of years later she was World Number 1.

I followed her career intently. I'd stay up watching any match she played, bought the same racquet she played with and had it strung and gripped identically to hers. I was so obsessed I was even a member of the Kim Clijsters online fan forum. Yes, how cool am I? Most fifteen-year-old boys run home from school to watch porn. Not me. I would run home every day from school to jump online and chat about

Kim. (I was also a member of the *Better Homes and Gardens* fan forum but let's not go into that.)

I met a guy on the forum called Alex. I didn't know much else about him, just that his name was Alex and he was a major Kim Clijsters fan too. After a few months we decided we had outgrown the forum so we swapped email addresses and emailed each other directly about our goddess and saviour. We eventually got bored of that and kicked things up a gear by giving each other our home addresses. As I said, I didn't even know what this guy looked like. What we would do, though, was cut out any articles from the paper about Kim and post them to each other. I wasn't 'out' at this stage as I was only fifteen, but I'm fairly sure that arrangement must've been a pretty big red flag for Mum: 'Mum, I'm leaving for school. Please don't throw out the paper! I need to cut out that article about Kim's latest eating plan for Alex. He'll love that. Actually, that reminds me. Can you make risotto for dinner? Kim says risotto is really good for you. Use brown rice though, I'm watching my carbs. What's that? A *girlfriend*? All right, I'll look into that next week, I am flat out at the moment, thankyouverymuch.'

I got to meet Kim Clijsters too. I don't want to blow you away with my celebriTAY this early in the book but I was a ball boy at the Hopman Cup in Perth when I was fourteen and fifteen. Yep, I was *that* good they asked me back. It's actually quite hard to get a gig as a ball boy, but Mum and Dad had family friends who helped me get the position.

I was so excited to see all these tennis players up close, but I was probably the most passive-aggressive ball boy they ever had. First of all, I had to wear a legionnaires hat – you know, one of those hats with a flap at the back that screams 'No hat no play'. I'm fairly sure I'd rather get actual Legionnaires than have to wear one of those fugly hats ever again. Not to mention if the player hit the ball too far away, I'd roll my eyes and mutter under my breath, 'I guess you want me to get that for you,' or 'Yeah, no, don't worry I'll do it . . . you just stand there,' or 'I hope you know I'm not getting paid for this. I'm volunteering my time.' Marat Safin, the Russian player who was infamous for his tantrums and throwing his racquet, probably thought I was a little shit. He once asked me to hand him his towel for wiping sweat and I said, 'Absolutely not. It's drenched. I don't care how famous you are, I don't want to touch your sweat. Thanks.' I didn't get to be ball boy for him again. Or at all, in fact. That was my last ever match.

The highlight of my ball boy career (can you call it a career?) was carrying the Belgian flag for Kim Clijsters. At the start of each game the player walks out behind their country flag while their national anthem plays. Therefore the ball boy carrying out the flag was top dog. Naturally, I was chosen. Leave it to me to turn this into a *Prisoner*-style Bea Smith-type scenario. Don't worry, I didn't shank any of the other ball kids. I did call one a 'bloody bugger' though. I'm also a very sassy flag waver, which wasn't required but I'd always throw it in to spice things up a little for the crowd.

I couldn't believe that not only was I going to get to carry a flag out (meaning at least fifty seconds of air time on the TV broadcast) but I was carrying it for Kim Clijsters. *The* Kim Clijsters. *My* Kim Clijsters. Not only that, but this was when Kim Clijsters was at the top of her game. She was the World Number 1, the favourite to win this tournament and, at the time, engaged to Lleyton Hewitt. I was never a fan of Lleyton Hewitt. He seemed grumpy, I hated his choices in sunglasses and he was male. Nil interest in all of these things. (The 'male' thing changed over the years, but bad sunnies are still a no-no.) I was also furiously jealous that he was engaged to the love of my life, Kim. I loved her so much, however, that I forgave her for her poor choice in fiancé. Soon she'd be wowed by my sassy flag-waving and be swept off her feet by my bald-pitted, teenage self.

So there I was at fourteen years old, standing in the wings of the Burswood Dome at the Hopman Cup waiting for Kim Clijsters to join me to walk out onto the court. Standing beside me was another ball boy holding the Slovak Republic flag. He was walking out the Slovakian player Daniela Hantuchová. Very beautiful player. Had honestly never seen her win a match. Sucked to be him.

Then I heard a procession of people coming down the corridor behind me. I could see coaches, publicists, Hopman Cup officials and then, bringing up the rear, Daniela Hantuchová followed by Kim Clijsters. Kim looked beautiful. White singlet, white skirt, white shoes and a brand new

Babolat tennis bag on her back. Shit, I didn't have that one. I made a mental note to get Jenny Creasey on to the case the second I finished.

Kim and Danielle stood behind me and my colleague (let's call him that). I couldn't believe it. My hero was standing behind me. I couldn't wait to write to Alex about this. I was so nervous I was paralysed. I couldn't turn to look at her. All I could do was try to keep hold of the heavy Belgian flag while my hands got sweatier and sweatier.

The voiceover was booming through the packed fifteen-thousand-seat stadium (theatre): 'Ladies and gentlemen welcome to the Hopman Cup and today's match . . . the Slovak Republic versus Belgium! First up, from the Slovak Republic. Please welcome the World Number 9 . . . Daniela Hantuchová!'

Off went the other ball boy and Daniela, onto the court to huge cheers and screams muffled by the Slovak Republik national anthem. Not a great tune, by the way, in case you were thinking about hitting the iTunes store later. Daniela and ball boy stood centre court for the anthem, and when it finished they moved to stand beside the umpire at the side of court where Daniela's rest station was.

Then it was our turn.

'Next up, please welcome to the court the World Number 1 from Belgium . . . Kim Clijsters.'

The crowd erupted. Kim Clijsters was a fan favourite all over the world, but particularly in Australia. 'Aussie Kim' the media would call her.

Kim bent down, gave me a hug, shot me a huge smile and whispered, 'Good luck.'

My brain basically exploded. *What?!* Why was she wishing *me* good luck? I wasn't playing! *Oh my God, she hugged me! Shit, does she think I'm Lleyton? We are both blond, I guess . . .* I couldn't believe it. I honestly couldn't process it. In fact, I was so busy taking it all in I forgot to walk out until some stressed stage manager hissed at me from across the corridor, 'Walk, idiot!'

My heart was racing, and my palms were so sweaty the flag was starting to slip, but out we went, onto the court, where the crowd got even louder at the sight of Kim. Why wouldn't they? She was fucking perfect. I somehow navigated us to centre court all the while thinking, *Respond to Kim, Joel. She spoke to you! This is your opportunity!* At the same time I was thinking, *Of course you can't say anything, you're on the court, you're on TV! She's listening to her national anthem. It's not very good, they really need to remix this.*

I didn't know what to do. I was shaking, I was so excited, *she* was standing next to *me*. For those few minutes we were a team. Kim Clijsters and Joel Creasey.

And then, well, I don't know what came over me. I knew this would probably be my only opportunity with this woman I had adored and admired for so many years. I knew this was my only opportunity to say something to her and I'd regret it forever if I didn't. Just like that time I sat next to Kim Cattrall on a plane . . . (But that's for another book.) So I snapped. The national anthem hadn't even ended and

44

I turned around to Kim Clijsters and words just started tumbling out of my mouth.

'Kim Clijsters, I love you, I've loved you forever. I love everything about you. I think you're so beautiful. The most beautiful woman on earth, in fact. I play tennis because of you. I've even made my tennis racquet look exactly like yours. I don't know if you ever check the Kim Clijsters fan forum but I post on there every day. I love you so, so, so, so much. And . . . I think . . . um . . . well . . . I think you're too good for Lleyton Hewitt.'

What? What was I thinking? 'You're too good for Lleyton Hewitt'? He was her fiancé! Who did I think I was? I was wearing a legionnaires cap, for fuck's sake!

I'll never forget that moment. Kim Clijsters knelt down next to me, smiled and . . . said something in Flemish. Not. A. Clue as to what she said. No idea. Don't speak Flemish. But it definitely sounded like it involved chocolate and beer, although I could be stereotyping there.

She stood up, walked over to her side of the court, and I exited stage left (yes, I know, not correct) and was berated by Hopman Cup management while Kim went on to win her match. Obviously – she was playing Hantuchová.

I've never met Kim Clijsters again to ask her what she said. I'd love to. I still adore her. Just saying, though, I do think my words might have gotten through to her – Leyton and Kim called off their engagement a few weeks later! Perhaps she knew she had other options, like sassy, flag-waving, sweaty-palmed fifteen-year-olds from fan forums.

My tennis career lasted a few more years into high school. But by late high school, tennis lessons meant time to flirt with boys, so I started to get distracted.

Plus, as I crept into my teen years, I quickly started to realise that it wasn't tennis I loved. It was the stage. The performance. And what better stage is there, than, well . . . an actual fucking stage?

4

BURGER FLIPPER IN THE STREETS, CASANOVA IN THE SHEETS

Something which I have not really spoken about publicly – or at all really – is what my parents do for a living. Apart from riding my coattails, I mean. Obviously I've spoken about my parents' time on the stage as models and actors and ballroom dance instructors on cruise ships, all those kinds of things all regular parents do. (I mean really – did they *think* they were going to get a straight son with resumés like that?)

When my parents had children they selflessly left their quest for fame behind (ugh, can you imagine?) and entered the corporate world. Sounds like an area of Disneyland: Jurassic World, Old West World, Corporate World. I reckon the rides in Corporate World would suck. Look, in all honesty, I don't think anybody actually calls it the 'corporate world' any more, but this was the 90s when pinstripe suits, PalmPilots (a terrible name for a little hand-held device – sounds like wristies for aircraft operators) and briefcases were a thing. Honestly, if someone rocked up to a meeting in a pinstripe suit and a briefcase these days I'd assume they were about to kidnap me. Either that or I'm having lunch with Diane Keaton.

In the 90s we were a very traditional family unit. Mum was a full-time mum (the best mum ever, in fact), and Dad worked at the Swan Brewery selling beer, so it's fair to say the love of alcohol runs deep in my family, or is possibly hereditary. Dad had other corporate-y type jobs too but they were nowhere near as cool as what I'm about to tell you. That said, he did run a sports management business for a hot second. Not sure who he managed, but based on my extensive knowledge of sports management, I'm pretty sure that Cuba Gooding Jr yelled, 'Show me the money!' at him at some stage.

We'd moved to Perth for Dad's job with the Swan Brewery and really weren't expecting what came next. One night Terry came home as we were all sitting down for dinner. We were big on family dinner – we ate together and there was strictly no TV. (Which always annoyed my dad – as an avid *Home and Away* fan, the 'no TV' rule really only ever applied to him.) This particular night we were having dinner in the formal dining room. I've always hated the term 'formal dining room' – it insinuates that somewhere in the house is an informal dining room, which I suppose there was in our house . . . if you count my bed. Obviously something big was afoot – the formal dining room was only ever reserved for special occasions or birthdays. Once we were all at the table my parents delivered the news. Dad was leaving the Swan Brewery. I'm sure in my already bitchy seven-year-old mind I thought, *Yawn. Who cares.*

And then they followed it up with this.

Dad was leaving the Swan Brewery *because my parents were buying a McDonald's store.* That's right. My parents were buying the single coolest thing on earth a two-, six- and ten-year-old kid could imagine. A fucking *McDonald's* store! Can you imagine my head exploding when I heard that? The only thing that would have been cooler was for them to tell us we were going to get Xena the Warrior Princess as our live-in nanny. I mean, I was six years old; everyone I knew was having their birthday parties at McDonald's. It was the best place *ever* to have a birthday party. And not only that, I'm sorry but Happy Meals? Fucking. Rock. And. Roll when you're six years old. Who the fuck doesn't want a collectible Snoopy figure dressed in traditional garb from every major continent?

We had to keep the news pretty hush-hush, as we had to wait for my parents to find out if they were actually going to be successful in acquiring a franchise, and then the company had to find a McDonald's store for them to buy.

A few months later I was finally allowed to tell people. That day was also the day of the Christmas nativity play at school. I was one of the three kings (I wish it had been queens) and I was standing backstage, or as the teacher liked to call it 'behind the pinboard covered in pictures to make it look like Bethlehem', waiting to walk on to give baby Jesus/Ashleigh's Cabbage Patch Kid his frankincense. By the way – what actually *is* frankincense? What a shit gift! If I was Jesus and someone gave me frankincense I would be pissed off – get me a David Jones voucher, or a cashmere scarf . . . something I can use! And what is a baby doing with frankincense? Get him a Bugaboo or something useful. How many newborns do you know rockin' round with frankincense in their nappy bags?

Anyway, I was waiting backstage next to a boy called Jeremy Cockran, who was playing one of the other kings. He was standing beside me with his myrrh, also eagerly waiting for our turn on stage. I decided that very moment was the *perfect* time to share my news so I turned to him and whispered, 'Jeremy, my parents are going to buy a McDonald's store!'

And, look, it wasn't the reaction I was hoping for, but Jeremy hissed, 'You're a liar!' and walked onstage to deliver his myrrh. And that was it. Way to ruin my big moment, arsehole.

My dad had to take a year of unpaid training before he was allowed to buy his first store. And then, all of a sudden, my parents were the proud owners of a brand new (well, new to us – the store had been there for some time) McDonald's Family Restaurant: McDonald's Myaree, Western Australia.

Burger Flipper in the Streets, Casanova in the Sheets

I remember the first day we went there as the owners – it was so cool.

The first thing my parents did was have a new playground installed. We're talking state-of-the-art playground, complete with ball pit. The ball pit didn't last very long – they ended up having to take the balls out because children kept shitting in there. An unexpected turd in a ball pit can really take the 'happy' out of a Happy Meal. At McDonald's in Myaree there was an old train carriage beside the playground that was used as the official party room, so our McDonald's was always known as the 'train store'.

It was so rock and roll for so many years. I'd have all my parties there in the train, I'd take in Macca's vouchers for the kids at school, and sometimes Dad would even bring home promotional food from the store. Remember the veggie nuggets or the McAfrica burger? No? I do.

I got my driver's licence in the last few months of Grade 12. After school, I used to drive boys from my high school to my parents' McDonald's for a free meal. I really used it as a way to flirt with boys I had the hots for – you can imagine how many free feeds Patrick Henning was getting. Nothing cemented my crush more than seeing a boy deep-throat a french fry. *I've got something you can McFeast on right here*, I would think. I was so naive though, I was usually referring to an actual McFeast. I'd love to see that on *The Bachelor*: some chick wearing a low-cut dress and Witchery pumps taken for a McNugget meal and a whirl on the playground.

Often I don't tell people what my parents do, just because of the reactions. Some people are like 'Er, gross!' and 'Your parents are making people fat!' Well, no, they're not. They're not forcing it down your throat or suggesting you eat it every day. Chill out. Everything in moderation right? Macca's is delicious. Have you ever been hungover? And no, it's not pig fat in the ice creams or horse in the burgers.

My parents have always been heavily involved with Ronald McDonald House Charities, and for ten years they ran the Ronald McDonald House Charities Ball in Perth, raising over two million dollars for families with sick kids. The ball was always in November and it meant we got to spend a weekend at Crown Resort while my parents staged the event. It was just an excuse for my sisters and me to swim and order room service and basically get in the way as much as possible. My parents have always been great at throwing a party and this really translated well to the ball. They had performers from John Paul Young to Guy Sebastian to Courtney Act perform.

My parents have always run their McDonald's store like they were originally intended – as a family restaurant. On the weekends, Mum would go in with little vases and put flowers on the tables. She and Dad would walk around with the coffee pot talking to customers and welcoming them. They also turned the store into the world's first sport-ing-themed McDonald's. They had sporting memorabilia on the walls, a genuine Olympic torch in a glass case and a 1st, 2nd and 3rd podium people could take photos on in the corner (and this was *way* before camera phones).

Unfortunately, cockheads would go in and steal things, smash things, rip the memorabilia off the walls and throw it around the room. Even on a Saturday morning people would smash the vases. Not just the dickheads – families too. I would watch parents allow their kids to just throw the vases on the floor. I guess they think of McDonald's as a giant, international, faceless (not counting Ronald McDonald) corporation. They didn't realise that, at this McDonald's, there was a person – my mum – who had been at home preparing all the little vases to be just right. My parents are invested in the relationships their business has created, to the point of even attending the funerals of regular customers and buying wedding cakes for employees who are getting married. Every time I'm on tour and walk into a truck stop and see the tacky plastic flowers glued to the wall, I think, *You've got the right idea.*

My parents were among the first in Western Australia to install a McCafé. That was super cool and incredibly convenient because it was around that time that I started working there in my very first job; I was about fourteen. I was a barista and I thought I was beyond cool. I was the only boy working in the McCafé – I worked with a heap of older girls who I adored, Amy, Jillian, Kristen, all fabulous nineteen-year-old chicks, so I felt very sassy. (To be honest it was a little bit of a gay job, but you know, start as you mean to go on, I say.) My specialty was the Chocco Frappe, which was basically just Oreos, milk, ice and chocolate sauce. I don't think I'm giving away any industry secrets there – it's not like I'm giving you the recipe for the eleven secret herbs and spices. But, fuck, did I know how to frap that frappe.

It was a great job working at McDonald's, I doubt I'll ever have a job as hard as that again. Eight-hour shifts on your feet, serving people non-stop. And the public are arseholes to people who work in McDonald's. If you are reading this, please remember next time you go to McDonald's: don't be an arsehole to the people working there. Those people have been on their feet all day, they are hot and tired, and they probably smell of special sauce . . . They just want to serve you your burgers, so don't be a dick. I feel like people walk into Macca's (or any fast food chain for that matter) and lose all sense of decency, forgetting that the people behind the counter are people too. Also, you're not paying enough to get to be a dick at McDonald's. A fifty-cent cone is not currency enough to allow you to be a dick. If it was one of the nine-dollar Ben and Jerry's numbers with the waffle cone and optional sprinkles, that's fair enough, be a dick. But a fifty-cent cent cone does not come with dick tax. (Dick tax, by the way, would also be a great theme for an end-of-financial-year gay party, wouldn't it? Remind me for next year.)

McDonald's was the only job I've ever had outside of the media industry. I worked there until the day I turned eighteen, and then I got a job at a radio station, Nova. I had started doing stand-up, and I'd already had my moment in the spotlight on *Today Tonight*. They did a feature on me as 'Australia's youngest comedian' when I was seventeen, so clearly I had some serious industry pull.

In all honesty, my job at Nova came about because my parents know Gary Roberts, who is a wonderful man and the general manager of Nova in Perth. I had grown up listening to Nathan, Nat and Shaun, the breakfast show on Nova Perth. They are brilliant and very funny, so I was so excited when my dad told me that Nova would employ me as a Casanova the day I turned eighteen, (Gary knew I was eager for a job in the 'industry'. Maybe Dad convinced him I'd be a good employee when they were drunk on a holiday together.) A Casanova is one of those people who drive around in a Toyota Hilux branded with Nova signage and hand out free shit all day long. You may have even encountered a Casanova in your time, as they are all across Australia. For those reading this who aren't based in Australia, you probably think I've lost my mind. Anyway, Casanovas most notably hand out 'ice-cold cans of Coke' and stickers. I mean, that was a cool job. I was eighteen, I had my P-plates and I was working for one of the top commercial radio stations in town. I was the youngest Casanova by a long way – normally you had to be off your P-plates, but they made an exception for me.

But it was the other people I was working with that really blew eighteen-year-old Joel Creasey away. They were my first experience of people within the 'biz'. Sort of – it was still Perth. But they were the coolest people I'd ever come across. I mean, they were in promotions, so like most people in promotions (read: Red Bull girls, Gold Coast meter maids) they were really hot and suave and cosmopolitan. Well, they were to me. At that age, I thought Vodka Cruisers were cosmopolitan.

I went in on my first day and met Paul, the boss of the Casanovas, and *totally* walked past breakfast show hosts Nathan and Nat in the hallway and got completely starstruck. Paul explained to me how the job worked, gave me a red Nova shirt and then sent me off to hand out free shit. How hard was this job? Well, it wasn't hard at all. It was an incredibly sweet gig. I didn't even have to drive. Not because I didn't want to, but it turned out I actually wasn't allowed to drive the Hiluxes until I got off my P-plates. It was an insurance thing but I think this really shat the other Casanovas, because they had to drive my arse around for a year. I'd make up for it by navigating poorly and suggesting places we could stop for lunch.

Our day would involve arriving at the office, seeing what we had to give away, splitting it up and then jumping in the cars. The cars had a huge sound systems and we'd pull up outside a Westfield or a train station or wherever we thought might have good foot traffic, and cross in to the radio station with a bit of 'Hey! It's Joel from the Casanovas! We're down here at Westfield Carousel, we're giving away chocolate milks and newspapers today, come down and say hi! We'd love to see you!' Then we'd pop the boot, turn up the sound system and hand out our goods for half an hour. We'd do this four times a day. And that was it. We'd have two hours between crosses to get to our next location. We're talking Perth, where nowhere takes more than twenty minutes to reach. So we'd often shop, have a manicure . . . Once I was so hungover I took a pillow and had a sleep on the beach.

I was a Casanova for about two years, working there pretty much up until I moved to Melbourne and became a full-time stand-up comedian. I had my first real taste of how disgusting the media industry could be while I was working there. Most of the office staff were fantastic, but one programming director kept insisting I sounded 'too gay' on air and if I could sound 'less gay that would be really great. Companies don't want their product spruiked by a gay man.' Shame we didn't get sponsored to give out any ice-cold bottles of amyl. He left the station only a few months after I'd been there. I was so happy once he'd left. Not sure why he went, though. Hopefully he was so homophobic he decided he couldn't be around me much longer.

About a year after I started as a Casanova the sales department employed a new sales rep called Simon. A few of my fellow gays came rushing into the Casanova office to ask me if I'd checked out the new babe down the other end of the building. Straight away I found an excuse to go down to the sales department to check 'what promotions were coming up' and have a good perve. Simon was at least ten years older than me and had a long-term boyfriend, and I was immediately in love. I do adore a challenge.

A few months later I said yes to buying a $150 ticket to the Fashion+Aid charity ball because I found out Simon had bought one too and we'd be on the same table. I bought a new suit and thought it was a good idea to streak my hair with bleach for the occasion. You've already got a boner, haven't you? Bear in mind I'd never spoken more than two words to this guy. The night was a disaster – I got drunk and spilt wine on him. Not to mention my hair made me look like Ellen DeGeneres. I left Nova not long after this. Simon and I are totally still Facebook friends and I saw recently he is now engaged to the same partner. Yeah, yeah, good on ya . . .

I made some best friends for life at Nova. One in particular being my gorgeous friend Janine Booth. I met Janine on my second day at Nova. She looked like Barbie and I instantly thought, *Right, well, I bet she's a total mole!* but I could not have been more wrong. She was one of the warmest, most fabulous people I'd ever come across. Janine had gone to my sisters' school, Penrhos College, and she was two years older than me, and we just hit it off right away. We used to ask for all our shifts to be together and, seemingly overnight, we became essential in each other's lives.

One day, when I'd been working at Nova for about a year, we went out on a miserable, rainy day. Janine and I had terrible shit to give away (like *really* shit – we were giving away a 'stress brick', which was a stress ball shaped like a brick because we were doing a promotion for a home building company), so nobody was coming down.

We were standing in the rain, soaking wet. The only person who did come by abused us because we didn't have any 'chockie milk or a newspaper'. After about ten minutes we figured nobody back at the office would know if we threw in the towel early and we went to a café called Sienna's in Victoria Park. Sitting there, we had one of those 'Well, what do you want to do with your life?' moments. Janine said, 'I want to be a chef,' and I said, 'I want to be a stand-up comedian,' and in unison we both said, 'Let's do it!' And that was it. We just . . . well . . . did.

Within a month, Janine had moved to Miami to start studying at Le Cordon Bleu, the most famous cooking school in the world. You may have heard of Le Cordon Bleu in the Meryl Streep movie *Julie and Julia* – and, really, if you haven't seen the movie by now, you and I probably can't be friends. Seeing Janine's determination, a few months later I registered to take part in the Melbourne International Comedy Festival. Obviously we'll be talking more about that later because it's kinda a major plot point in my book, but Janine is doing so well now – she finished studying at Le Cordon Bleu, went on *Top Chef America*, made the finals, met one of the mentors on the show, fell in love with him and had a baby with him. Actually, writing it out, I think I'm a little jealous of her life. They've opened three restaurants in the States, one of which is consistently ranked as one of the top ten restaurants in Manhattan. She's killing it and she's still one of my dearest friends. I like to think that, in a way, Janine is still handing out ice-cold Cokes, just in really, *really* fancy glasses. And they're certainly not free.

I had done my first open mic gig about eight months before starting work at Nova, and the other Casanovas were really supportive, regularly attending my gigs and helping me fill the crowd. My rapidly growing experience behind the mic led to me MCing the half-time game at the NBL Basketball during Perth Wildcats home games (Nova were the radio sponsor). I loved going out in front of five thousand people at those games. And I loved getting to sit backstage with the Wildcats cheerleaders – all called names like Jade, Crystal and Celeste – even more.

I remember sitting backstage one night with my favourite cheerleader, Kourtney, who'd just finished a particularly fierce Janet Jackson routine. Curious as to where cheerleading might lead, I asked her, 'So what do you want to do with your life?'

She said, 'I just want to be famous.'

'Don't we all, babe?'

That's when I knew I had to leave Perth and take my stand-up more seriously. I didn't want to MC the half-time game forever. I wanted to *be* the game.

5

THE MAKINGS
OF A MONSTER

I decided I was going to be a stand-up comedian about halfway through Grade 12. The academic life was just not for me, plus studying algebra wasn't exactly going to help me as a stand-up comic . . . so, goodbye homework! Although I think the idea of becoming a comedian had been sitting in the back of my mind, dormant, for some time. As you've probably worked out, once I get an idea in my mind, I will usually execute it. The quality of execution has varied, however . . . like the time I decided I needed a fake tan before I went on my Grade 11 school camp. Think sassy Donald Trump on a budget . . . but with worse hair. But with stand-up I've been lucky that it's, well, sorta worked out all right. My sheer insecurities stop me from saying, 'Yep. I'm nailing it.'

Admittedly, I've always known I was funny. If someone asks me if I think I'm funny, I say yes. I never understand comedians who get asked that question and are unsure how to answer. Obviously you think you're funny if you're getting up on stage to tell jokes to an audience. Especially if you're expecting to be *paid*!

I've also always known I could use humour both as a weapon and as a defence mechanism. I realised from a young age that I could make adults laugh – definitely more than other kids around me could. Other kids could make adults laugh, but they were doing it in a 'kid' way. I could genuinely make them laugh the way their funny adult friends did, whether it was a spirited aside or a comment about someone we were walking past. Plus I knew the added shock of it coming out of a child's mouth would enhance the joke. I also understood delivery and timing, which are two of the most important ingredients in jokes and stand-up.

Essentially, I started my life in comedy as a prop comic (vomit). When my parents were having dinner parties, with Mum serving her signature creamed veal, I would put on a show as 'Magical Mafisto' – a magician who couldn't quite get it right. I had a briefcase of magic tricks, although I didn't know how to do any of them. But that didn't matter – they were all just vehicles for me to deliver my improvised comedy. I remember my parents and their friends falling around the dinner table, laughing. My delivery was perhaps not quite so refined and perhaps at times they were actually laughing at me and not with me. And perhaps they had polished off the equivalent of a Dan Murphy's stocktake sale (Mum's creamed veal wasn't for everyone).

None of that mattered, though, because the attention was still working out for me . . . it was well and truly past my bed time and they hadn't noticed.

In school productions I always wanted (ie demanded) to take the lead as the comedy character. As I would in drama class. Unlike most kids, who wanted to play the dramatic role and the over-the-top death scene, I was much happier providing the comic relief. If it involved being a fuddy-duddy old woman or wearing a wig, even better. Life is always better in a wig (that's the title of my next book, actually).

In Grade 7 for our school assembly item the drama class performed *Snow White*. I took the script away after school and completely rewrote it – notably my part. I modernised the story and changed the magic mirror to a magic TV, making myself the TV news anchor. I also painted all the sets by hand, using all the tips I'd picked up on the *Better Homes and Gardens* fan forum.

The performance slayed (that's a drag queen term for 'the show went really well'). And by this point I was already addicted to the drug that is the sound of laughter elicited from a live audience.

A year before, I'd auditioned and successfully won a part at North Lakes Children's Theatre. This was a co-curricular program for children in Grades 6 and 7. On Tuesday and Thursday afternoons we were allowed to leave school at lunch time and attend this special theatre group of thirteen students who had auditioned and been selected out of hundreds from the surrounding schools. Here we learned drama and advanced English – including language, pronunciation and diction – and would perform a two-week season of a show at the end of the year for school groups, family and friends. Attending North Lake Children's Theatre was the highlight of my week. Otherwise I'd sit in school staring out the window, bored out of my mind and wondering whether I should try a perm or not.

A man called Clyde Selby took the classes. He was a gentle but sharp older man who really helped shape my early performance life and taught me so much about stage-craft that I still use every time I step on stage. He was smart, funny and dry. A Dumbledore-esque figure, if you will.

My friend Ashleigh Prosser (a different Ashleigh to the one I've mentioned earlier), who also attended my primary school, had won a spot in the theatre group too and she and I adored going each Tuesday and Thursday and being allowed to accelerate our performance. We were involved in our school's drama program but it wasn't enough for us, we wanted to perform morning, noon and night – with other kids who took it as seriously as us.

I loved the end-of-year productions at the North Lake Children's Theatre. Each year the play was written by Mr Selby, and would always deal with topics like bullying, self-esteem and self-discovery. We would do hair and make-up and have a live audience every day and night. At first I thought it was purely an educational experience for the audience. But looking back, I realise it was as much a learning experience for us. It's only now I see that Mr Selby didn't just select necessarily the best actors for the program, he chose people who were perhaps a little different, and didn't always fit in with the Australian norm of a sports-focused, rough-and-tumble primary school. He chose kids who needed an escape and an outlet for their talents, to be with like-minded people.

Through the children's theatre I got a huge taste of the performance lifestyle – I was hooked and knew I had to be a performer. I just hadn't quite put my finger on what *kind* of performer. I thought I was going to be a very serious actor or a fuddy-duddy old woman in a wig. Unfortunately back then there weren't many roles going for a young, limp-wristed actor living in Perth. And Margaret Court has the fuddy-duddy old woman market cornered.

Clyde Selby also taught me a lot about modesty, like how to check your ego and never allow yourself to get consumed by your own self-importance, which is an important early lesson for performers – and humans in general, for that matter. It can be hard not to be consumed by yourself at times. After all, your product is yourself. My business is literally being Joel Creasey. I earn my money by playing Joel Creasey.

And finally, Mr Selby truly taught us the importance of books and reading. He would often pull particular students aside and recommend a book he knew would be perfect just for them. It's only writing this now that I realise how proud I am to write a book that could potentially take up a prestigious position on his bookshelf. (Note to self: offer Mr Selby 10% discount on book.)

I attended high school at Wesley College in South Perth, a prominent private boys' school that features alumni like Ben Cousins and Buddy Franklin. It always makes me laugh – on their Wikipedia page, under 'Notable alumni', it reads: Ben Cousins, Buddy Franklin . . . Joel Creasey. Hmm, pick the odd one out. (Not sure what you were thinking, but obviously it's Ben – Buddy and I still have careers.)

At high school I was part of the drama program but Wesley was so focused on sport that drama really took a back seat – I had to hustle to get anything out of the drama department at all. The class was held in a dilapidated old building at the back of the school and we went through about six teachers in my time as a student. Perhaps it was the lack of funding or perhaps it was the pressure placed on them by me. No other subject truly interested me the way drama did, so obviously I wanted my drama teachers to take it seriously.

In fact my first drama teacher was a Chris Lilley/ Mr G-type character who was so distraught by the way the school treated him that he wrote a rebellious note for us to take home to our parents, outlining how utterly shit the school was and urging them to pull us out and send us to another school. The day after he sent that letter home he was absent from class – in fact, I never saw him again. I like to imagine him being dragged, kicking and screaming, from the drama department yelling things like, 'I NEVER GOT TO TEACH THEM THE STANISLAVSKI METHOD!'

(Nerdy side note for all my drama peeps reading this: Stanislavski can get fucked. His 'methods' were ridiculous. Captain fucking Obvious.)

Midway through high school I decided that most of the teachers truly did not give a shit. Don't get me wrong, I had the odd gem of a teacher. Like Mrs Rafferty, my Grade 9 English teacher, who was utterly fabulous. She swore at us, cracked jokes, would heckle students if their English presentation wasn't interesting . . . She actually cared. At the end of the year, she took a few weeks off to have a breast reduction. Naturally, we threw her a Happy Breast Reduction Party the day before she left. She loved it.

Or Ms De San Miguel. She was my Political and Legal Studies teacher and always my favourite. I initially fell in love with her because she looked like a cross between Rikki-Lee Coulter from *Australian Idol* and Schapelle Corby. She was younger than most of our teachers and more on our wavelength and genuinely engaged her class, coming in each day with something new and interesting, even when it came to mind-numbing topics like the Australian Constitution. Tough read, let me tell you.

Looking back now, I can see she recognised I was gay the minute we met. And she became somewhat of a fabulous friend for me throughout high school – I'd go flouncing into her office whenever I had a problem: 'I just cannot seem to get the lighting right for our production of *Julius Caesar*!' We'd sit in her office and, over a couple of flat whites, chat, constantly getting off topic and gossiping about whatever was in the news.

Ms De San Miguel re-married and is now Mrs McGivern, but I call her Lynette. She has remained a close friend since I left high school and is a huge supporter, even staying with me when she visits Melbourne. I still bitch to her about lighting I'm unhappy with, too.

In a way, I thank my high school for being an uncomfortable fit for me because I learned an incredibly valuable lesson – create your own shit. If there's nothing for you to do, make something yourself. Make yourself an opportunity and then fill it. And that's exactly what I did. From about Grade 10 on, I decided that if most of these teachers didn't give a shit about me then I didn't give a shit about them. So I busied myself either putting on shows, competing on the school mock trial team or working as the editor-in-chief of the student newspaper.

Previously, the student paper had been a double-sided piece of paper quickly thrown together with a few of the sports results and a brief mention of academic results. It came out sporadically, twice a year if we were lucky – whenever whoever was in charge could give a fuck. When Grade 12 rolled around for me, I didn't ask any questions, I just took over. Under my reign (if you will), we upped the student paper to a glossy fifty-page colour magazine and rebranded it the *Wesley Inquirer*, complete with an agony aunt section and gossip column. If I could have squeezed in a few full page ads for Louis Vuitton or Rolex, I bloody would have! By the end of Grade 12, I was publishing a September issue à la *Vogue* with a completely black cover and 'WI' for *Wesley Inquirer* in gold. Sadly, none of my sub-editors backed me in changing the magazine's title to *Just Joel* but you can't win them all. It's not a coincidence that *The Devil Wears Prada* movie adaptation came out a year prior – I clearly took the wrong message from it. After the September issue was released, a note was passed around the staff saying, 'Once Joel Creasey graduates in a few months, let's cut down the size of the student paper . . . And definitely no more completely black covers, the school has run out of black print cartridges.'

Another area I immersed myself in was the Young Achievers program, a shit name for what is actually a pretty cool concept. Young Achievers is a national school-based small business program; the apprentice *The Apprentice*. You sign up to be part of the group at your school, start a small business, make a product, sell shares, sell the product, and at the end of the year split the profit among the shareholders.

I was of course the General Manager of Wesley's Young Achievers company. Now, I can't remember if I had to win that position or if, like the *Wesley Inquirer*, it was simply a matter of me telling everyone I was the boss, but I suspect it was the latter. Our company was called PsychYAdelic as you had to have 'YA' in your company title. The company name suggestion of 'Fuck YA' saw me fire my first employee. Our company sold novelty TV shirts and a few other boys and I took control, designing, sourcing printers and marketing our product. It was very *Project Runway Junior*. Across the year we presented our products at Young Achievers trade fairs, competing against other schools' companies. Naturally, I loved the competition. I roped in Mum and Dad to drive me in early and help me set up our stall and I would stay there all day, watching over the other boys in our group like a hawk – making sure there wasn't a second where they weren't making a potential sale. I was like *Undercover Boss* without the undercover part.

As a result, PsychYAdelic was the most profitable national company, both at the high school and also at university level.

Then I went on to compete in the Young Business Person of the Year competition, also run by Young Achievers, successfully becoming Western Australia's Young Business Person of the Year after presenting to a judging panel of prominent WA business people. I delivered a funny but informative presentation of our company (I knew I had comedy up my sleeve), and was flown to Sydney to compete nationally against each state's representative. Ultimately I lost to some chick from Canberra whose company sold buttons. Frankly, I've never lived it down. Selling fucking buttons. From fucking Canberra. Get. Fucked!

Of course I was Wesley's drama captain from about Grade 10. Technically you could only be the drama captain in Grade 12 but I somehow twisted the rules and (channelling my inner Meryl) became somewhat of an Iron Lady figure, having a reign that spanned longer than it should have. In 2007 the pinnacle of my time as drama captain was, the Grade 12 production. Although I'd been involved in other school productions, this year I didn't have any pesky seniors to rain on my parade. And you'd better believe that song was my anthem.

As much as I controlled the drama department, our drama teacher (number six by the time I was in Grade 12) got to choose the school musical. She chose *Charlie and the Chocolate Factory* and I was fuming. *Charlie and the Chocolate Factory*? Seriously? I was thinking more along the lines of *Madam Butterfly* or *War of the Roses*. How the fuck were we supposed to stage *Charlie and the Chocolate Factory*? And how would we do that creepy scene with all the grandparents in the same bed like some weird senior orgy? Not to mention Slugworth, who is without doubt a paedophile. Yeah, sure ... you're after the recipe for the Everlasting Gobstobber. If I had a dollar ...

Naturally I wanted the lead role of either Charlie or Willy Wonka. Our drama teacher took this moment to exact some revenge on me and cast me as Mike Teevee's father. The day the cast was revealed I was furious. I quietly excused myself from drama class, went to the bathroom and screamed at the top of my lungs into my school blazer. Think Diane Keaton in *First Wives Club* when she bashes the shit out of Marcia Gay-Harden – that level of crazy.

71

And as I said, the drama building was pretty run down, so the rest of the class *definitely* heard me.

For the first few weeks I turned my back on the production but when I saw there was no control and no direction, I couldn't help myself. 'Maybe you could go get us some coffees?' I said to the teacher as I turned to the rest of the class. 'Right, I'm back. Where do we begin?'

Luckily, given that I was also the editor-in-chief of the student paper, I gave the production tons of free advertising space. I also organised for PsychYAdelic to sell the merchandise in the foyer. I had a monopoly on that fucking school.

At this point I still had my heart set on acting, but as I discovered who I was, I also quickly realised that there aren't many roles for camp, limp-wristed sixteen-year-olds living in Perth. I'd watched stand-up for several years but I didn't understand until Grade 12 that I, too, could do that. And it wasn't until I sat up late one night on my laptop watching Joan Rivers YouTube clips that I recognised that that was me. Admittedly, I was never the class clown and I think boys in my year would have been surprised when I got into comedy. It wasn't so much that I wasn't funny at school, it was just that I had already decided that I had more to do in life than kick a footy on the oval each lunchtime, so I didn't really bother wasting jokes on my classmates. Most breaks I'd hang around with the staff, making them laugh. I'd love to target a particularly grouchy staff member. If I complained about a grumpy teacher, Mum would say to me, 'If anyone can crack them, you can!' And I always loved that challenge.

At the end of Grade 12, Ms De San Miguel, being the brilliant teacher she was, gave all the students in her Political and Legal Studies class a Mr Men book that matched our personality. I got *Mr Funny*. That was the confirmation I needed. If she thought it, then I definitely was. That day I went straight home from school and signed up to the RAW Comedy Competition.

The RAW Comedy Competition is a national stand-up contest run by the Melbourne International Comedy Festival. They hold heats in each major city, then semi-finals and a state final. The state finalists then head to Melbourne for the national final, where the winner gets crowned and sent to Edinburgh. It's like *Australian Idol*, if you will, minus Marcia Hines handing out irrelevant feedback. Remember that episode of *Idol* when Marcia said to a contestant 'Well done. You came out here . . . you sang. Well done'? Yeah, no shit, Marcia.

I signed up to RAW Comedy not knowing how to construct a stand-up set or really what I was doing at all. A few weeks later, I told my parents about the competition, as I was going to be needing them. Literally: the Perth heats were being held at the Charles Hotel in North Perth and as I was underage, I would need my parents to sign me in. How very fucking rock and roll!

In true Terry and Jenny Creasey style they invited about twenty mates along and 'made a night of it'. They were probably still pissed from a dinner party, to be fair. But still – no pressure. So less than three months after graduating high school, in early January of 2007 at seventeen years of age, I was backstage waiting to go on to perform stand-up comedy for the very first time. Little did I know it was to be my first of, oh, so very many . . .

When I first performed stand-up my set was actually a character (as cringey as that is to admit). I did a routine playing 'Glenn Suave', a Qantas flight attendant who was hellbent on taking over the world. Interestingly, I had performed this same character for my final Grade 12 drama examinations, which gave me one of the top scores in the state. Suck it, Willy Wonka. But this time, I repurposed Glenn and turned him into stand-up.

I promise you, I cannot remember a single line of that material. It's so awkward to think back on it that I've wiped it from memory, kind of like your first time having sex. There's a video of it somewhere (Glenn Suave – not my first time having sex) but I just cannot bring myself to watch it. I know I didn't quite commit to the character. Instead of dressing in a flight attendant's uniform, I dressed normally. Well, sort of: I wore torn jeans, white slip-on sneakers and a 'comical' shirt. (Mega cringe.) I thought this was edgy and urban and 'comedy'.

Side note: it really irks me when comedians walk on stage in a sloppy shirt or a hoodie. It shows a lack of effort and a lack of respect for your audience. Unless of course they're playing a character. A T-shirt and jeans is fine but at least *iron* the shirt! So often I hear comedians complaining about not getting ahead in the industry. I usually say, 'Buy a nice fucking shirt then!'

I can't remember much of that first night on stage. It was all such a blur. I just remember standing backstage at this dirty old pub. I don't think I was even nervous, I was so numb and blind with determination. Once again, much like my first time having sex.

But my RAW performance went well and I made it through to the semi-final. I think a lot of my success was based on my age, because I was extremely green – and probably the fact that half the audience were there to see me. I then made it to the state final at His Majesty's Theatre. This meant my third time ever performing stand-up was in front of a sold-out audience of fifteen hundred people. I didn't win – nor come close, to be fair – but I was hooked at that point and knew stand-up comedy was my calling.

A few days after making the state final of the RAW Comedy Competition, I sat in the car park of Curtin University, where I was studying Political Science and Foreign Affairs, knowing that I was destined for a life of fame and fortune. I'd done three gigs. I was basically Chris Rock. Now, you might be surprised to hear I was going to uni. I hadn't gotten the required mark for my first preference (Law), because I hadn't bothered to study. I only wrote Political Science and Foreign Affairs down on my university application because I was so in love with Ms De San Miguel and figured that if I couldn't be a stand-up comedian, I'd be cool like her.

Sitting there in the carpark, I couldn't stomach the idea of getting through another day of mind-numbing politics, so I rang Mum. I Meryl Streeped the shit out of it, put on the water works, begging her to let me drop out. I knew she wanted me to study and get a degree, but I also knew she wanted me to be happy and follow my heart (she, like Celine Dion, knew it would go on).

Mum said I could take a year off from uni and pretty much left it at that.

Sweet. Hollywood, here I come! I thought and hung up the phone, wiped away the tears and went to find best friend Ashleigh to help me celebrate with a coffee and a game of Wheel of Goon. Hollywood would have to wait until tomorrow.

And after I'd been doing stand-up for a few months, Mum never brought university up with me ever again. In fact, my parents have been nothing but supportive of my stand-up career, which I'm not sure every comedian can say, sadly. They've often been a little *too* supportive. They've flown all over the world to see me perform and, like a recently evicted *Bachelor* contestant, will accept any and every after-party invite they can get their hands on. Terry and Jenny Creasey: the ultimate groupies. They do genuinely just love

76

the lifestyle and being around other comedians. Every year during the Melbourne International Comedy Festival, my dad generously puts on a drinks function after my show one night and I invite a bunch of comedians along. Mum and Dad love holding court, surrounded by professional funny people. And they totally hold their own.

After making the RAW final, I did little open-mic gigs around Perth. I decided to drop the Glenn Suave character and started forming the early stages of the stand-up I do today: observational and pop-culture driven. My first paid gig was about a month after the RAW heat. I performed at the Charles Hotel, where the heats had been held. This was probably the first time I got nervous. That numb first-timer feeling had worn off and now I was getting paid! That's pressure! A lovely man called John McAllister runs the Comedy Lounge. John has always been a huge supporter of mine and handed me my first pay cheque. An actual cheque – that's how long ago it was. Fifty bucks for a five-minute spot. Mum told me I should keep the cheque and not cash it in. I told her I would and then immediately went down to the bank, cashed it in and spent it on a night out with friends. Now that I was a superstar I could only drink fancy cocktails, right?

For the record, in Perth, fifty bucks can buy you approximately one and a half fancy cocktails.

Not long after, I decided to take myself on a little stand-up tour of Australia. Hilarious, thinking about it! A stand-up tour! I only had fifteen minutes of material – if that! And by 'tour' I mean I did a couple of open-mic gigs in Melbourne and Sydney and stayed in backpacker joints. I think you're meant to earn money on a tour? I didn't. I spent money I'd saved up working at Nova on flights and trains across town to the shows and got paid in beers and laughs. As you can imagine, backpacking wasn't quite my thing, and I kept telling myself I had to get successful so I could be flown around the world. Or at least successful enough that I didn't have to share a bathroom with twenty German men. (Look, there's a joke there ... but it's too easy, surely.)

I accidentally double-booked myself for one of my gigs in Sydney. I called the lady booking the second gig to apologise and she screamed at me down the phone, saying, 'You'll never work in this town again!' I was mortified and felt so ashamed. I do sometimes wonder if she remembers this. I clearly do. I'll ask her, if she ever serves me at a Starbucks.

The following year, I competed again in the RAW Comedy Competition and made the final but didn't advance beyond that. In 2010, after working up enough material from two years of gigging wherever anybody would possibly have me, I applied to do my first show at the Melbourne International Comedy Festival. A lot of comics rough it the first year but I'm impatient. I'm like the Veruca Salt of comedy. I know what I want and I want it now ... or yesterday, in fact. I decided to go all out and make a huge impact.

The Makings of a Monster

I ended up saving up around fifteen thousand dollars by handing out ice-cold cans of Coke with Nova during the day and then squeezing in the odd shift at Macca's where I could at night (when I wasn't gigging). I also approached my dad's friends to sponsor me in exchange for a logo on my poster. I knew, having all been so supportive of me my entire life, they would've given me the money and not asked for a logo on the poster of a no-name comedian doing his first show at the Comedy Festival that nobody would attend. But PsychYAdelic had certainly taught me a thing or two – business was business and I proudly stuck the logos on my poster.

Using the money I'd saved up, I hired some friends to produce my show. Once again, most people self-produce their first year, but not me – I knew I didn't have the skills to maximise my debut outing on the national festival circuit. I even splurged on a publicist, a fabulous Melbourne PR expert whose business card I'd kept when I met her on my mini tour. I also spent money on advertising. I didn't realise that you kinda have to be known for advertising to work, but I also knew that it was important for perception within the industry.

I rented a tiny two-bedroom apartment in the city with my Perth friends Laura, Bonnie and Natalie. Nat and I shared a bed and Bonnie slept on a mattress in the lounge room.

My show was at a cocktail bar on Little Collins Street called the Kitten Club, which wasn't an official festival venue but I was stoked to be there due to its proximity to the centre of the festival. Every day around 4 pm we'd get huge pieces of chalk and draw arrows from the Melbourne Town Hall (the main hub of the comedy festival) to the venue: 'JOEL CREASEY'S SHOW THIS WAY'. It's a tactic I've seen so many new comics use since and it always makes me smile. I remember being on my hands and knees in the middle of Melbourne CBD with a piece of chalk, looking like a crazy person while people left work for the day. We handed out popcorn to the audience each night and the bartenders mixed a specially designed Joel Creasey cocktail.

The show was titled *Slumber Party* and was essentially all about celebrities. (See how much I've evolved?) At each show I would make the audience play Pass the Parcel and when the music stopped the audience member holding the parcel had to unwrap it to reveal a picture of a celebrity, like Christina Aguilera or Justin Timberlake, who I'd then tell a story about. For example: I once interviewed Christina Aguilera and was genuinely asked to not look her in the eyes during the interview. I asked her manager, 'Are you serious?' And her manager was like '*Yes!* Do *not* look her in the eyes!' I was like, what is she? The fucking basilisk from *Harry Potter*?

As for Justin Timberlake: I met him at a meet and greet when I was eighteen with about fifty other people. As I was leaving the room I realised I hadn't made much of an impression so I decided I should make a joke. I turned around and yelled, 'Justin! Justin! Just so you know . . . *I actually brought sexy back*!' Then I realised how lame the joke was, panicked and immediately exited the room. Essentially, I hit-and-ran Justin Timberlake with a shithouse joke he probably hears every day.

I did twenty-four shows of *Slumber Party* and sold maybe fifty tickets across the whole season. We would give away free tickets to anybody we could, because we knew it was more important to get people in to see the show and create some buzz. This meant my audiences were relatively full every night, even if I was haemorrhaging money like crazy (I guess it was good practice for future relationships). Plus it also meant you would have the odd night where you'd accidentally given all your free tickets to fifty Swedish backpackers who don't understand a word of English. That makes for a tricky show, albeit a very attractive one.

One day during the third week, a manager named Andrew Taylor came to see my show, bringing with him two of his clients: Jeff Green and one of my biggest comic idols, Fiona O'Loughlin. I knew Andrew was coming along to check out the show but had no idea about the other two.

During *Slumber Party* I would stand at the door to greet people, saying things like 'Welcome to my party' and handing them popcorn. Andrew, a very tall and imposing man, walked up the stairs to my little theatre. He looked just like you'd imagine a manager to look, so I knew it was him. Then I saw Jeff and Fiona enter the room behind him and I almost fainted. They were the last people to arrive and stood up the back of the full room (we made sure there wasn't a spare seat that night to leave a good impression) while I waited to walk on stage. I'll never forget that moment. Fiona didn't say anything but gave me a really reassuring smile and a cheeky wink and then I walked on stage to do my thing. I can still remember standing on stage and hearing Fiona's laugh. I was elated. Fiona O'Loughlin thought I was funny? Then I must be!

It was an awesome show, and the next day Andrew signed me to his books. I now had a fucking agent. I was a signed comedian – I could finally start saying things like 'You'll have to contact my agent'!

Andrew ended up being my manager for the next seven years and became one of my best friends.

Although I lost fifteen grand on that first comedy festival season, I gained a career. And a nomination for the 'Best Newcomer' award. The day I was nominated, my friend and producer Bonnie put on 'Defying Gravity' from *Wicked* and we ran around our apartment screaming and laughing.

At nineteen years old I was pretty stoked and it meant, with the help of Andrew and his agency, work started coming in.

A few months later I relocated to Melbourne at Andrew's insistence. He said, 'It's gotta be Melbourne or Sydney.' Given that I knew a little more about Melbourne – and that it seemed to have more musicals more frequently – I decided that had to be it. It's how I base most decisions, to be honest. I was nervous, however, as it meant moving away from all my friends and, of course, my family. I'd had a pretty sweet life at home, plus a great job at Nova, and now I was throwing it all to the wind to move to Melbourne and become a famous comedian. Scary shit.

I mean, that's something you hear Reese Witherspoon–type actors say in movies as they flee their small town, guitar in hand: 'I'm moving away to become famous!' It's not something anyone actually *did*. I never second-guessed my decision, though; I knew this had to be done. So in mid-2010 I packed my very limited belongings and off I went.

In Melbourne I started gigging solidly for little to no money. For that first two years I survived off the money I'd made selling my car in Perth and whatever money I could get from telling jokes. I spent a lot of time eating baked beans and recall putting on weight because I couldn't afford to eat healthy food. Healthy eating is fucking expensive, okay, Jamie Oliver? So go fucka your pukka tukka.

I also spent a lot of time taking long tram and train trips to suburbs and towns you've never heard of, performing in dingy pubs for people who had never heard of me. I've performed on stages that aren't stages. I've performed on pool tables, bales of hay and in the middle of a field at a rum distillery in far north Western Australia. And I've spent too much time convincing the person running the room that 'Yes, *I'm* the comedian!' A young, blond, gay kid isn't exactly your stereotype of an Australian comedian. I still say that to this day – I'm not what you picture when you think 'stand-up comedy'. I'm more what you picture when you think 'sassy retail assistant'.

In my first year signed to Andrew, he got me my first televised stand-up performance: on the Comedy Channel in *The Breast Darn Show in Town*, which was a comedy gala raising funds for breast cancer. I wore a blue leather jacket and unloaded about three cans of hairspray in my hair. It really is a sight to behold. But I'll never forget that gig because I was finally on TV. The clip is still floating around YouTube somewhere.

My second year at the comedy festival I performed a show called *Political Animal*. My management suggested I try to veer away from the celebrity-based stuff to show I could do more than that, plus it would highlight my interest in politics. The show wasn't great, however – I definitely had 'second-album syndrome'. If I were Lady Gaga – this was my *Artpop*. The show was poorly researched because my heart wasn't in it and the venue I played in Melbourne was a thirty-seat room in the Forum Theatre, which, outside of the festival, they use for storage. I was essentially the Harry Potter of comedy. The room had such terrible ventilation, an audience member even fainted one night. Another night someone in the second row spent the entire show farting, gassing everyone behind him (admittedly the audience was so small there were only about four people).

After that show I swore I would stick to my guns and not let anyone try to influence how I should perform stand-up. To Andrew's credit, he agreed.

I really felt like I had set myself back with that show and halted the momentum from my first, very successful, year at the festival. So, in 2012, I decided to go all out with my third show. Andrew had also managed to secure me a venue in the Melbourne Town Hall, the official hub of the Melbourne International Comedy Festival. I knew I wanted to make a splash and titled my show *Naked*. The poster featured me, completely nude, with a sign saying 'Naked' covering my junk. You know, subtle. Sex sells, right? At that point I didn't care why people were coming along . . . I just needed an audience to show them what I could do. I knew word of mouth was my most powerful tool at this point.

I went back to my strength and focused the show on myself and pop culture. It featured one of my favourite stories, which I still tell in stand-up shows to this day, about the time I went to the Celine Dion concert in Las Vegas.

So I might as well tell you here, right?

The night I went to the Celine concert (on a $345 ticket by the way) Celine decided to dedicate 'My Heart Will Go On' to an audience member. A special fan. At that ticket price, we're clearly all special fans, Celine. Anyway, instead of performing 'My Heart Will Go On' with the full, epic, *Titanic*-esque staging, she sang it *a cappella* and stood beside the audience member. But because I was seated in the balcony, I couldn't see her. And the fan was so overwhelmed by Celine's gesture that he screamed the entire time, thus drowning out Celine's voice. It was a gay man's Vietnam.

I was furious. The only reason anybody goes to see Celine Dion is to hear 'My Heart Will Go On'. And she knows it too, that's why she does it at the end of the concert. If she sang it at the start people would get up and walk out after it, leaving Celine on her own in her six-thousand–seat Celine Dion-atorium.

This story might seem trivial, but I managed to mine that experience for gold ... and got a fifteen-minute stand-up set out of it that I still regularly perform.

Going back to irreverent, celebrity-focused stand-up worked. My show sold out every night and it was the first time I was making money out of performing a festival show, albeit not a lot. But I was no longer eating baked beans morning, noon and night. Now I was throwing the odd bit of parmesan cheese on top. This show also toured to Adelaide, Sydney and Perth. I finally felt like I was a performer and could officially call myself a full-time professional comedian.

That show also got TV producers interested in me. The second 'sold out' stickers start appearing beside your name, the more people want tickets. Off the back of *Naked* I was offered my very first stand-up special on ABC2. It was filmed in a warehouse in Fitzroy, aired on the ABC and released as a DVD. With three shows now up my sleeve, I performed a 'best of'. Celine Dion of course made the cut. As someone who doesn't get particularly nervous, I was shitting myself (that's an industry term) for the taping of the DVD. The enormity of the situation had set in. Never before had I had a crew of twenty or so working on something solely for me. I remember being on stage for the first fifteen minutes of the special and telling myself to just concentrate on my breathing and to *slow the fuck down.*

I was so elated after the taping. People sent me champagne and flowers to celebrate. I was on a high. But soon after I came off stage, the guy I was dating cracked the shits and told me he was bored and hungry and that the night had been 'too much about you'. I apologised to my management and said I was going to go home with him. I bought him McDonald's (he had no money) and then stood in the rain, arms full of flowers and champagne, trying to hail a cab while he stood under the shelter eating his Macca's. It was such a come down from the glamour of taping my first stand-up special. And I'm so annoyed with myself that, while I'm so confident and self-assured in the rest of my life, I used to be so weak with guys. I should've told him to shove a cheeseburger (that he'd paid for himself) up his arse and fuck off. Unfortunately, instead I apologised to him for it taking so long to hail a cab then sat in silence the entire way home. I didn't even have the balls to tell him when we got home that the second cheeseburger was meant to be for me.

By the middle of 2013 I was off and racing, making regular appearances on panel shows, radio shows and TV shows. I had a good year that year, gigging solidly. I backed it up with another well-received stand-up show the following year,

The Drama Captain – all about my time as the führer of my high school drama department – and appeared at my first Melbourne International Comedy Festival Gala. At the end of 2013 I was offered my first regular TV gig on the show *A League of Their Own*, which was an Australian version of a hit show hosted by James Corden that is still on air in the UK. It's a comedy program where sports stars and comedians answer sports-themed quiz questions and compete in stunts. Our show was hosted by Tommy Little (who had moved up through the comedy ranks at the same time as me) and featured Pat Cash and Eamon Sullivan, whose team I was on. My job was to be the comic relief to the sports stars and to basically fuck up every challenge. As someone who had shunned sport in school (minus my early successes in the pool and on the tennis court) and was picked last in every PE class, it was quite hilarious that I was now working with Australian sporting legends on a daily basis.

The show was filmed at Fox Studios in Sydney and it was my first experience of the glamour of television. I was being chauffeured around set, had my own 'star trailer' and felt fucking rock and roll. By the way, in reality, those 'star trailers' are not remotely sexy. They're like being in your grandparents' caravan: it's hot, dingy, moves every time you move, and reeks of toilet detergent.

On the show, I went from being plunged into ice baths and cycling around velodromes, to having the shit beaten out of me by two female wrestlers, all the while trying to make the audience laugh. I'm not sure if Eamon Sullivan got the memo that I was meant to be incompetent at all the games, as he was always furious with me when I was the reason our team lost – once he forced me to stay in the ice bath longer than I had to. I totally know what those people on the *Titanic* went through. At least they got to hear Celine Dion's 'My Heart Will Go On' uninterrupted (she was there, right?).

Unfortunately the show 'took it up the arse' in the ratings, as we say in the biz (and occasionally other professions) – it completely flopped. But I seemed to come out of the show unscathed and it had still raised my profile and meant more offers came in.

It also meant I started to get recognised on a more frequent basis, including my first time being recognised overseas! It happened in New York. And it was after I woke up next to a guy after an incredibly big (read: blotto/wasted/smashed/drunk) night. He rolled over and said, 'Good morning! I thought you were really funny on that show *A League of Their Own*.' I thought, *Fuck, that's creepy. Is this guy a stalker?* So, trying to act calm, I said, 'Oh . . . did it air on TV over here?' And he said, 'No. You made me watch two episodes before we went to bed last night.'

Shit.

In 2014 I was playing a venue at the Melbourne International Comedy Festival where I could make decent money. That year's show was called *Rock God* and it was all about trying to desperately get famous and working with Joan Rivers (whom I had begun working with that year). My tour was now clocking up around sixty stops nation-wide and we had such a successful season, I ended up adding shows everywhere we went. It was a simple show, but Janelle Koenig, my writing and business partner, and I had worked out a successful format for my stand-up shows: Just make them laugh and stick to what you know. So many comedians do beautiful shows about their life and their troubles. They tell stories that'll really challenge the way you think about and view things. Some comedians do shows that are very politically minded and share a deep message. I know my limitations. I can't do any of these things. I always say to my audience, 'You're not going to leave my shows having learned something. If anything, you'll probably leave dumber . . . but we are going to have a laugh.'

That year I also made my first appearance on *The Great Debate*, a comedy debate that aired on Channel Ten as part of the comedy festival and that I had adored growing up. I was teamed with Tom Gleeson and my now dear friend Fiona O'Loughlin. The topic was 'It's Good to Fake It' and we were the affirmative team. I ended my debate with shirt-less dancers and drag queens – obviously! That appearance also meant I was cementing my position in the industry. I used to watch all the comedy festival specials growing up – now I was on them!

The Makings of a Monster

Off the back of my *Rock God* season I continued to film TV shows and tour. It also meant I had money to spend for the first time in my life. At the end of that year I signed on to appear on *I'm a Celebrity . . . Get Me Out of Here!* – don't worry, that shit is getting a chapter of its own – which led to me being asked to host the after-show, *I'm a Celebrity . . . Get Me Out of Here Now!* the following year, as you'll read about too.

When I returned from hosting the after-show, I went straight into a new tour titled *The Crown Prince*. I had launched the tour before I'd left for Africa, so I knew it worked. I really enjoyed the hour I had on stage each night with my audience because I was doing what I loved and controlling the outcome. I could be myself again.

I began partying each night after the show. I never drink before a show because it's the most important, sacred hour of my day, but, foolishly, I was going out each night post-show for the validation. I think I subconsciously wanted people to recognise me and praise me because I felt like my career had completely fallen apart after that second trip to Africa. Partying so hard also meant that by the time the Sunday show rolled around I was performing on autopilot, my brain completely fried.

To be fair, a lot of comedians party after their shows, I just hadn't up to that point. It's such a trap – we're already performing in bars and pubs. And truth be told, alcohol is an incredibly effective way to manage that adrenalin buzz that lingers long after you walk off stage. I don't know many performers who can finish a gig and go straight to bed.

I feel so privileged to get to do what I do. For a while I was stumbling through, accepting anything that came my way and rolling with the punches. Now that I've realised it's a job, and it's become my life, I can focus a lot more. Of course, the thrill of anybody actually wanting to buy a ticket to see me talk has never worn off and will never get old. Stand-up has been my therapy and my way of dealing with the shit life throws at me. Whether it's a personal or professional problem, I've always managed to laugh through it and tell the story to my audience, no matter how frivolous. I hold nothing back. People who have been coming to my shows for years know everything about me. When people say to me, 'I feel so silly saying this but I feel like I know you,' I always say, 'It's not silly, you actually do!'

And as I arrive to perform each night and see people lining up to see me, I genuinely beam and have to pinch myself. I remember chalking the pavement in Melbourne for my first show, praying that it might entice even one paying customer to come. It's not lost on me that some people haven't just paid for the ticket to my show; they've paid for parking, a babysitter, time off work, dinner before-hand and, in some cases, flights and accommodation. That is why I strive to never phone in a performance or not give my best, because I have been that person in the audience so many times growing up, admiring the people on the stage and thinking, *Fuck, I wish I could do that! They are* so *lucky!* And now that I get to do it, I will never take it for granted. Even writing this just made me stop and think, *Fuck, I can't wait to get on stage tonight!* Also, *Must iron a shirt.* If you're going to pay me to tell you stories from my life, and about my silly little problems, and the different celebrities I've encountered – if you're going to *pay* me to do that? – well, I am going to give you my all every single time.

It truly is the weirdest job on the planet. People often ask me if it's terrifying. I know that, after actual death, public speaking is most people's greatest fear. I always say that stand-up for me is like going to an office job that I love. The stage is my office and that is where I work.

On the flipside, there are people who say I have the easiest job in the world. Well, in some ways that's true. I get to do what I love and make people laugh for a living. But often it's because they think as comedians we only work sixty to ninety minutes a night. Or if we're playing a comedy club, a mere twenty minutes. What people don't see is the time and effort behind the curtains. I am constantly writing material and testing that material. Or I'm recording radio or TV interviews, or filming spots on TV shows, sometimes a year before they actually go to air, and filming pilots that never even *make* it to air. I'm forever going to auditions and often waiting for a phone call that never comes. I also do corporate gigs for companies at charity lunches and awards nights. I do private gigs for people and events. I maintain my own social media. I have endorsements and sponsorship deals.

But I love it all. Every single last bit of it. It's pretty fucking fabulous.

6

COMING OUT

People love to ask gay people 'When did you come out?' or 'When did you know you were gay?' or 'Should I buy this dress?' The answer to the latter is usually 'No, Jessica, your mother should have told you about horizontal stripes in kindergarten.'

I guess I've always known I was gay. There was never really any question. In my stand-up I say I knew when I was four years old, when my mum sang me 'Mary Had a Little Lamb'. I stopped her and said, 'Do you know anything from *Chicago*?' And also, 'You're a little bit pitchy.' Or when I was three and I decided the Tellytubbies were a little too butch. Or when I was a baby and Mum tried breastfeeding me and I said, 'Let's just be friends.'

Or perhaps it was when I was eight and would cry at the end of *101 Dalmatians*. Not when the puppies were finally reunited with their owners – when Cruella de Vil *didn't win*. I used to bawl my eyes out. I was so upset she wasn't going to get the beautiful puppy coat. Eight-year-old Joel was like, 'Fuck the puppies! Give Glenn Close the fur!'

I also say on stage that I told my parents I was gay when I was eighteen: I sat them down and told them, and they said, 'Cool. We're having pasta for dinner.'

To which I said, 'I don't think you heard me. I said I'm *gay*! I can't eat fucking carbohydrates any more!'

In reality, it's far more complex than that. But that's the general essence, and I was pretty lucky in that respect. But I do want you to know that not every coming out is a horror story. (Although admittedly it would've made for much juicier reading – fuck you for being so reasonable and cool, Mum and Dad!)

I started questioning my sexuality when I was in primary school. While I had crushes on plenty of girls, they weren't necessarily romantic crushes, they were more the early stages of my complete and utter adoration of women. As I write in Chapter 13, 'Women Who Inspire Me', I have always loved women. I've *idolised* them. And I think I confused early crushes on girls in primary school with just thinking women are fucking fabulous. It truly bugs me when people say, 'Oh, you just love women because you're gay. That's a gay thing.' I don't think that's necessarily true, I just think I've been lucky (or #blessed) to grow up with really positive female role models in my life, from my mum and my grandma, to my sisters, teachers and friends. And Sandra Sully, obviously.

I knew I liked the fellas in primary school, but didn't know the word for it till I was in about Grade 6. That's when

96

Coming Out

I started to hear the word 'gay' being used in a derogatory way. Up until then I'd only ever heard the word in Enid Blyton books. (By the way, what was Enid smoking when she wrote that shit? Saucepan Man? Dame Wash-a-lot? Girl, you're smoking too much weed. I knew it was a magic faraway tree, I just didn't know it was a marijuana tree.)

The word 'gay' never really bugged me. When people said it, I started subconsciously connecting the dots and thought, 'Oh, they're talking about me.' But I have always relished being different; I couldn't think of a bigger snub than being considered 'normal' or 'average'. I've always thought of being gay as being special, something that differentiates me from the pack. I get to be part of an exclusive club full of very cool people. I mean, come on – how many shit gay people have you met? Not many, right? Milo Yiannopoulos being a major exception.

I was about thirteen when I first acknowledged to myself that I was gay. I remember thinking, *Wow, that's big – this time last week I was thinking about Mario Kart and Sara-Marie's bum dance.* And then I thought, *I'm going to park that and come back to it in a few weeks.* And sure enough, a few weeks later I tackled it again – and I more or less shrugged my shoulders and went, *Well, that's settled then. I'm gay.*

I'm incredibly lucky to never have had that internal struggle that so many gay men have. Some have it their whole life and can't quite come to grips with it. It's sadly not surprising that the suicide rate is four times higher in LGBTIQ people than in the general population.

On my very first day of Grade 8 I met a boy called James Hodgins. I knew instantly that he was part of the club too. While we didn't tell each other for a few years, it was an unspoken acknowledgement. I've never asked James, but I think he felt the same way about being gay as I did: it was never a problem, just something that we had to work out. It was just a fact, like being right handed, or figuring out what you want for dinner – you know you want something, but it's not until your stomach is rumbling with anticipation and that particular something is rapidly approaching that you work it out. Gosh, what a metaphor.

James was important in my life because we operated on the same wavelength. Like me, he loved women, and we laughed our entire way through high school, talking about all our female teachers. Making up fake storylines about their lives, discussing what they'd wear each day, what we thought they got up to in their private lives. To us, they were our own personal versions of the Real Housewives – the Real Teachers of Wesley College.

At the same time I was exploring my sexuality online – thank God I'm Generation Y. I would google things about being gay. 'What is gay?' I'd type and up would pop images of Ellen and Elton John. I'm pretty sure if you google 'What is gay?' now, a selection of my headshots will appear. I had to resort to the internet back then because there was no education about it in school. None whatsoever. In fact, I don't believe there is much more now.

Coming Out

Even in sexual education we never learned anything about gay sex. I think that is abhorrent and that the education system has a lot to answer for. I can count at least twenty gay men in my year alone, many of whom I've kissed since leaving school . . . and that's not even including the teachers. For a private boys' school, that is insanity. But it is one of the many areas in which I think my very expensive high school let its community down.

As well as googling, I would trawl the internet and start chatting to random gay men in chat rooms. Nothing seedy, just kinda getting a grasp on the situation. Are chat rooms even a thing any more? Actually, is chatting even a thing any more? It's all been reduced to swiping left or right these days, hasn't it?

I don't actually remember the first boy I kissed – it was all a bit of a blur. But I have no doubt James was the first boy I kissed that actually meant something more than 'I've seen people do this in the movies so I guess that is what we're supposed to do'. When I kissed James, it was the first time I thought, *Wow, kissing boys is actually awesome.*

Outside of James, the first person I told I was gay wasn't my best friend Ashleigh. It was my friend Dani Du Plessis. Some girls are just born fag hags. And I don't mean the phrase 'fag hag' in a derogatory way. Some people take offence to being called it, but I mean it as a total compliment. If the terms 'fruit fly' or 'queer peer' make you feel more comfortable, well, you can use them instead. But some fag hags truly understand the plight of gay men. Something within them knows how hard coming out is and they provide an outlet for us to say those words that seem so hard to say out loud for the first time: 'I'm gay'. I told Dani after too many Bacardi Breezers at a New Year's Eve party in the summer holiday break between Grades 11 and 12. She said something really sensitive and compassionate along the lines of, 'Duh, dickhead!' Which seemed to be the most common reaction, truth be told.

Why weren't people shocked and outraged? I had glamorous dreams of running away for two weeks and when people found me, I'd be singing 'It's a Hard Knock Life' in an orphanage run by Anthony Warlow and/or Irene from *Home and Away*!

Speaking of musicals, it was no surprise that, in the year after we graduated, Dani and I would save up money to take trips to Melbourne and Sydney to see musicals like *Chicago*, *The Rocky Horror Picture Show* and the ultimate gay musical, *Wicked*, which we once saw twice in the same day. Dani would then happily wing-woman for me at gay bars, covering for me with our nosier friends while I kissed boys. We would go out and say I was a famous comedian. I had done maybe four stand-up gigs in my entire life by this point. Start as you mean to go on, eh?

Coming Out

A major part of my growing up and coming out occurred in the summer just after I'd graduated high school. I was seventeen and, like most people that age, unsure as to what I was going to do and where I was going in life. I was meant to be starting a Political Science and Foreign Affairs degree at Curtin University. I had also registered to compete in an open-mic competition in a few weeks' time so, just like the 2002 cinematic flop starring Britney Spears, it's safe to say I was at a crossroads. Become the Foreign Affairs Minister or tell dick jokes for the rest of your life? Choices!

As soon as we'd graduated, Ashleigh had flown overseas to work with her brother Heath Ledger, who was an outrageously talented and famous actor. I had met Heath many times over the years, since Ashleigh was not only my best friend, but also my neighbour. I had watched his career boom completely wide-eyed and in awe. But I was also inspired, knowing that if one Perth boy could make it in Hollywood, then so could I.

Before Ashleigh flew overseas, Heath had spent Christmas at home. Ashleigh and I (along with our other good friend Matt) were basically living in the granny flat at the back of her house at this point. We called the apartment JAM (Joel, Ash, Matt) and it became our sanctuary to be ourselves. Heath would often come up to say hi late at night when he was having a smoke. Ashleigh, Matt and I would hurry to hide our goon bags or Vodka Cruisers when we heard footsteps coming up the stairs. We were always relieved when we saw it was Heath and not Ashleigh's parents.

After Ashleigh headed off to the States, I spent the summer partying with Matt and other mates and working at my parents' McDonald's. One morning, shortly after I woke up at a friend's house with a splitting headache – we'd spent the night playing drinking games (I still cannot face pear vodka) – I rolled over to check my phone to see a hundred or so missed calls. Heath had passed away in the night and nobody could get in touch with Ashleigh. My family, friends and Ashleigh's family were all contacting me to tell me the devastating news and also to ask if I'd heard from her.

Everything that happened after that is a bit of a blur, to be honest, but I remember Matt came to pick me up and take me to Ashleigh's family home which was only three doors down from my parents' place. When we arrived, media crews were already camped out the front.

Ashleigh's mother, Sally, whom I'd known and adored my entire life, was utterly distraught. I remember giving her a hug and not even being able to comprehend what was going on. I also felt terrible, thinking I might be reeking of alcohol and how inconsiderate that was; I hadn't had a chance to shower. All I remember was saying to Ashleigh's family, 'If you want me to fly over to be with Ashleigh, I will.'

Then I left and went to meet the rest of our friends. We sat around the TV watching the news unfold on the news, all feeling numb and unsure of what to do. By then I had spoken with Ashleigh briefly and she was getting on a plane from Vancouver where the film shoot was to fly down to LA and, we thought, home to Perth. My friend Emma cooked us spaghetti bolognese and the combination of the news with the pear vodka from the night before became too much and I threw up all over her bathroom before someone drove me home and I got into bed.

Later that night I got a knock on my bedroom door from my mum, who said, 'I need to talk to you. Ashleigh's family want you to go to LA with them.'

I immediately agreed without having a chance to truly process the enormity of the situation and twenty-four hours later I was being escorted onto the tarmac of Perth Airport, up a security tunnel and directly onto the plane. A customs officer came aboard and processed our passports on the plane. We didn't see any other passengers.

Although I was extremely close with the family and Ashleigh's mum Sally is without doubt my second mother, it all felt a bit odd as I wasn't a blood relative and I had zero experience dealing with grief. Even now I'm pretty terrible at it and avoid it as a rule. I don't watch sad movies for that reason. Apart from *Beaches*, of course – you don't get your gay badge unless you've seen that. All I knew was that I had to be a strong and loving presence. And, of course, do my job as Ashleigh's best friend and Sally's second son.

Twenty hours later we were in LA, being escorted out of the airport by dozens of security guards as paparazzi surrounded us. We sat quietly in the SUVs as we drove through the streets of California on an uncharacteristically gloomy day to the Beverly Hills Hotel, where Ashleigh was waiting for us. I'd been to LA with family several years earlier but that was an entirely different experience: in a Winnebago with my parents and sisters, screaming our heads off at each other as we bitched and fought our entire way to the Grand Canyon.

We met Ashleigh in the foyer and she and I went up to our room together. Forty-eight hours earlier we'd been living our lives. Ashleigh was at work; I was sculling pear vodka. Situation normal. Suddenly I was standing in a luxurious Hollywood hotel suite with my best friend whose brother, an internationally adored actor, had tragically died.

Ashleigh and I did the only thing we could do. We looked at each other – and burst out laughing. It was manic. We fell over ourselves. We had no other way to deal with the situation, it felt completely crazy. We just laughed and laughed and laughed. There were possibly tears, who knows? But we just couldn't believe what was happening and where we were standing.

I think laughter has always been my coping mechanism in times of shock. Or any situation, really. I find it far easier to laugh than be serious. And Ashleigh is much the same, which is why we've been such close friends all these years. It sounds so clichéd but laughter really is the best medicine. Well, laughter and Xanax.

The week that followed was tough and surreal. My job was to distract Ashleigh from what was going on by taking her around town and seeing sights. We got a private tour of Disneyland, were chauffeured to dinners and went to fancy parties. It was meant to be the Hollywood trip you dream of, but it was a nightmare, like somebody had drained all the colour out and we were watching a black and white movie. All the while, though, Ashleigh and I coped in the only way we knew how – with humour. We still laugh telling the story about how one night we returned home to our glamorous hotel and decided to play a game of knock and run along all the hotel doors on our level. Who knows which celebrities we disturbed?

The truth is, I was unsure whether to include this story about Ashleigh and LA in my book as it's not my story to tell. But it's important I tell you my part in it because I left Perth a boy and returned from that ten-day trip absolutely a man. I was suddenly thrust into the most grown-up environment under the most tragic and heartbreaking circumstances and I had no choice but to man up or crumble. I also had to really step up to support my beautiful, lifelong friend, who had never wavered in her support of me and for whom I'd do anything.

I also want to tell this story in the chapter about my coming out because (and I know this is now getting beyond cliché) it was when I first saw the musical *Wicked*. Seeing it with Dani wasn't my first time. Growing up, I had always adored *The Wizard of Oz* and would watch it obsessively as a child. I'd always loved witches and adored the fabulous, over-the-top acting of the Wicked Witch of the West. Give that woman a fucking Oscar. I know it was years ago. And she's dead now. But, my God, that was a brilliant performance.

Muriel, my grandma on my father's side, always told me she was a witch when I was younger and instead of being horrified I was delighted. We used to play witches in her caravan for hours when I was growing up. I loved it. Although I don't know many witches who have fallen on hard times and resorted to living in a caravan.

But despite my love of *The Wizard of Oz*, I had never heard of *Wicked*. It was playing in LA when we were there for Heath's funeral and I kept seeing posters and flyers for the show everywhere around town. I still don't know why I said it but I remember turning to Ashleigh one day and saying, 'We should go and see that.'

She said, 'Yeah, we could.'

Thinking it would take our minds off things, I really put the pressure on and said, 'Let's do it. I really think we should.' We had been assigned a personal assistant of sorts to help us out with plans, so Ashleigh inquired if we could get tickets. The show was sold out but we managed to score three house seats and a few nights later, Ashleigh, her other sister Olivia and I were off to see it, completely unsure of what to expect.

By the end of the first act we were gobsmacked and by the end of the show we were in tears. I think we had so many emotions building up that we didn't know how to release and the show was the perfect vehicle to help us get them out. It just seemed like the appropriate time. *Wicked* finally cracked us open. Because *Wicked* is all about being ostracised for being different but accepting who you are and loving yourself and your own skin, no matter the colour.

Coming Out

Although, as I said, I was always comfortable with my sexuality and was never bullied to the extreme, watching *Wicked* was exactly the boost I needed to come out.

And just as it's stereotypical to love pop music or soft furnishings, watching 'Defying Gravity' sung live in LA, in the circumstances we were in, beside the little girl I met on my first day of primary school (and one of the true loves of my life), who had just lost her brother, was the moment I knew we weren't the little kids, best friends and neighbours from Applecross any more. The two best friends who would scoot down to primary school each day. The same Ashleigh and Joel who got busted for opening a lemonade stand outside the local IGA one weekend and thus infringing on their business and breaking several laws. We were still Ashleigh and Joel, but we were now grown-ups. Furthermore, I was exactly who I wanted to be. And now I had to show people.

Once we'd returned to Australia it took a while for things to go back to normal. It truly was a strange time. I still think of Heath all the time, and remember the unfillable hole he left in the hearts of those who knew and loved him, not to mention in the entertainment industry.

I told the rest of my close group of friends that I was gay at a party I had at my parents' place while they were away. There's nothing like a game of Wheel of Goon to bring out the truth; I'm not sure why the Federal Police haven't adopted this system over the lie detector. It'd certainly be cheaper. I can't even remember how it happened, but an argument had broken out and, in an attempt to regain the spotlight, I announced I was gay. Probably before performing an excerpt of 'Defying Gravity' and having Ashleigh lift me above her head as if I were flying. It was about midnight and phone calls were made to other friends insisting that they had to get out of bed and come over because 'this is a really big moment for Joel'. We ended up having a meeting where everybody told me, 'Yeah. We knew.'

Ashleigh was upset I hadn't told her first and very sweetly said, 'You know I would have looked after you.'

I replied kindly, 'Way to make this moment about you, Ashleigh!' But she was right.

And she got her own back several years later when I was one of the last people she told she was a lesbian. Well played, bitch. I guess that explained why she loved Bunnings so much. No one is *that* keen on a sausage sizzle.

Once I was eighteen I started to attend gay clubs in Perth. 'Attend' is possibly the wrong word – it's not exactly maths class or community service. Until then, I truly hadn't known much about gay men or the world of gays. My knowledge was James, *Wicked* . . . and the gay couple on *The Block* in 2004.

I never did do the wild thing of getting a fake ID. It truly never crossed my mind. My first experience of a gay club was the Court Hotel in Northbridge. I was dropped off there after a friend's birthday party one night to meet Dani. We drank Malibu and lemonades and danced all night. I was a little intimidated, though, and definitely stuck to one corner of the club. I was also not very sexually adventurous in my early years of clubbing and being gay. (Don't worry – I've certainly made up for lost time.)

Eventually, James and I found ourselves frequenting Connections Nightclub, which is the biggest gay nightclubs in Perth and one of the oldest in Australia. At first I found it all slightly overwhelming but we quickly found our way around the club and formed our own little clique. I also always loved the drag shows and to this day can be found at the front of any stage cheering along as a man in a wig mimes to 'I'm Every Woman' or having a heated conversation about the latest episode of *RuPaul's Drag Race* while gesticulating with a vodka soda. However, it wasn't long before I moved to Melbourne so I never really established myself in the Perth 'scene'.

I met my now best friend Thomas (Ashleigh aside) soon after moving to Melbourne. He was dating a friend of mine whom I knew through the comedy scene, but when they broke up I told Thomas he could move in with me while he found his feet. Thomas was and still is one of the most spectacular human beings I have ever met. He's only a few years older than me but is someone who has clearly known who he is since day one. He is gloriously, unashamedly camp, loud and brash, and has a heart of gold. He is a mad fan of the royal family and has Queen Elizabeth II tattooed on his arm. He also occasionally performs drag as his alter ego, Rhonda Butchmore, and once a month with two other friends he dresses as an old lady to run Granny Bingo, a gay bingo night that has become a cult hit.

Thomas taught me absolutely everything I know about the gay world. These days, with gay culture becoming more and more mainstream and accepted (which is fabulous), the younger generations of gays don't realise what our community has been through and the battles the older gay generations fought on our behalf. Thomas put those words in my mouth. He is immersed in the gay culture and scene of Melbourne and I am thrilled that he welcomed me into the fold, teaching me about everything from the Stonewall riots, to the first Sydney Gay and Lesbian Mardi Gras, to why Miss Candy is the best drag queen in Melbourne.

It's Thomas who made me realise how lucky I am to be gay. I get to be part of such a brilliant community that you just don't get elsewhere. I get to attend gay bake-offs, lesbian mud wrestling, drag bingo, gay camping festivals (like, actual camping with tents and stuff – not just a weekend of limp-wrist workshops), protest marches and the only clubs that still book *Australian Idol* contestants. And at the centre of every single one of these events is the huge heart of the gay community, a friendly, loving and just plain fucking fun place to be. And you'll probably always find Thomas out the back with the smokers, Carlton Draught in hand.

Thomas knows every detail of my personal life inti-mately. He is the person I text when I've woken up at a stranger's house and he is always the person to counsel me through a break-up. Thomas's opinion certainly carries a lot of weight in my life. When I was a contestant on *I'm a Celebrity . . . Get Me Out of Here!* it was Thomas and Ashleigh who ran my social media, taking it in turns every night to watch the show and tweet along.

But the gay community isn't without its flaws and I feel my generation of gay men (I make us sound like an iPhone) has contributed to problems in the community in a big way. Body-shaming in the gay community is at an all-time high with the rise of apps like Instagram and Grindr. Don't get me wrong – I love Instagram and Grindr. I love social media in general and I hate hearing older people attacking it. I always say, 'That's fine, don't use it. You keep calling your cabs. I'll get an Uber (Black, prefer-ably).' But it's almost as if every young gay man feels like they have to be a product, and your social status is only as high as your follower numbers. Every gay man has to be ripped with washboard abs or they're just not consid-ered cool. I know a clique of gay guys in Melbourne who wouldn't be caught dead associating with anyone without these features. And it feels as if you can't meet a man at a club any more because they have already checked your Instagram and judged you.

There's a disgusting saying in the gay community: 'No fems, no fats'. It means: 'No feminine gay guys and nobody remotely out of shape'. Guys will put this on their profile but can you imagine saying this to someone's face?

Last year someone took a photo of me getting undressed at my gym, then uploaded it to their Facebook page and gay men wrote comments underneath like, 'Wow, that's disappointing, I thought he'd have a better body than that.' But I'm probably preaching to the converted by telling you this story. I doubt people who write this shit would be picking up a book – or can read.

I have scoliosis, which means I have a twisted spine. My ribs stick out at the front and my body is completely uneven and looks quite odd. I feel totally uncomfortable taking my shirt off in public. And the thought of taking my shirt off in front of a room full of gays? Mortifying.

I think we are so much better than this, but I'm certainly not innocent of some of this behaviour. I've dated guys only for their looks, or judged somebody before I've gotten a chance to get to know them. But I really worry that we are losing the best part about our community – our empathy and heart. Who cares if you don't go to the gym every day? Who cares if you don't have a social media presence? Who gives a shit if you are feminine, limp-wristed and so camp-as-fuck your lisp could open the Chamber of Secrets? The toughest man I know is Thomas. He is also the campest man I know.

I always feel very honoured and flattered when people message me saying they watch my stand-up to make them feel like being gay is fabulous and something not to be ashamed of. I do get asked for advice for young people struggling to come out. I often get asked by the people themselves. I always start by saying I am absolutely not a role model, in any way shape or form. I don't sell myself as a role model; I am a performer and comedian who tells frivolous jokes about celebrities. I don't live my life in the healthiest, most Gwyneth Paltrow-y, GOOP-y way I can.

So my advice to anyone grappling with their sexuality is always this: Coming out is the best feeling in the world. In most cases that feeling will be instant, but not always. Judge your situation and the people around you. If you're living in a city then you're probably going to be all right. Gays – we're everywhere. We're like BPs or Ubers. If you're living more rurally where being gay might not be common-place, then get out, even if only for a weekend. Maybe not now, but make a plan and do it. Find your tribe! The best part about being an adult is getting to surround yourself with people you want to be with. It ain't school – if some-one's a fuckhead, get away from said fuckhead. Find people who will make you snort-laugh, who will drink cocktails with you till six in the morning, who will be on your doorstep the second you need them. Find those people and live your fucking life . . . and don't let anyone or anything tell you who or what you should be. Find your Ashleighs and Thomases.

And in the meantime, if you're struggling and you can't get out, you're still living at home, you're stuck in a dead-end job, *make the plan*. But find an ally. In every tiny town or workplace there will always be one. It's 2017. Hint: It's probably the lady wearing the most jewellery. Find that person and get it off your chest. Say the words 'I'm gay' out loud to them. You'll feel better.

And then get to Melbourne, find me on the dancefloor at Poof Doof and let's have a drink. I'll probably pash you.

Because if I could choose, I would choose to be gay every time. Hands down.

And if you can read the final sentence of this chapter again but finish with your best Elphaba-from-*Wicked*-at-the-end-of-'Defying-Gravity' 'Ah-ah-ah-Aaaah!', that'd be even better . . . and gayer!

7

WHEN IT ALL GOES WRONG

Comedians absolutely love talking about their worst gigs. (To be honest we reaaallly love talking about other comics' bad gigs. That's our *favourite*.) Bad gigs are something we love talking about backstage, it's something we love talking about in interviews, it's something we love writing about. I'm not sure why. Perhaps it's because a bad gig is so excruciating that the only way of dealing with it is by laughing. At least we can if the bloody audience doesn't! Imagine it, standing in front of a room of people and trying to make them laugh . . . and they don't. Normally when people say the phrase 'it's the stuff nightmares are made of' they're exaggerating. But comedians aren't. One of the most famous fears in the world is public failure. And a bad stand-up gig is public failure of epic proportions.

Often the worst gigs aren't because of hecklers. A lot of people assume this but, to be honest, in this day of modern stand-up comedy, hecklers aren't such a big thing. I think stand-up has really evolved through television and YouTube, and audiences are far more savvy than they used to be. I will say some comics are more partial to hecklers than others. Some even actively encourage them. But I don't think I've ever really had hecklers at my solo shows, probably because my audiences are always so attractive, and classy, and intelligent. (Oh, for Christ's sake – what am I trying to win you over for? You've already bought the fucking book.) I also talk extremely fast on stage – so it's hard for a heckler to even find an opening.

Don't get me wrong. I don't mind the odd heckle. And I've certainly had my share. Sometimes it's been dumb shit like 'Faggot!', which is just the most stupid insult and sets you up for such an easy come-back. 'Yes, thank you, I *know*! You're just stating the facts! Everyone knows that – it would be like if you walked out on stage and I heckled you by calling out, *"Cunt!"* – we *know*!' Zing! Saucer of milk for table Joel Creasey!

But I do think we learn more from our worst gigs than our best gigs. Joan Rivers even told me about a few horror gigs she'd had. And now whenever I'm having a particularly tough gig, I tell myself, 'This could've happened to Joan Rivers too.'

Often a bad gig is your fault – your timing might be off, or you may have made a bad judgement call on a joke early on and gotten the audience offside. Sometimes a bad gig can be the audience's fault. But all too often, a bad gig can be the event organiser's fault – sometimes a booking is badly matched to the comic and they just don't like *you*. (Let's just say I won't get invited to perform at Margaret Court's Christmas do.) Just recently, after performing stand-up at a travel agents' awards evening to a crowd who were far more interested in drinking than listening to me talk, I had the following conversation with the event organiser post-gig.

Them: Would you like to stay for a drink?

Me: I would genuinely rather stab myself in the face.

Always the consummate professional.

One of my worst gigs was the latter – event organisation crisis. I think sometimes people think you can just grab a microphone and start performing stand-up wherever, like a musician. But you can't, there's a science to comedy; people need to be seated, engaged, there needs to be a mic, a stage. At this horror gig, I was twenty years old and my dad had got me booked to perform at the Duxton Hotel's staff Christmas party. This is what is called a 'corporate gig'. The fee is a lot higher at a corporate gig, but that's because there's a lot more room for error and a hell of a lot more pressure. At a comedy club people are expecting and *wanting* to hear comedy. At a corporate . . . well, they usually just want to drink and possibly fingerbang a receptionist.

The hotel had hired staff from another hotel to run the place for the night so that the entire Duxton staff could attend the party and get fucking loose. They used the hotel ballroom as the function space and they really went all out. Sadly, my own yearly staff Christmas party usually involves me alone on the couch necking a bottle of red wine sans glass and heckling Rhonda Burchmore and Marina Prior on *Carols by Candlelight*.

Back to the hotel gig – I know what you're thinking . . . what could possibly go wrong? An extremely inexperienced comedian performing stand-up to five hundred drunk hotel staff at Christmas? A lot, as it turns out.

I rocked up with Ashleigh for my sound check in the afternoon while they were still setting up the room. I immediately noticed there was no stage – and it didn't look like they were constructing one either. Problem number one. The organiser said, 'Well, you can perform in the middle of the dance floor.' Only being visible to a quarter of the room is not ideal for stand-up. Look, it's fine for *Jesus Christ Superstar – Arena Spectacular*, not fine for twenty-year-old Joel Creasey. A lot of stand-up requires a connection with the audience, and being able to make eye contact with people really does help.

But I didn't have the confidence then to back myself as the expert and say, 'No, look, it'll work better with a stage.' So I instead thought to myself, *Okay, I'll make it work, I'll keep turning so everyone can see me, I'll just. Make. It. Work.*

Problem number two: the microphone didn't work. The sound guy said, 'Don't worry, it will work for the gig.' But this was a cheap microphone, and you can always tell a cheap microphone: if it's really light, that's the giveaway. If it feels like a SingStar microphone, it's probably not going to be great for stand-up or vocals or any kind of performance that requires a *decent fucking microphone*. But the guy said again, 'Seriously. Don't worry, it will be fixed by the time you come back.' So I thought, *Okay*. As I said, I couldn't and didn't want to argue, as I was also only twenty and it was one of my first corporate gigs and I was getting paid fifteen hundred dollars, which for me at that time was amazing money. (Janelle, who has done all the edits on this book, read that bit back and said, 'Is fifteen hundred dollars not amazing money to you any more, arsehole?' Just to be clear – yes, it is. That's three thousand Macca's cones!)

So after my rehearsal I went across the road with Ashleigh to grab something to eat and wait for the gig. I was due to perform at 6.15 pm, which I thought was a little early for stand-up, given that the event itself started at six. But once again I was young, so I didn't think too much of it.

All the hotel staff were waiting eagerly in the foyer when they opened the ballroom at 6.05 pm. They all flooded in, full of excitement, very busy saying hi and grabbing drinks and telling each other, 'Oh my God, Trish! You look amazing!' (Obviously they weren't used to seeing each other out of their hotel uniforms.) To be fair, Trish did look great. I could tell immediately there was going to be a bit of frisky Christmas party action behind the bain-maries later that night. (Side note: I once hooked up with someone at a Christmas party in a bush. Never behind a bain-marie.)

No one was even close to sitting at their tables when I was due to go on, and the room was big, a proper ballroom.

119

At 6.15 pm on the dot, though, the hotel CEO – who was clearly a stickler for punctuality despite opening the doors five fucking minutes late (probably from years and years of experience refusing people complimentary late check-outs) – wanted to get started with the entertainment portion of the evening. So he jumped on the mic – which, surprise, surprise, had not been fixed – and said, 'Ladies and gentlemen, please welcome to the stage comedian Joel Creasey.'

First of all, nobody knew who the fuck 'comedian Joel Creasey' was. Second of all, no one could hear the CEO thanks to the microphone, which might as well have been a carrot or a shoe. And third of all, nobody was even sitting down in a style suitable for being a receptive audience for a live comedy performance.

Not to fucking mention the balloons ... (Sorry, having some serious PTSD here.) What they'd done, between me going in for my sound check and the guests arriving for the event, was fill the ceiling above the dance floor with helium balloons. Normally that would be fine, except for the fact that attached to each of those helium balloons was a length of ribbon. Long, curly ribbon that hung from the bottom of each balloon to about the height of my knee. So on top of the fact that no one knew I was performing and they couldn't hear me – they couldn't see me either as I was literally enshrouded by a jungle of fucking multi-coloured ribbons. Seriously, all you could see was my feet. It felt like that scene from *Finding Nemo* when Marlin and

Dory are trapped in the school of jellyfish – only this was more painful.

The only person watching me was the CEO and he was glaring at me through the ribbons. He also happened to be the person who was paying me, so at least *he* got to enjoy the show.

I didn't know what to do. I was eyeballing Ashleigh up at the back of the room and she was just staring back at me, wide-eyed. I started panicking, and in that panic I decided the best thing to do was to start bagging the hotel. I started going on about the hotel next door and how much better it was than this one, thinking that would be a good way to get a rise out of people. That didn't work. The staff clearly did not give a shit – there were free drinks to be consumed (or they agreed).

So then I decided it would be a good idea to just start screaming at the top of my lungs, thinking that might make people pay attention, but I didn't really think it through beyond that. I just started screaming and when they did turn around, I panicked, dropped the microphone, grabbed Ashleigh's hand – and ran! So all any of the staff at the Duxton Hotel saw at their 2010 Christmas party was the feet of a young gay boy as he screamed his head off in a thick sea of helium balloon ribbons and scampered out of the room. I've had similar sex dreams.

To be honest, no, it wasn't a great gig, but I've never been paid faster before or since. And it's taught me to demand a strict no-balloon policy in my live performance contracts and to always – *always* – wear good shoes on stage. Just in case they're the only things the audience can see.

What might pleasantly surprise some people to learn is that I've never really experienced a great deal of homophobia on the road as a touring stand-up comedian. I mean, yes, it has happened, I've had the odd gay heckle, or someone has posted online saying they're uncomfortable with me being gay, all the standard stuff. 'Go die, faggot', all those really impeccably crafted, Shakespeare-esque slurs. They don't faze me though. To quote my favourite drag queen, Jinkx Monsoon: it's really just water off a duck's back.

But never on the road has it been particularly bad. I mean, obviously I was once literally chased out of a town by homophobes, so maybe that took up my own personal quota of homophobia for the next fifty (thousand) years.

Sorry, what? You got chased out of a town by homophobes?

Yep. Totes did. But I'll get to that in the next chapter.

First let me tell you about the strange, thinly veiled but quite malicious homophobia I experienced to my face from a man in a small rural town. That sounds like fun . . . right?

I was on tour with the Melbourne International Comedy Festival Roadshow, which is a really awesome gig for comedians. It's a mini gala that tours to over one hundred cities and towns across Australia each year. They pick five top comedians who have performed at the festival that year – one MC and four comedians, a mix of up and comers and comedy legends. The cast changes depending on the comedians' availability, and there are often multiple casts touring different states at the same time. I did my first roadshow when I was nineteen and toured with the show for the next couple of years. Being part of the roadshow was an absolute career highlight. I got to experience towns in Australia you've never even heard of. Not only that, but I got to perform in them. As an avid fan of vanilla slice, it also really helped me review the entire vanilla slice spectrum Australia has to offer. Yackandandah is my pick of the bunch.

In 2013, the roadshow ended up in a teeny tiny town in rural New South Wales, very much a farming community. We stayed at the one motel in town and the venue we were performing in was a shearing shed. Someone rocked up on horseback. Another person arrived on a tractor. One guy even turned up on a ride-on lawnmower fuelled by casual racism and Carlton Draught . . . this is how regional we're talking.

I do like performing in odd venues, I've performed in burlesque bars, in rum distilleries, on stages where the lighting has been provided by construction lights, in tents, on beaches. After a couple of drinks, I've performed unrequested at every single nightclub I've ever attended.

On that tour I was the headline comedian and during the day I was asked to go and do an interview at the local radio station. Our tour manager, the gorgeous Katie Minchin, took me to meet a local businessman, an older guy with grey hair, who locked up shop, went next door and grabbed a pair of keys, then walked me down the street to a small shed which happened to be . . . the radio station. He unlocked the place, flicked on the fluorescent lights and then turned the radio station *on* for the day. Which means if you happened to be listening to the local channel that day, apart from my five-minute interview, all you would have been listening to was static. I like to imagine people sitting in their cars . . . waiting . . . wishing . . . for anything to be broadcast.

Katie and I were standing around casually preparing for the interview. It was all very relaxed and, to be honest, I was already thinking about the nap I was going to take later that day, post-vanilla slice. But then just before the interview began, the businessman/radio broadcaster/possibly local mayor and headmaster said to me, 'Now, I hope there won't be the same nonsense we had last year.'

The roadshow had being going to this town for a couple of years, but I had no idea what he was talking about so I asked, 'What do you mean?'

'Well, look, a few people were a bit upset about the topics discussed on stage last year.'

I said, 'Oh, okay . . .' having no idea who had been on the tour the year before. As he was talking and going about setting up I started to google the tour from the year before to see if it might come up. 'Well, what were the topics discussed?' I asked, thinking it might have been something really horrible or inappropriate. I know my limits when performing for a country town, I'm not going to give them my most graphic material. Perhaps one of the previous year's comics had. In a way, I started to empathise with him as it does bug me when a comic doesn't know their audience.

The old man said, 'It was one of the female comedians.'

That's when I got the first red flag that this wasn't going to end well, but I took the bait and asked what she had been talking about.

He said, 'Well, she was talking about her –' and he got really uncomfortable '– lifestyle.'

I said 'Sorry, what?' but by then Google had downloaded (thanks, country internet), and I saw that he was talking about DeAnne Smith, a brilliant comedian from Canada who just so happens to be a lesbian.

This guy continued, 'Yeah, you know, lifestyles ... people around here aren't really comfortable with that kind of strange, you know, weird behaviour. We had a council meeting afterwards and we decided we aren't comfortable with it.' Then he disappeared back into the studio to start setting up in there and begin the interview.

At this point I turned to Katie, speechless. She looked equally shocked but immediately said, 'Look, Joel, you don't have to do this interview if you don't want to, we can call it off, you don't have to be anywhere near this guy at all, he's disgusting.'

And yes, I did feel gross, as well as a little embarrassed. I felt extremely nervous because I was the headline comic and it was pretty clear I was gay. I don't think this guy had worked it out yet because obviously he was one of the dumbest of fucks to ever exist. But the audience there in the shearing shed were sure going to work it out pretty quick smart. Y'know, when I started talking about having sex with men ... (Pro tip: that's a good way of telling if someone is gay. Also a Grindr account is a bit of a giveaway, too.)

Thinking again of the desperate farming community waiting for its five-minute daily broadcast, I decided I would go in and do the interview. And it was very uncomfortable, because he eventually clicked that I was gay – probably when I spent five minutes talking about Bette Midler being a major influence in my life.

I left the interview and Katie said, 'Don't worry, I'm going to get to the bottom of this.'

I went back to my room for that nap I had totally forgotten about.

Before the gig that night, Katie said, 'So guess what? I spoke to that man's wife ...' God, I love regional towns, 'and she is furious with him. He's not allowed to attend the show tonight and he wants to call you to apologise.'

'*What?*'

'The wife also said that the council never had a meeting to discuss the show, no one complained, no one was uncomfortable, only him. In fact they all loved the show last year. Hence why they've asked us back. Anyway, they're really sorry and they really want to personally apologise to you.'

I didn't need to receive a personal apology, I just wanted to do the gig. So I declined. Plus confrontation makes me uncomfortable. Unless it's a *Real Housewives*-style scenario and I have a glass of French champagne to throw.

I rocked up to the gig that night and it was wonderful. The Country Women's Association had made us a delicious curry and a cheesecake, the gig was brilliant and afterwards they even gave us these quirky hand-crafted metal statues of the Melbourne International Comedy Festival logo, which were very nice but not something you could have taken in your carry-on luggage because they definitely would have been classified as weapons.

As I was leaving the gig and people were getting on their horses and their tractors, the guy from the radio station approached me and shook my hand and said, 'You were brilliant,' and scurried off into the night.

Here's a horror gig that is a bit more tricky and one of those hard-to-navigate nights. I was performing at the Adelaide Fringe Festival. It was a Wednesday night of the festival, which is always dubbed by performers 'Suicide Wednesday'. This is because we don't generally perform on Monday nights, Tuesday nights are at 'Tight Arse Tuesday' prices so you usually get good crowds and Thursday through to Sunday are considered the weekend. But Wednesdays ... *oof.* Now, I really can't complain, I still had a pretty good audience and I felt bad whining to another comedian earlier in the day that I only had a couple of hundred people in that night. He told me he was cancelling his show because he literally hadn't sold any tickets. Whoops. Admittedly, I'd possibly have preferred a cancelled show that night to what happened.

I rocked up to the venue at about nine for my 9.30 pm show. Dave Hughes was up before me so I listened to the end of his show, which sounded great as usual. At the Adelaide Fringe Festival you perform in big circus tents, properly fancy ones, though, with air-conditioning, no carnies and comfy seats that don't smell of circus pony shit. Dave finished his show and his audience cleared. I saw Dave briefly backstage but we didn't shake hands. He had gastro the entire week so we had to stay a safe distance from each other. Gosh, I hope he doesn't mind me putting that in my book . . .

My tour assistant and I went into the venue to do a quick sound check before heading backstage (and to sanitise the microphone Dave had been holding). The stage manager said to me, 'We're just going to be setting up some sound and light equipment for another show while you're on stage tonight.'

I wasn't thrilled by that thought given the only thing separating myself and backstage was a curtain, so the audience and I would hear everything through it. But I also didn't want to seem like any sort of diva, so I said, 'Oh. Okay.'

Then the stage manager said, 'And we've got a few people with wheelchairs in tonight so we're just reconfiguring the chair layout to make some space.'

This didn't register as anything new to me as we have people in wheelchairs at the show most nights and I make a point of always trying to work in venues that are wheelchair accessible.

I headed backstage and had my pre-show ritual of a long black (coffee – what were you thinking?) and got ready for the show. All was pretty smooth sailing. I walked onstage and looked out at the audience. Within a few seconds of starting, though, I heard some moaning and yelling to my left and looked down to see a group of people in wheelchairs who were both physically and intellectually disabled. Normally when someone is making noise in your audience you can immediately address it, get a laugh and move on. This, however, really was the exception to the rule. I am absolutely thrilled when people of all abilities come to my shows, but there is no way you can really address disabled people making noise and make it funny or appropriate. Your only option is just to ignore the noise.

As the group got progressively louder, I continued with the show but I couldn't really leave too many pauses otherwise the yelling would get louder. So I upped my performance levels by about twenty per cent and pressed on, under the pump a little, a slight sweat starting to break out across my forehead. (I'm not usually much of a 'sweater'.)

Soon, though, I spotted a girl holding her phone in her lap but with her camera pointed towards me. I kept looking down and checking and seeing it not move, and she wasn't smiling. I then started wondering why she was filming. Or worse – who she was filming for. I'm the sort of person who always thinks he has some grand enemy out to get him. Plus, given that I talk shit about a lot of people in my stand-up shows, I really don't like people filming. Also ... *why*? I never get people who go to concerts and film the whole thing. Just enjoy the show. Live in the moment, man!

I started having an internal debate over what to do. I decided she might eventually stop, so I pressed on with the show. I was already incredibly distracted so couldn't spend too much time focusing on the girl, I had to dedicate my brain juice to performing. I was getting sweatier. Twenty minutes in, however, she hadn't put the phone down. I thought she might've just been trying to get a little footage for Instagram or something, but that wasn't the case. I eventually stopped the whole show and asked her why she was filming. She quickly minimised the video camera screen and said, 'I'm not, look,' and turned her phone around. But I wasn't going to physically grab her phone and go through the videos, there's nothing funny about that. Also it was a fucking Samsung – who knows how to operate that shit?

I had no option but to carry on and hope that one of the venue ushers would've seen me flag the situation and go and speak to her. The second I launched into another story,

I saw her phone facing me again, filming, the venue ushers nowhere to be seen. And there was still the noise coming from the audience members on the left of the stage.

I started to feel a little stressed. And that's when I heard a huge crash from backstage. I immediately turned, as I thought someone was about to run up on the stage and tackle me. This has happened to me before and it's really scary, so that's always my first thought. It turned out it was one of the venue technicians setting up backstage for the circus show bumping in in a few days' time.

I started to get frustrated. I was already up against it on stage, now I had a show setting up and making noise behind me. We were paying for that venue for that one hour of the day . . . why couldn't they wait for me to finish?

It was a seriously tough show. But you cannot stop. There is no point at which you can stop and ask yourself how best to deal with the situation at hand. I wanted to be respectful of the people in the wheelchairs, meanwhile I really wanted the girl to stop filming and I also wanted to turn around and scream at the people backstage. You have to keep going, keep smiling, keep delivering material and split your brain in half – half working out what to do with the situation and half keeping yourself on track and processing the words coming out your mouth. Plus I wanted to give the paying audience a great show, the show that they deserved.

I normally float off stage in a great mood, having had the best time. That night I walked off and, the second I hit the wings, I stormed back to my dressing room, so annoyed that although the show had gone fine, I couldn't make it reach the heights of a normal show – that audience didn't get my proper performance. I got backstage to find my stuff had been moved by the circus troupe and they were all back there rehearsing. It was now 11 pm. They didn't open till the following week.

I went to leave the venue but the circus troupe were moving huge set pieces around backstage. I ended up snapping at one of them and saying, 'Can I please just get the fuck out of my venue first?' before hailing the first taxi I could see, going home and eating an entire tub of ice cream.

The show I performed was *Poser*, which was nominated for a Helpmann Award that year for Best Comedy Performance. I'm guessing the secret judging panel weren't there that night.

8

GAYCRASHERS

So yes, arguably the worst gig of my life was when I was run out of a small country town by thirty angry homophobes. How's *that* for the best heckle you've ever heard? Just to be clear, I wasn't literally 'run' out, I was chased and then I got into a car and drove away. Running wasn't an option – I'm not a savage – plus I was in the wrong shoes.

I was once again on the Melbourne International Comedy Festival Roadshow. This was the 2011 tour, I was twenty and had been on road for about six weeks. I was feeling pretty good. I was learning that stand-up was a bit like tennis – you've got to be match fit and it's always better if you're wearing all white. After six weeks of touring and gigging every night with the roadshow or a month of gigs at the comedy festival, you feel pretty indestructible on stage. Your timing is a lot more in tune and you can catalogue your material in your head faster.

We had ended up in regional Victoria. We'd done Warrnambool, Aireys Inlet and Bendigo, you know, all of the rock and roll comedy capitals of regional Victoria, and we eventually arrived in the town of Colac.

Aaah, Colac, Colac, Colac . . .

First of all, 'Colac' isn't a particularly enticing name for a town – sounds like a throat infection, or an STD. In fact, I'm fairly sure I got a pretty bad case of Colac after sleeping with a closeted engineer at an airport hotel recently. The town is about a two-hour drive west of Melbourne. And it's built on a lake called . . . wait for it . . . Lake Colac. The lake itself is, sorry to be blunt, a total shithole. I think it's completely fine to call it that because I'm fairly sure the promotional pamphlet at the local visitors' centre calls it that too. Well, it was either that or 'gorgeous tourist attraction, great for couples and families'. Look, it was a few years ago, I can't remember everything.

We discovered, upon arriving in Colac, that we were performing in a cinema because the theatre in Colac was being renovated. It seemed that everywhere we went on that particular tour we were never playing in the actual theatre because apparently most of the old theatres in these country towns have quite severe asbestos problems, which is fun. Gives it a bit of character, right? Plus nothing makes your audience enjoy the thrill of live performance more than the threat of asbestosis! This could be your last laugh guys . . . so make it count!

Gaycrashers

Actually, in Warrnambool we played the local high school and nobody thought to warn us that half the crowd was deaf. When I saw the interpreter on stage I just thought it was a wildly gesticulating woman who'd gotten lost on the way to the bathroom.

Physically finding the exact cinema we were performing at in Colac was quite tricky as there were about six in the complex. I found that out the hard way when I walked in the wrong door and ended up blocking the projector that was showing *Mr Popper's Penguins*. You better believe my CV has me listed as starring in that film. It's technically not lying. I did. It was just in one very specific screening of it.

On this particular leg of the tour I was third in the line-up. In stand-up, third is always considered a pretty prime position. It means you're on after the interval, so the audience have had time to get in the groove, then have a little break and now they're refreshed and ready for you. They're well lubricated, if you will. But you also don't have the pressure of closing the show.

I went on stage and had quite a good gig, although I did accidentally refer to Colac as Warrnambool. As I said, I'd been on the road for about six weeks and it was my total Britney Spears moment. Do you know that Britney Spears famously gets the town she's performing in wrong, like, nine times out of ten? I remember going to see her *Circus* tour in Perth, which was a complete atrocity, but I feel like that's what you're paying for when you go to see Britney. No one wants to see lucid, coherent Britney – I want to see

2007-style, broken down, bald, infant-behind-the-wheel, fanny-flashing, nutso Britney. Anyway, she walked out on stage and said, 'Hello, Sacramento! How's it going?' And I remember leaping to my feet elated thinking, *This is going to be a good night!*

My Britney moment didn't go down *as* well in Colac. But I managed to win them back and it was a very pleasant gig.

Every night after the roadshow gigs we'd stand in the foyer and pose for photos and sign merchandise, which I actually quite enjoyed doing. As I'm sure you've ascertained already, I've been practising my autograph since I was old enough to hold a pen. If I ever get to sign this book for you – let me assure you the pleasure is all mine, and don't worry, I'll be carrying a Sharpie. Actually, only very recently, at a fan's request I signed someone's arm, not knowing she would return to my show the following night having had my messy scrawl tattooed forever onto her skin. If I'd known she was going to do that I would have taken a bit more care. The tattoo looked like the signature of a serial killer . . . or a doctor. Or a serial killer doctor. Embarrassing.

On that particular tour I was with musical comedy duo Die Roten Punkte, Daniel Townes, Greg Fleet and Anne Edmonds. Greg, Anne and I would normally group together and make each other laugh while we said hello to people and thanked them for coming. The foyer in Colac wasn't huge, but it wasn't a huge show, probably only a couple of hundred seats. As I was standing there, a young guy in his mid-twenties approached me with his girlfriend.

His opening gambit was, 'Hey, mate, I think you're really funny . . .' which I thought was nice (because it is – duh). I was about to say thank you, but before I could, he continued with, 'But I just want to let you know . . . I still hate faggots.' And with that he turned on his faggot-hating heel and walked out.

I was really thrown by the whole thing – on one hand he was telling me that he thought I was really funny. On the other hand – well, he hated me. Do they cancel each other out? I was as confused a chameleon on tartan.

I didn't quite know what to make of it. To be honest, I wasn't overly fazed and I kind of shrugged it off. But I do remember Greg and Anne got quite worked up and upset about it, far more than I did. Their reaction was really sweet and endearing. I felt super special and safe having my comedy family around me, knowing they had my back.

I didn't really think much about what happened until I found out the story had been published in the local newspaper, the *Colac Herald*, a few days later. Just by the by, I have *definitely* caught a bad case of *Colac Herald* before. I think that was on a business trip to Spain.

So! As it turned out, a reporter had been standing in line behind the guy who loves my stand-up/hates my sexuality (hot combo) and had heard the whole thing. The reporter then wrote that I'd been abused and put it in the paper. Which is nice, I guess? And it must have become a bit of a talking point in the town, with people trying to work out who the guy was.

Flash forward a few months later and I had completely forgotten about the whole thing, but a community group called DYNAMIC (a local group for young LGBTIQ teens) called and asked if I'd like to go back to Colac and host an anti-homophobia event. I said of course, I'd love to, and also I was thinking of the boxes of T-shirts I had left over from my days as managing director of PsychYAdelic in Grade 12 going mouldy in Mum and Dad's garage that I might finally be able to pawn off. This group would be teaming up with a similar bunch from Warrnambool who were driving up for the day. These groups are so important for LGBTIQ youths to be able to interact and feel safe with other like-minded people, particularly in regional towns where homophobia is rife – I really thought it was a brilliant cause.

I am always impressed by how brave the kids in those groups are to organise and attend events like that in these towns where there really aren't any gay people hanging out, it's just not the norm. It must be so tough and my heart really goes out to them. There were about twenty other gay guys in my year alone at my school. Imagine being the only gay guy in an entire town. Your Grindr options would certainly be limited.

So off I went back to Colac. I decided to make a bit of an afternoon of it, taking Ashleigh along (I needed someone with a car) and our friends Kate and Andy. The drive there was really fun, listening to musical soundtracks and stopping for lunch in Geelong. I know! My life is *so* glamorous!

Gaycrashers

Around early afternoon we arrived in Colac for the event. The function was being held in a local bar called Straight Shooters (Christ, the irony, I cannot *begin* to tell you!). I think it was a bar – but who knows? It had a bit of a saloon-type vibe. The actual bar itself wasn't open, so that was a bit of a bummer. I mean what's a trip to Colac without a cocktail, I always say.

There was quite a big turnout there, and I thought, surely all these people can't be the local gay kids? Turns out they weren't. There were also a lot of . . . what would you call them? Hoodlums, thugs, ruffians? Little fucking shits? They were walking around the event giving the LGBTIQ kids a really hard time. They were easy to spot too, in their hoodies and Globe shoes, reeking of Lynx Africa and broken homes.

I aired what I had seen with one of the people running the event, but they were a bit snowed under themselves – there were only two organisers, and it was such a tough job, their hands were already full. So I took it upon myself to have a bit of a word with some of these little arseholes. What was going on at that stage wasn't too major and the event was still in full swing, it was just the odd comment made here and there and nobody really standing up for themselves. And look, fair enough. Why would they want to? They probably had to go to school with these bullies.

But I did my bit and MCed the event and it all went well. Besides, by the time I got on stage most of the bullies had left, it seemed. I was there for a couple of hours and then it was time for me and my mates to leave. We had ice-creams to purchase in Geelong! We said goodbye to everyone and left the venue.

Unfortunately we didn't get the Golden Gaytime we were after.

When we got outside Straight Shooters there were about twenty kids, sixteen or seventeen years old – basically grown men – waiting on the street to pick a fight. They started yelling at me and my friends, calling us faggots and telling us to burn in hell. We ignored them and kept walking, but they started to really press in on us. It seemed like more and more of them were appearing. In the end there were about thirty of them.

It didn't quite register with me what was happening. It was surreal.

We were keeping our heads down as we tried to walk through them to get to the car, but they started shoving us, and it was really hard not to snap back. Then they started pushing and shouldering us.

Finally Ashleigh, summoning the verbal strength she had exhibited at that schoolyard tennis match of our youth, told one of them to go fuck themselves. I think it's essentially become her catch-phrase.

They didn't take that well. Two seconds later, we were running to Ashleigh's little Holden Astra as a couple of plastic Coke bottles were thrown at us (thank God – imagine if they had glass?). They missed. It's a sad day when a faggot has better aim than you. We jumped in the car and were off. I remember turning around in my seat and seeing these thirty kids yelling homophobic, disgusting abuse at us, every vile thing under the sun. Mostly one-syllable words though, let's be honest.

It's a strange feeling to turn around and see a group of people yelling, 'If you ever come back we'll kill you, faggot!' Like, stop being so obsessed with me. Who has that sort of time?

In all honesty, I was shaking. I cried a bit. But the thing is, I'm Gen Y, I have priorities, so I still found time to tweet about it. And it blew up immediately. It went *crazy*. It was in every paper, all over the news, I had to do radio interviews about it (and you know how I hate attention). It even made international news because my friend saw it in a magazine in Changi Airport in Singapore, which totally counts. It was a big deal. My profile was only on the start of a rise at this point, but it was a big story. A gay entertainer was chased from a town – the irony being he was chased from an anti-homophobia event.

I probably should've told my mum. She called me, panicked, having read it in the paper. She called during the intermission of *Love Never Dies*, the sequel to *Phantom of the Opera*, and the show was about to start again and I had to quickly explain to her what had happened before hissing, 'Mum, I've got to go, the Phantom is about to come back.' She was even more confused.

The silver lining of the whole incident, and something these homophobic cocksnaps didn't realise, was that my exposure went through the roof as a result of that incident and I scored an invite to the *Sex and the City 2* premiere in Sydney, where I totally met Sarah Jessica Parker and told her she had fabulous shoes and she replied, 'Thanks, girl-friend!' and we sassy clicked at each other.

So essentially those homophobes were the direct cause of the gayest thing that had happened to me up to that point. Thanks, boys, if you're reading this. Hope you're doing well and you're really happy with all your life choices. P.S. Please don't reproduce. Joel x

You'd think I was done with Colac at that point, never to return. But at the end of 2013 I went back with one of my best friends, a brilliant comedian called Rhys Nicholson, who is also gay (he *says*, but apart from being engaged to a man I am yet to see proof) and a film crew to make an anti-homophobia documentary, because after all the press about what had happened to me, Colac had earned the reputation as the most homophobic town in Australia. I actually think it was on Colac's Wikipedia entry for a while, but some local councillor probably frantically edits it off every time it goes up.

The film crew we went back to Colac with was headed by the brilliant Tom Rohr and Nel Minchin (sister of Tim Minchin and Katie Minchin, my tour manager in that rural town with the radio station). They had won a grant to fund the idea and were filming the doco for ABC2. I'm not sure how they specifically pitched it, but I'm guessing 'Let's put these homos in serious danger' would probably have gotten it across the line.

The doco was called *Gaycrashers*. It really is one of the pieces of work I am most proud of and it was amazing to experience it with such a fabulous person as Rhys. We were in Colac filming for a week and Rhys and I did things like working at the local timber mill and the pub. Then at the end of the week we put on a show, having sold tickets on our rounds of the town's businesses. The test being – will the town be comfortable enough to buy a ticket to support and watch two gay comedians?

It was interesting because nobody was really openly homophobic to us on camera but it was also frustrating because people would drive down the street and shout out, 'Faggots!' or 'Homos!', and because it was such a small film crew it was really hard to capture that stuff on camera. It takes a brave person to yell abuse at someone out of a car window and drive off. I'm sure they have *huge* penises and *great* jobs and *really* happy home lives.

Other people we encountered, though, were on their best behaviour after an article appeared in the *Colac Herald* almost instructing locals not to fuck up while the cameras were around. We read that and thought wow, what a way to brush the issue under the carpet. What happens when we're not around?

One of the really shocking things that happened during my time there was that I spoke to Emma, who ran DYNAMIC and had been involved in organising the anti-homophobia event I'd been chased from. We had a coffee on camera and it was extremely uncomfortable. She told me that as a result of my actions in the media, the group had lost its funding and had disbanded. Even worse, she told me it really hadn't been good for the LGBTIQ kids in the town, resulting in further bullying.

It broke my heart that my actions had had a carry-on effect for those kids, because I really didn't want to make their lives any harder than they already were.

When the incident happened and I went to the media I was only twenty, and perhaps it was ignorance on my part, but I truly believed that getting that media attention would help the cause and shine a light on the issue. And perhaps locals would be more vigilant and keep an eye out for any bullying. But instead the locals turned against the anti-homophobia group. They were anti-anti-homophobic, if you will. During the whole media frenzy following the Colac incident, I was taking advice from publicists, from managers, and yes – part of me was trying to look out for my own career. But I truly thought I was championing these kids by being in the spotlight.

In the end, Emma and I had to agree to disagree. I remember leaving the chat with Emma furious. We were on the same page, both fighting homophobia – why on earth would she attack me and bring that up on camera? But now, a few years on, I totally understand what Emma had to say. And I thank Meryl Streep that Colac has someone like Emma looking out for these kids.

Filming with Rhys was such a fun week though, especially working at the local pub where we spent a night pulling beers (but as expected, no roots). The reactions of the locals in the pub were interesting: some people really wanted to be served by us, and some people clearly did not – as if they would catch 'gay' if they bought a beer pulled by us. At the same time we were trying to spruik and sell tickets to our stand-up show in town a few nights later. I vividly remember one thing that a local waitress who'd been showing us the ropes all night said that was kind of shocking. Up to this point Rhys and I had really been getting on with her – we sort of thought she was the local fabulous fag hag and we'd become quite chummy. That was until she said, 'So . . . do you think this will be a full-time thing?'

We both immediately thought she was referring to our stand-up careers, which truly would've been a valid question. Because at that point it could've gone either way. But instead she clarified with, 'No, no, being gay. Do you think when you're forty or fifty you'll still be gay?' It was just so shocking because she wasn't being mean or homophobic – there was no malice in the question, she was just uneducated. She didn't realise that being gay is not a choice. Anyway – spoiler alert – Colac was still homophobic. And that *is* a choice.

But there were some positive changes that had been made between my first and second visits. The mayor who was there when I was first chased out of town had been replaced. This is the same mayor, by the way, who, in an ABC interview to defend his town during the media backlash, said, 'Well, it's not like there were any sticks or bottles thrown or any bones broken!' I think even the town knew this was a bonkers thing to say because he was voted out at the following election and replaced by new mayor Lyn Russell. Rhys and I met with Lyn and she was gorgeous and exactly what the town needed.

The end of the documentary shows our local stand-up night, which we had been selling tickets to over our week in Colac. The show was quite bittersweet: not many people turned up to see us perform, only about thirty, which was really sad. I think more people would have come if the cameras hadn't been there. Perhaps they didn't want to be seen publicly supporting two gay guys.

What was really sweet was that the mayor, Lyn, gave a speech at the start of the show before welcoming Rhys to the stage. It was a really beautiful speech, saying that people should be free to love whoever they like, and nobody should be allowed to get in the way of that. That was really fucking cool and I have so much respect for Lyn for doing that. I think if regional towns had more people like her leading the community, then issues like homophobia, racism and sexism wouldn't be as prevalent. And I know Lyn wasn't just putting it on for the camera.

What a poser.

My family:
Mum and
Dad, me, Alice
(centre) and
Holly (right).

A typical
Creasey family
photo with my
grandparents.

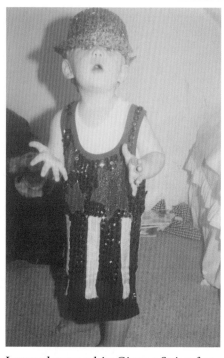

Hair game on fleek.

I was always a big Ginger Spice fan.

Wearing my sister's uniform better than she did.

My short-lived career with Applecross footy.

Keeping busy.

Livening up my parents' dinner parties as Magical Mafisto.

Check out the popped leg with Daniel and Ashleigh.

On stage at North Lake Children's Theatre.

I loved tennis for years, until it got in the way of my quest for stardom.

Mixed doubles dream team with my partner Holly Brindle.

Just a ball boy at the Hopman Cup, about to profess his true love to Kim Clijsters.

My first Montreal Gala, televised and everything!

The fierce world of Hong Kong karaoke. L to R: Me, the mic-hogging host, Anne Edmonds, Luke McGregor.

My 'shirtless spread', still doing the rounds on other peoples' Grindr profiles I might add.

Costume party with my friend Kyle.

After a Gala with Mum.

My business partner, comfort blanket and writing soulmate Janelle Koenig.

With Thomas.

With Thomas (in drag).

The gay coven. (Gay comedians assemble!) L to R: Craig Hill, me, Stephen K. Amos, Paul Foot, Rhys Nicholson.

A night at Adele with this power posse. L to R: Nazeem Hussain, me, Urzila Carlson, Julia Morris.

My best friend Chrissie Swan.

Pashing Magda Szubanski.

God.

Cuddles with Carrie Fisher.

On stage . . . What was I saying?

Hosting Eurovision 2017 with Myf Warhurst.

Gaycrashers

We donated the couple of hundred dollars we raised from ticket sales to DYNAMIC so they could have a catch up after disbanding the previous year. And it was really nice that Emma, despite our differences at the time, attended the show, sat in the front row and accepted the cheque on their behalf.

Now that I've gotten the heartfelt part of that story out of the way I can tell you the most shocking thing that happened that week.

I got pregnant.

To a cow.

Or rather – a bull.

Well, I don't know if you can get pregnant from getting *bull jizz in your mouth*. But that is what happened to me.

Before you call the RSPCA, please allow me to explain.

One day during our week of filming we went out to work on a farm for a few hours with a farmer, Oliver (who was a total babe, by the way). The second we saw him, Rhys and I were like two schoolgirls at a Justin Bieber meet and greet. Unlike the Biebs, Oliver turned out to be super cool. Oliver also turned out to be a big supporter of the homosexuals. He was unfortunately also married with a pregnant wife, which was a bit of a boner killer. Pregnant wife = biggest cock block of all time.

At one point during the day, Oliver asked if we wanted to artificially inseminate a cow, a task I immediately nominated Rhys for, knowing it would (a) make for great TV and (b) be hilarious for me. Half an hour later, Rhys had a long plastic glove on and was fisting a cow up to his armpit with shit all over his arm. I don't know myself of course, but I assume this is how it happens for hetero-sexual insemination too. I was laughing so hard at this, thinking, *This is so funny! I don't have to do this, I've literally put him in the shit!*

Obviously karma came around to bite me on the arse – or spray me in the mouth, if you will – pretty fucking quickly, because after Rhys's fist-athon, Oliver the farmer asked us if we would like to watch a cow and a bull have sex, and of course we said yes. Who on earth would say no to that question? Actually, most people – you're right.

So off we went to watch the cow, Helen (which seemed an appropriate name) and the bull, Kai (which does not sound like a name for a bull – that's much more like a personal trainer from Fitzroy who's really into reiki) get it on. So Kai – I'll put this politely – mounted Helen and they were having a good old time. The crew filmed Rhys's and my reactions. The whole time I was having flashbacks to Mardi Gras the previous year.

Helen and Kai were really going for it but then it became all a bit odd, especially when Kai suddenly pulled out a little bit too early and Helen sort of freaked out and fell over. (I could totally relate. I have fallen over during sex at least three times. Twice I was already on the bed, which is impressive.)

Anyhoo, it felt like everything suddenly went into slow motion. Kai pulled out. Helen fell over. I gasped. Kai's bull dick was like a fucking super soaker and in the excitement and panic, Kai shot his load into the air and, my God, it was like a fucking confetti cannon. It went into the air like some kind of silky lasso, missing Rhys, missing Oliver, missing any of the crew, and landing on me, all over my head, all over my jacket and perfectly in my mouth. That's right – I got bull semen *in my mouth.*

YES , YOU ARE READING AN AUTOBIOGRAPHY THAT INCLUDES THOSE WORDS.

BULL.

JIZZ.

IN.

MY.

MOUTH.

There is footage of this, by the way, for you sickos out there. You can actually watch me, Joel Creasey, national treasure and gay icon, who has performed on Broadway, experience hardcore bull bukkake.

I lost my shit. Everyone was falling around laughing. Rhys was doubled over and struggling for air. Our producers Nel and Tim were roaring with laughter – I could see how stoked they were to get such a moment for the documentary. The cameraman had a hard time even keeping the camera on me he was laughing so hard.

In my mind I knew I had to give them something, I knew I couldn't completely lose my shit on camera. So I gave a thirty-second 'airable' freak-out where I sort of laughed with Rhys about it happening. And then I said, 'Turn those fucking cameras off right now.' I threw my farming apron on the ground, jumped in the car and sped off – remembering we only had one car an hour later when I emerged from the shower having cried and scrubbed myself raw.

So sorry, Colac, but perhaps your water shortage in some serendipitous way is your trade-off for me being called a faggot.

Kai never called, by the way.

9
HOPELESS ROMANTIC

People are always surprised to hear that I want to get married. I also would love kids, either by adopting Angelina-style or asking Emma Watson to be my surrogate (I haven't decided yet), and live a normal life. Just a really normal, simple life, with a minimum household staff similar to that of Downton Abbey, and be insanely rich and famous.

That's my spin on normal anyway. I think Elton John and I have the same idea. Also, like Elton, I too am trying really hard to become BFFs with a princess (just in case Kate Middleton is reading this – hit me up, Your Royal Baeness).

When I tell people about my desire to lead a pretty traditional family life, they always say, 'Really? You?' I think that's because I divulge so many embarrassing sex stories on stage and at times have been a bit of a mega slut. It's not slut-shaming when you're talking about yourself – it's bragging.

I'm not embarrassed to say I just want to be loved. And that shouldn't come as a surprise. *Hello?* I stand on stage asking people to laugh at my jokes and clap for a living! That being said, I'm a very closed-off, guarded person. I'm not someone who enters relationships purely for the company. I live alone, work alone and travel alone and, for the most part, enjoy that. I don't need to be arguing with someone over what we watch on Netflix, or whether Thai is a 'healthy good group', or whether carrots are carbs or not.

I've been on so many first dates that have been just that – first dates. They could have made that reality show about me – could've gone for seasons! I've found myself on dates with guys who have clearly just wanted to say they've been on a date with me. I can usually pick them when they've asked for a selfie before they've asked for a menu. In those instances I've made an excuse and left. I've been on dates where the guy has rocked up with a pair of Oakleys on his head at night and a Velcro wallet and did not have a chance in hell. I've even been on a date where I was so bored I just told the guy I was going to the bathroom and left through the back door. For once this is *not* a euphemism. Not that I'm a dreamboat on dates either, I'm sure. I swear too much, drink too much and talk about myself too much. (*No shit*, I hear you think as you sink yourself into the ninth chapter of my memoir.) I've seen people doing the same as I've done, checking their watch to see when it is an appropriate moment to bail.

But I really am a hopeless romantic. When I've fallen, I've fallen hard. And although it hasn't worked out for me *so* far (brb – just checking Grindr) I am proud of that fact.

Having said that, I *think* I've only been in love once. And although that ended in a complete clusterfuck as you'll soon read, I also can say openly that I cannot wait to fall in love again. (Please note: forward all applications to my manager's email address.)

My first crush was Chloe Lewis. She was a family friend and one of the girls in my class from Grade 1. She came from a posh Italian family and I thought everything about her was beyond glamorous. For show and tell on the first day of school she brought in these fancy china dolls wearing vintage dresses that her mum, Rina, had to help her carry. I thought it was beyond pretentious and was immediately obsessed with her. I'm still friends with Chloe and her mum. Not sure what happened to the dolls.

I always joke (through my tears) that I've been dumped by every guy I've been in a long-term relationship with. On stage I used to say, 'I'm going for the trifecta. Apparently you win a bottle of lube and a copy of *The Notebook*.' I'm a comic genius, right?

And it's true, I sorta have been dumped three times. All you get is bags under your eyes and greasy take-away. Of course I dumped every girl I ever dated in high school – I dumped them the second we moved beyond kissing and sending flirty texts on our Nokia 3315s. There was *no way*

I was touching vagina. No thanks. I feel the same way about vagina as I do about *Dr Who*. I love that people are super passionate about it . . . but it's just not for me.

For a week in Grade 9, I dated a girl called Kitty. She was really pretty with red hair and no china dolls à la Chloe and was, conveniently, the only girl in my year who hadn't worked out I was gay. I dumped her via text, and she ended up taking a few months off school because she was sick. I still like to imagine it was from heartbreak, but it was probably from sheer embarrassment.

The first guy I dated was when I moved to Melbourne. I was nineteen and we dated on and off for a while. He was a total stoner but looked like my primary and high school crush Patrick so I was immediately obsessed. He lived in a really cool share house in Brunswick. Brunswick, for those outside of Victoria, Australia, is our stereotypical hipster suburb. It's one of those suburbs where the locals wear glasses without prescription lenses – or without any lenses at all – and they all ride bikes, claiming to be environmentally friendly, but really because they can't afford a car. I thought I was super hip dating this boy. I felt like I was in an episode of *Girls*, or at least *Offspring*.

He, in turn, I think, sorta hated me but tolerated me because it was easier. Plus I always brought around snacks. Anyone who has been 'tolerated' in a relationship will know how I felt. You know full well what's going on and you keep trying to fix it, but your desperate attempts to fix it only make you more annoying. It's a weird cycle and you hate yourself the entire time. It feels similar to performing stand-up comedy when you get an audience offside by saying something that's perhaps considered a little 'too soon'. In a situation like that, it's better to ignore it than try to fix it. I was on stage in London during the Lindt Café siege in Sydney and I had a very ex-pat-heavy crowd who were all aware of the horrors that were playing out in Martin Place. I made a joke at the start of the show about the incident, which didn't go over well (no shit, Joel). I kept trying to fix it but just ended up with ninety minutes of me scrambling to win back the crowd. That's how that first relationship felt. And just like that crowd in London, I never won that boyfriend back either.

My policy is to stand by every joke I make, though, so I'm still not backing down. Nor will I ever, no matter how wrong I am. That's my policy with relationships, too.

That same guy also called my dad a cunt at dinner the night I introduced them to each other. Mum was particularly furious that he'd got in first – usually that's her domain. I stuck at that relationship though, because I didn't know that many people in Melbourne and needed the company. It wasn't a particularly good relationship. Shock horror! But it was what it was and I'm glad for that. We've actually remained better friends than we were boy-friends. Plus he's handy when I'm looking for someone to help me 'pack a bong'. Okay, fine – that's not what people say, is it? I'm trying to look cool and seem like I'm into weed, but it's just not for me.

Next up I made the mistake of dating a best friend, a fellow comic. (Which one? Josh Thomas? Tom Ballard? Hannah Gadsby? I'll never tell.) We met soon after I moved to Melbourne and I became instantly infatuated. I'd go running to him whenever I was having problems with the stoner. When the stoner and I finally broke up for the twenty-eighth time, I dated around but kept going back to my friend. He was beyond charismatic and one day we suddenly went from being good mates who occasionally slept together to being boyfriends who didn't leave each other's side. I was paranoid about becoming too needy from my previous relationship, though (or possibly from all the weed I had passively smoked), so I ended up being even more neurotic with this guy. It ended with him saying, probably rightly, 'Thanks but no thanks,' and me crying on the floor of my apartment as he walked out.

It's so odd, but in bad situations I always feel as though I have to give a 'performance'. I didn't need to be on the floor of the apartment, but in my mind there is always a hidden camera watching. Even in that moment I knew being on the floor would look way better. I knew the director would be watching on, *Truman Show*-style going 'And . . . cut! We got the shot! He's coming back next season!'

After that relationship breakdown I was fairly upset. I was also annoyed that I'd ruined what had been a great friendship . . . and a patch of my carpet.

Carlos, my stylist at the time, suggested I start seeing a personal trainer – not for sex, for personal training. I hate myself for saying this, but it totally worked. I had never been to the gym before but it got me to think about my health and I sorta started to . . . love it. Don't worry, I hate me too. Tear this page of my book out if you like. Make sure you warm up properly and have a protein shake before you do, though.

But Andy Brand, my trainer, has also inadvertently become my counsellor, someone I tell all my problems to while lifting rubbery weights women in their seventies use during water aerobics classes.

Carlos then suggested I work towards something, like a shirtless photo shoot. I'd been offered money in the past to do one and ignored the offer. When Carlos suggested it I initially resisted the idea but when he said, 'It would really annoy your ex-boyfriend,' I said, 'Absolutely. I'm in.' If there's one thing that'll get me out of bed each day, it's revenge. Anybody who says they haven't seriously enjoyed a bit of retribution at some point is full of shit and shouldn't be trusted. I essentially have the temperament of Cersei from *Game of Thrones*. We also drink the same amount of wine.

So I got myself in shape and a few months later I did a shirtless, black and white photo shoot on a rooftop in Melbourne while Carlos threw water at me to make me look sweaty, and a photographer screamed, '*Tense!* But don't *look* tense! You're looking far too tense! *What is making you tense?*' It was a lot to take in at the time. And can I just say, for someone who is supremely insecure about his misshapen body (cheers scoliosis) – this was a big step for me.

But I can unequivocally say I have been in love. Proper head-over-heels, I-want-to-marry-the-shit-out-of-you love.

It was doomed from the beginning given that he lived in LA and I lived in Australia. But I was so intoxicated by him that I didn't care. I'd had previous relationships with guys who'd made me laugh, guys who had made me cry, and guys who had made me constantly crave Kit Kats and a kebab. All those boyfriends had each made me both excited and nervous. But I had never had someone who could make me feel the way Jeffery did. This was next-level, *The Notebook*, Romeo under Juliet's window–type shit. I realised I had never been in love until I met Jeffery.

I met Jeffery in Sydney during Mardi Gras, 2014. By pure chance I was in town for one night to perform in a stand-up show that my best mate Thomas was hosting.

Despite being gay since birth, where I shot out with jazz hands, a marching band and Celine Dion on backing vocals, I'd never been to Mardi Gras before and I was pretty excited. I'd flown in from Tasmania that morning and my original plan was to stay for the Friday night and go home the following day, thus missing the parade. I'm actually not great around crowds . . . unless I'm on a stage and I have their devoted attention, plus a moat and security guards between us, then I bloody *love* a crowd. At other events I get claustrophobic – and jealous that the crowd aren't there for me.

That same day my first 'shirtless spread' was published in *DNA*, Australia's biggest gay men's magazine. The photo shoot that Carlos had me work towards ended up being released in the Mardi Gras edition. *Well, this'll be a great profile pic for Grindr*, I thought. (Turns out it was – I've seen loads of people using it as their own!) Walking through Launceston Airport trying to find a copy of *DNA* magazine was pretty tricky. The publications there were more along the lines of *Cheese Maker's Monthly* and *The Abalone Almanac*. But arriving in Sydney for Mardi Gras, I remember feeling great – I was feeling good about myself physically for once, I was happily single and my profile was on the rise. I even remember thinking, *Enjoy being on your own for a while*. I didn't expect to fall head over heels in love that night.

In true laid-back Thomas style, he had inquired about booking the venue for his show several months before – and hadn't followed it up any further, resulting in the venue telling him it was booked for another show when he went in to do the sound check a mere three hours before curtain up.

The solution to the venue being double booked was that Thomas negotiated with them to give us the front lounge area of the upstairs bar to perform in, as well as a free drink for anybody with a ticket and unlimited free drinks for all the artists. It resulted in us getting really quite drunk and inviting everybody back to Thomas's Airbnb around 10 pm for a kick-on party.

I can't remember the exact timing of events and who messaged who, but my friend Roberto (he's a 'Robert' but somewhere along the line has Italian relatives so has given his name an upgrade) sent a text saying that he was going to meet us at the party and that he'd bring his friend Jeffery, who was in town from America doing his sketch show for Mardi Gras.

I didn't know anything about Jeffery. Thomas, however, was really excited that he was coming because he had been a fan of Jeffery and his comedy sketch partner, Cole, for quite some time, having watched their work online. In true generous Joel Creasey style, though, I rolled my eyes and said to the closest person, 'Pfft ... some American "comedian" is coming over.'

Then Jeffery arrived and I thought, *Oh, he's really handsome. That's so annoying.*

He was very much what I'd always dreamed of in a guy: tall, thin, great jawline, amazing hair; almost a stereotype. On top of that he was incredibly charming, very funny and we connected instantly.

We all ended up going out to a club. Jeffery invited me to stay the night at his place as we were leaving, and I said yes. We went home, hooked up (put your boners away), he offered me a Xanax before I went to sleep and I thought, *This guy's fucking great.* As a rule, unless we are in love, I probably don't want to sleep the night at your house. Nor do I want you to sleep at mine. There's no grey area with me. It's normally, 'Let's do the deed and then immediately live our own lives and pretend this never happened.' But ever so rarely (once) it's, 'Oh my God, I think I've fallen

160

in love with you, let me cook you breakfast and make you immediately reciprocate my love with my amazing scrambled eggs.'

I woke up shocked that I had slept the night. Incredibly well, might I add, thanks to the Xanax.

I asked Jeffery if he wanted to grab breakfast and he said yes. I frantically texted Thomas because I knew he'd be stoked to have breakfast together and we met up in Surry Hills. We sat at the café for a good two hours, laughing. Not only was Jeffery beautiful but he was genuinely hilarious. And American! How exotic! I was already imagining my life split between Australia and America. I fancied myself as a gay Nicole Kidman: I could see myself telling people, 'Sorry, just off to visit my American boyfriend,' and developing a fake hybrid accent. We even joked about becoming an international comedy power couple. As he joked, I mentally did the math on what *New Idea* might pay for that story.

Breakfast ended and I said goodbye and went back to Thomas's to pack up my stuff, all the while saying, 'Fuck, Thomas, what do I do?'

Tom told me, 'Stay! You could see him again tonight!'

But I kept thinking it was going to be a complete waste of time – Jeffery was flying back to America the following Monday.

Thomas, who was in the parade (of course he was), had to get ready and get down to Oxford Street, but as he left he said to me, 'Have a nap before your flight and think about it.'

161

I took a nap, perhaps too long – on purpose – and completely missed my flight.

I ended up seeing Jeffery again. 'I missed my flight!' I told him, hoping that he didn't know there are flights between Sydney and Melbourne every fifteen minutes. We went home together again that night. And the night after. When Jeffery left for America the next morning, I said goodbye and how great it was getting to know each other.

My flight was a few hours before his. I sat on the tarmac at Sydney Airport quite confused, trying to make sense of the seventy-two-hour whirlwind. I ended up thinking, *Fuck it!* and sent him a text along the lines of, 'This may sound really dumb and a little bit hopeless. But I really like you.'

I got a short message back: 'Chat when I get back to the States.'

And I thought, *Ah, well . . . that's that then*, and headed back to Melbourne to grab my bags and fly to Brisbane the next day to open my show there. I wondered if I should send him my topless *DNA* photo and then decided that was getting a bit desperate and I should just put the whole weekend out of my mind.

True to his word, however, Jeffery contacted me when he got back to America. And we spent every waking minute (that lined up with the time difference) texting back and forth. I don't think a night passed without us FaceTiming before he went to bed.

Less than two months later, in early April, Jeffery was on his way back to Melbourne for ten days. For no reason other than to see me.

I was nervous. When we had last spent time together it was during the buzz of Mardi Gras – it was intoxicating and fast. Now he would be in my home, with me as really the only person he knew, and barely at that – and it was during the Melbourne International Comedy Festival. I was performing my 2014 show, *Rock God*, which is still one of my favourite shows, and it was getting great reviews. I remember snapping one of the reviews and sending it to Jeffery. He replied, 'You are killing it. I hope you don't think I'm some loser when I come down to hang with you.' I remember my insecurities becoming overwhelming and genuinely thinking, *It'll probably be the other way around.*

I had all my friends on high alert. They were across the Jeffery situation and instructed to 'make me, my life and Melbourne look fabulous at all costs'.

I love that humans do this. Everybody has, at some point, said to their best friend, 'Can you big me up to him/her?' Imagine if you took a date to meet your friends and they said, 'Why the fuck are you dating Helen (not the cow from Colac – another hypothetical Helen)? She's a cunt.'

Jeffery arrived and the chemistry was instant, as if we hadn't been apart. He came to my show each night, I took him to parties and introduced him to people, we went to great Melbourne restaurants and he was amazing the whole time. He was incredibly charming – able to make anyone he came in contact with laugh in an effortless way. And so unashamedly camp that it was empowering to be around, his flamboyance and confidence ironically made him seem incredibly strong. His stories of growing up in a small town in America were captivating and for once I was quite happy to sit and listen without saying a word, completely enthralled. I didn't have to be the one who was 'on'.

We decided we were a couple that week. We were boyfriends. Buckle up, tabloids! International comedy power couple here we come!

The Comedy Festival closed and we went down to a house in Red Hill on the Mornington Peninsula that I had booked for us; we were going to have a night on our own before Thomas, Ashleigh and a few other friends joined us. The house was amazing (probably because I was paying an insane amount but was totally pretending I wasn't) but I was kind of bummed that my mates were joining us the following night because things were going so well. I had only really invited them in case things hadn't gone so well and I needed them to help me bury the body.

Before the troops arrived, Jeffery and I went into town and had an incredible lunch and walked out onto the pier with ice creams. Jeffery said, 'I know this is crazy and we haven't known each other that long, but can I tell you something?'

I said, 'Yes ...' praying to Meryl Streep he was going to say what I wanted to hear but never had before. I also remember thinking, *Knowing my luck he's probably going to tell me he's lactose intolerant after I've paid fifteen dollars for this artisanal ice cream . . . Maybe I finally will dump someone after all.*

'I've fallen in love with you.'

Things had been utterly perfect but I couldn't quite believe it. 'Really?' I said with the same shock I had when I wasn't picked last for a sport team in school.

'Yeah. Is that crazy?'

'I don't think it is. Because I love you too,' I said.

I was so happy. After a few false starts with other guys, it was at twenty-three years old, on a jetty in Sorrento in Victoria (so pretentious and so perfect), eating very over-priced ice cream, that I knew what it was like to be in love with somebody. You were right, Tina Arena – that Sorrento moon is very sweet indeed.

We kissed on the jetty and it was totally a movie moment. Somewhere, off-camera, an overweight producer in a beret and ill-fitting polo shirt was smoking a cigar, saying, 'There's the money shot!' Well, it was the glamorous money shot, until we both got boners and thought it best to leave.

When Thomas and Ashleigh arrived a few hours later, I pulled them aside the second they walked in the door and whispered, 'Jeffery told me he loves me!' We had a silent party in the corridor for a few seconds before composing ourselves and walking casually into the lounge room to join the others.

We had a few more amazing days in Red Hill and then one final night in Melbourne before Jeffery was due to go home.

It was an emotional morning as I drove him to the airport to board his flight back to LA. He took my head in his hands, kissed me and said, 'I'll see you soon. I promise. I love you.'

As fate would have it, I was due to be in America three months later to perform shows in New York and take meetings in LA. (That's industry speak for you – in America, you don't 'have' meetings, you 'take' them. But Australians don't 'take' meetings. We take the piss, take the mickey and, depending on how much fibre is in our diets, regularly take shits.) And a few days after Jeffery left, I got booked for the Just For Laughs comedy festival in Montreal, Canada. Just For Laughs is considered the most prestigious comedy festival in the world as it's a curated event, meaning, unlike Melbourne or Edinburgh, you have to be invited to perform there. This was perfect because it also meant arriving in North America earlier. So Jeffery and I worked out that I would fly to Montreal from Asia (where I would be touring), then fly down to New York where Jeffery would already be doing his sketch show with his mate Cole. Thomas would then join us in New York to do my show at the New York Fringe Festival before we all flew to LA. All up, Jeffery and I would have about three months together. You following? Good? Let's press on.

The time between Jeffery leaving Melbourne and me going to Asia was excruciating. But I knew once I had left Australia it would get easier as I would at least feel like I was on my way to him.

In this time I was quite busy filming *It's a Date*, written by Peter Helliar, in which I played my friend Tom Ballard's boyfriend, as well as continuing to tour my stand-up show. However, Jeffery and I still FaceTimed every second we had free. Never in public, though. I often see people FaceTiming in the lounge at the airport. Please don't. We don't want to listen to your conversation, let alone see and hear the person on the other end of the line.

In early July I headed off to tour Asia as part of the Melbourne International Comedy Festival Roadshow and I had struck gold with a pretty epic cast of amazing comedians who also happened to be good friends – Anne Edmonds, Harley Breen, Luke McGregor and Ronny Chieng.

We began the tour in Kuala Lumpur, which was the Comedy Festival's first time touring there. We stayed across the road from the local karaoke bar and we spent every moment we weren't on stage there, drinking outrageously potent Long Island iced teas. Harley and I also took a comedy workshop with some of the local comics, culminating in a performance that afternoon that they could invite their friends along to, plus the rest of our cast came. I've always remembered that as one of the cooler things I've had the opportunity to do in my career: giving advice to aspiring comedians in another country. And they were fantastic. Our own shows each night were awesome, too.

Then we headed to Singapore, which I was nervous about, given their strict laws concerning homosexuality. Plus I'd heard they'd been a bit strange when gay comedians had been there before. Not the audience, but the administration of the Arts Theatre. On our first day we were given a briefing by the head of the theatre, who was this very severe Singaporean woman: tall, sky-high heels and hot pink nails (obviously knew *some* gays).

She sat opposite me and went through everything we weren't allowed to talk about. When she got to 'permissive lifestyles', she eyeballed me. I eye-rolled back at her. Well, I did on the inside. She was fucking terrifying, and probably knew a martial art.

I was only twenty-three and a bit overwhelmed. The meeting finished and I held it together until I got to my room, where I burst into tears. How the fuck was I going to do the show? Gideon, our tour manager (also gay and very fabulous), was great and just told me to 'do what I do'. So I thought, *Fuck it*, and went out and delivered the gayest set you've ever seen. Full gay-man-on-ketamine-on-the-dancefloor-when-Kylie-Minogue-comes-on-at-Mardi-Gras style. To be honest, I've never considered my material as being specific to a 'gay comedian'. I just discuss relationships and my life on stage. If a straight comic were to do it you wouldn't describe them as a 'heterosexual comedian'. But for some reason the second a gay man references their sexuality, a partner or a sexual experience on stage, we become 'gay comedians'. It's a total double standard.

However, the gigs went so well in Singapore that I ended up getting to close the show for the final leg of the tour in Hong Kong. In the industry, that's a big deal. And Hong

Kong was great. We were doing shows at the Arts Theatre and they were going off. Plus I didn't realise Hong Kong had such a great gay scene. One of the big gay clubs got wind that I was in town and invited us to come along and judge their karaoke competition. I ran it past the other comedians and we decided to make a night of it. There were only three spots for judges so Anne, Luke and I took those spots.

We didn't realise quite how seriously the locals took their karaoke competition. We were there to get drunk, and suddenly we had people begging us to keep them in the competition. We loved the power trip. Anne ended up doing five numbers herself and getting in a fight with the drag queen who was hosting the show when she asked for the microphone back. I'll never forget the sight of them, each with a hand on the mic, yanking it back and forth, with Mariah Carey playing in the background all the while (which was to be Anne's sixth number). It's truly one of the best nights I've ever had on tour. And the most hilarious.

I was also getting excited because the Asian tour was coming to an end and that meant I had only one week until seeing Jeffery. On the night of our final show I went straight to the airport to head up to Montreal while most of the other comics were going to Edinburgh the next day.

Landing in Montreal was exciting. Not only was I now finally on the same continent as my boyfriend, I was also at the biggest comedy festival in the world for the first time. And I had also been booked for one of their televised galas, which an invite to Montreal doesn't necessarily guarantee you, and is particularly rare in your first year. The galas in Montreal are filmed at the Place des Arts Theatre (that's French for 'Place of Arts', by the way. I'm very multilingual, I'm basically Shakira), this ginormous theatre housing close to four thousand seats. And I was to be on the gala hosted by the legendary Chevy Chase.

I had an amazing debut performance, playing it safe and going with material about Perth and shark attacks, which I'd been doing for years and could count on. I was named a highlight by the *Montreal Gazette*. Chevy Chase didn't review so favourably. Not particularly surprising given I'd heard him walk past my dressing room on his way to the stage and grumble to his minder, 'I am not in the mood for this shit.'

I was also part of the all-Australian show. The line-up consisted of me, Dave Hughes, Adam Hills, Wil Anderson and Felicity Ward. It was really a pinch-myself moment, being part of this legendary group of Australian comedians. Having watched all these performers growing up, I was honoured to be performing alongside them. But I also wanted to hold my own and – in my typical selfless, charitable style – potentially outshine them if I could. We were performing in an eighty-seat theatre called the Montreal Improv. It was warehouse style and really run down. But it was quite funny, because there were nearly more performers than audience members some nights. Little did the audience know that any of these comedians back in Australia (or the UK, for that matter) pack out giant theatres. The backstage was about two metres by two metres and the five of us squished in there while chowing down on the backstage rider (potato chips and coffee – glam) and listening to each other's sets. I fucking loved it.

Suddenly Montreal was over and my manager Andrew and I went out for a celebratory dinner. He took me to a restaurant that Celine Dion supposedly loves, so naturally I did too. *Magnifique!* (Side note: As I've mentioned before I love Celine Dion. But I also find it hilarious how she's lived in America pretty much her entire life now and still has that thick French–Canadian accent. Get *les* grip, Celine!)

The next morning I jumped out of bed and basically ran to the airport to board my flight for New York, where Jeffery was staying at his friend's gorgeous house in the West Village. I reckon I could've run all the way from Montreal.

🎤

Seeing him after all this time – three whole months apart – was incredible. The first night I was in town he was booked on Andy Cohen's *Watch What Happens Live*. It was really cool, but also an unusual experience for me to be the one in the audience. I felt a bit overwhelmed. I also questioned if my ego could take it if this ended up being a regular occurrence. What if I were permanently the one in the audience?

It was only a fleeting thought, however, as I topped myself up from the open bar. Another of the guests that night was one of *The Real Housewives of OC*. I sat next to her stylist in the audience, who had also been helping himself to the free booze. He was about sixty-five years old, had peroxided hair, black and white pinstripe pants, white shoes and a lime green blouse-type shirt. Halfway through the show I found his hand on my thigh. That was a . . . nice . . . welcome to New York. Turns out the Real Stylists of OC are a little bit handsy.

Jeffery and I had a few weeks of seeing shows, eating at great restaurants and being disgustingly in love before Thomas arrived. As Jeffery had previously lived in New York there was never a search for where to eat or where we should go – he has great taste and knew exactly what we would both like. We drank Negronis at probably every bar in New York, laughed till our cheeks hurt, walked through the streets holding hands and telling each other how in love we were (controlling our boners this time) and Jeffery even introduced me to meatloaf – the food, not the singer.

I was loving it. I was infatuated and living a dream. But I couldn't work out what I was doing. I wasn't being myself. I mean, I wasn't doing a Lindsay Lohan–style German accent or anything crazy like that, but I couldn't relax completely when we were around his friends. I could only let my guard down when it was just Jeffery and me. I couldn't quite understand why. Maybe it was sheer insecurity I'd never discovered I had: I was suddenly nobody in the most powerful country in the world standing beside my boyfriend, who seemed to know everybody. Not to mention that he was always the loudest one at the party; always in control and always with something funny to say. That was normally me. And I'm not saying I was standing there fuming in silent, unfunny jealousy – I would laugh too. But I couldn't quite get my comedy timing calibrated in social settings. It was so odd, and happened every time we were with people I didn't know. I kept imagining them thinking to themselves, *I thought Jeffery said his new boyfriend was a comedian . . .*

I felt like a competent tennis player who kept getting knocked out in the third round of a grand slam. Essentially I was Samantha Stosur, *sans* those weird wrap-around sunnies she always plays in. Even during night games. Samantha, what you doing, girl? You better not have a Velcro wallet.

Soon Thomas arrived and we all moved into a fun Airbnb in the East Village. I was stoked to have Thomas in town because it felt like I had an ally. Not that I needed one, but it was nice to have someone who could be as confused as I was when Jeffery and his friends were talking about a casting executive from LA I had no idea about. But I was also so smitten with my relationship I probably didn't give Thomas a lot of attention.

Jeffery and I took Thomas around to every gay bar in town to find him a husband and had a particularly awesome night seeing *Cabaret* starring Alan Cumming and Michelle Williams. We ended up backstage at a private party with Alan and the cast in his swanky dressing room called *Club Cumming*, which was actually sponsored by Campari. I'm dying to have a dressing room sponsored by an alcohol company. That's when I'll know I've made it. It can even be VB or Midori Illusion, I'll take anything.

Around the same time, my manager, Andrew, and my parents arrived in New York. My show opened at the Fringe Festival at a theatre in the West Village called the Players Theatre. I'd never heard of any other comics performing at the New York Fringe Festival before, and probably for good reason: the Fringe is a pretty poorly run festival. It felt shoddily put together and the line-up basically consisted of myself and two Norwegian contortionists who'd had the same idea as me, thinking they'd be ahead of the curve if they signed up.

The Players Theatre were shocked that I required a microphone for my first sound check. The theatre manager (who admittedly was a volunteer from the festival) could not have hated us more. And although they had a theatre technician on hand, we had to supply our own technical support. We at least knew this part in advance so came up with an idea. We'd decided Thomas would be my support act. In drag. We came up with a character called 'Tracy from Toowoomba' – Toowoomba's local theatre technician who had been sent with me by the Australian Government. Tracy would open my show by doing ten minutes of very Australian-centric gags and then literally walk up through the audience, get into the theatre technician's box and begin the show. So . . . theatre technician sorted!

Tracy wore head-to-toe khaki and boots and a tool belt, from which an unnecessary number of keys, mini toy kangaroos and Australian flags hung. Thomas decided Tracy was a distant relation of the Irwins and he told stories of growing up in Northern Queensland with Steve, and all of the supposed productions Tracy has 'teched' in Australia prior to mine. (*Phantom of the Opera* starring Deborra-lee Furness as the Phantom, apparently.) It was so hilarious watching people in the heavily American audience believe him, completely wide-eyed and in awe. I am laughing even just writing this, remembering the night we rolled around my lounge room in Melbourne dreaming Tracy up, never predicting she would be on stage in America, let alone having some in the audience thinking she was a real woman and not my best mate Thomas in drag.

We also decided that, although quite a rough-looking woman (Thomas would do full prosthetic sunburn and peeling all across his face for the character), she would have an amazing pair of breasts that were simply never referenced. So Thomas bought a $1500 professional drag breast plate.

As I said, it really confused the audience some nights. Some in the audience truly believed she was a real Australian theatre technician with an extraordinary pair of boobs who had come across to America with me. But, my God, sitting in the wings of that theatre listening to Thomas interacting with the audience, I would laugh.

Our New York Fringe run truly could not have gone better. Aside from the nightmare staff and the disorganisation of the festival, we received a five-star review from *Time Out New York*. I woke up on my birthday to see the review sitting in my email inbox from my US manager, Jodi.

I rolled over to Jeffery and said, 'Hey . . . is this a big deal?'

He said, 'Fuck, yes. Congratulations, babe.'

I was stoked. My boyfriend, best friend, family and friends were in New York while I performed my show, which was now getting some proper buzz and actually selling tickets thanks to this great review. On my birthday. And that night I was opening for my hero Joan Rivers. Not to mention I had Tracy and her (gravity defying) bosom of support.

As I'll write about later on, that night with Joan Rivers was so special because it was her last performance in New York. Well, special for me. Not so much for her as she sorta, kinda . . . died afterwards. By the way, how's the suspense I'm building? I've totally learned that from my years of watching *Masterchef.* If this were a TV show we'd go to an ad break right about now.

What happened that evening was strange. After Joan Rivers' show, Jeffery, Thomas and I said goodbye to my parents and decided to go to some of the gay bars in midtown. We were all in odd moods. Jeffery was acting strange and Thomas was acting strange, purely because Jeffery was acting strange. And, as a result, I was acting strange.

Things were tense and we decided to go home. Then Jeffery and I had a blow up in our bedroom as Thomas, in his room, tried to drown out the noise with Netflix cranked up to full volume. On second thoughts, it was probably porn. Anyway, he was trying to distract himself.

I was drunk and going for a 'movie moment' so I started to put my shoes back on as if to storm out of the apartment.

Jeffery said, 'Seriously? What are you doing?'

I said, 'Going for a walk. I can't be here right now.'

He said, 'Don't be an idiot. Come here.'

I got back into bed and he put his arm around me, apologised and said, 'I'm sorry. I'm just not used to being the one in the audience.'

(Look, he said it way cooler than that . . . but I'm writing this part of the book at forty thousand feet on my way to do a gig in Darwin and I think it's playing with my emotions. Also, I need another G&T . . .)

But I knew I couldn't be mad at him. Hadn't I had that exact same thought watching him at *Watch What Happens Live*? Perhaps he was just more honest than me.

I later found out my dad had tried to be supportive and turned to Jeffery just before I'd walked on stage at Joan's show and said, 'I'm so glad Joel has you to support him.' Dad meant it one way, Jeffery took it another . . . but I wish I had known this earlier.

We closed our time at the New York fringe with a sold-out show thanks to Ms Joan Rivers insisting everybody come along. Jeffery and I flew to LA the next day.

Jeffery lives in a house once owned by Buster Keaton and now owned by his very generous friend who we'd also stayed with in New York. Thomas arrived a day later and Jeffery happily played tour guide to us both, including driving us up to San Francisco for two nights. On our way we stopped at the Madonna Inn, a kitschy hotel halfway between LA and San Francisco. If you ever do that drive, I insist you stop there for a night. It's in the middle of the desert and every room is themed to within an inch of its life. The hotel's restaurant has gaudy, hot pink booths and the food portions are huge (and unlike Madonna, not all vegan, thank God). For dessert, they roll around a cake cart with cakes made of colours that are surely not natural nor good for your body. The champagne cake we chose (the size of a small car) was practically glowing like phosphorus. The three of us sat in a booth and laughed, cracked jokes and drank wine, and I remember thinking I couldn't possibly be happier. I was with my two favourite men, eating a ridiculous meal, in a ridiculous location, laughing like fucking crazy.

Soon enough, Thomas left LA and I was once again alone with Jeffery. We spent our time together eating dinners, hiking and telling each other how in love we were. I also began doing some gigs in LA and taking meetings with my US manager, Jodi.

In America, casting agents and network executives do something that I've not found in the rest of the world – they have meetings with talent to kill time. I've honestly met with every casting director and network executive in Hollywood. The meetings are completely fake and phoney. They roll around laughing at your jokes, tell you you're a star . . . and you never hear from them again. Two days later they've completely forgotten you and you've completely forgotten them. It's all so strange. But at least they pick up the bill. Or – sorry, it's America – the 'check'.

Jeffery was very sweet and obliging. He would drop me at these meetings, go to Starbucks to work on a novel he was writing (I'm not plugging it, we have different publishers) and then pick me up afterwards. He'd ask how it went and I'd shrug and say, 'Pointless.' But I was so in love that I didn't really care. I found the meetings irritating because I'd rather be spending time with him.

I think it was starting to irritate him, however, that I refused to drive. I'm not a great driver at the best of times and the thought of driving in LA (still) makes me want to puke. I'd rather get an Uber. When we took trips to Palm Springs and Las Vegas, Jeffery drove, of course. My roles on those trips were simply 'DJ' and 'wide-eyed tourist'.

In Vegas we were invited to the opening of the US tour of *Kinky Boots*. We went for the night, but had to get back to LA the following evening as Jeffery was doing a stand-up gig. We left Vegas with plenty of time for the three-hour drive back to LA, but about twenty minutes out of Vegas we hit standstill traffic. Proper bumper-to-bumper, *The Walking Dead*-style, what-the-fuck, someone-better-have-died traffic.

I frantically googled options for other routes we could take as I didn't want Jeffery missing his gig. Otherwise I could've had an extra night in Vegas. I'm like an old lady when it comes to gambling . . . give me a glass of cheap wine and poker machines and I'll be entertained for hours.

I said, 'I think I've found a side road a few miles back.'

He said, 'Really?'

And I said, 'Yeah, trust me.'

He shouldn't have. But he did.

So we did an illegal U-turn across the ditch separating the two stretches of highway and headed back towards Vegas and this supposed side road I'd found online. We turned on to said road and hit a sign that said 'Do not pass'. I thought, *Oh fuck*. However, as we sat there wondering what to do, a car that I'd seen in the traffic jam beside us earlier came flying past, drove past the sign and continued on down the road. Maybe they knew something we didn't, so we risked it. Off we drove for a good half-hour, just us and the other car in the distance. We started to feel smug and laughed at how stupid the thousands of other drivers caught in the jam were for not thinking to try another route. We were even audacious enough to crank Taylor Swift's *1989* for the forty-billionth time, the only album we'd brought with us.

But our smiles were wiped off our pretty faces very quickly when we saw what must've been thirty cars parked all over the road, and people having concerned conversations. We pulled up and I got out to chat to some other drivers and find out what was happening. That's when I saw the road had ended and there was a thirty-metre crevice separating where the road ended and started again with a twenty-metre drop in between. My first thought was, *We could probably jump that if we got a good run up.* I then remembered there was a reason I wasn't driving in LA.

I looked down the side of the embankment and saw a few people had taken matters into their own hands, deciding to navigate around the gap in the road, which meant driving down the hill, through what seemed like swamp, and up the other side. Nobody seemed to be having much luck, however – a Maserati was already stuck in the mud and, as I watched, I saw a big family van with about eleven people attempt the same thing and also get completely bogged. I've used the term 'completely bogged' before, but this is the first time it's described a motor vehicle and not my Saturday evening.

I was about to go back to the car and tell Jeffery we were probably going to have to go back and join the traffic jam (or, fingers crossed, cancel his gig and head back to Vegas to see if we could get tickets to Cher) when I saw the one thing you want to see in an emergency situation, a beacon of hope when times are tough: two lesbians, their border collie and their Jeep four-wheel drive.

Gay men and lesbians rarely interact but come together like yin and yang whenever there's a problem. Think Captain Planet: 'With our powers combined . . .'

I quickly approached and massively played the gay card. 'Haiii, ladies.'

After requesting I call them women, not ladies, they explained to me that they too were about to attempt the swamp crossing (again not a euphemism, although I have heard that phrase used in reference to lesbian sex). Apparently the key was to absolutely floor it. They said, 'You boys can follow us if you like.'

I immediately agreed, jumped back in our car and said words I had literally never uttered before: 'Follow those lesbians!'

I should point out the vast difference in our cars. The lesbians were in a spotless, ivory-coloured Jeep four-wheel drive. We were in the cheapest two-door sedan we could find at the local car rental back in LA. This didn't stop us. We followed the lesbians, who flew down the side of the swamp. A crowd significantly bigger than any of our Australian showcase shows had attracted in Montreal had gathered to watch us attempt the crossing. Plus a few people had seen the confidence with which the lesbians got in their car and took off, so we had about another three cars following behind us.

The lesbians flew across the swamp, past the bogged Maserati and people mover, where all eleven family members were now trying to push the car up the hill with no luck, and made it to the other side. Without even looking back, the lesbians flew down the road towards LA (and towards a protest march or working bee or whatever it is they had on that afternoon). Look, if their tattooed heads hadn't been shaved their hair would've been billowing in the wind. I was completely infatuated and I will never forget them. Ladies – sorry, women – please adopt me.

The rental car Jeffery and I were rocking was having a little more trouble, however. Lights were flashing as mud was getting stuck in the tyres and up the side of the car. Alarms I've never heard in a car were going off, Jeffery had his foot to the floor and I was providing crucial assistance by screaming hysterically at the top of my lungs. All the while Taylor Swift's 'Out of the Woods' blared on the car stereo – 'No, we are fucking not, Taylor!'

If we'd had a metre more mud I have no doubt we'd have been stuck but with one last splutter, our car crept up the side of the opposite hill and starting flicking mud off the wheels like crazy as we built up speed. We'd made it! As we took off like lightning down the joining road, I looked back to see that the family immediately behind us had gotten completely bogged halfway, thus blocking the path for anybody else.

A good day for the gays. Suck it, breeders!

We headed down the road for another half-hour, laughing about how lucky we'd been and the hilarity of only the two gay couples making it through the swamp. We hadn't seen a single other car in this time in either direction until, in the distance, I saw a large vehicle moving towards us.

I turned to Jeffery and voiced still more words I never had before that fateful day, 'Does that look like an army tank to you?' What I actually thought was that of course the lesbians had gotten home, picked up their other car and were coming back to help us. He replied, 'I think it *is* an army tank.'

It was, in fact, an army tank ... followed by about another fifty tanks full of men in army uniform, camouflage, guns – the whole get-up. I recognised it immediately because I'd seen an almost identical float at Mardi Gras eight months earlier.

With the crazy traffic jam happening on the main highway and suddenly a convoy of military vehicles *heading straight towards us*, we turned to each other and said, 'What the fuck do you think is happening? Is the world ending?'

I frantically googled and realised the mistake I'd made. I sheepishly turned to Jeffery and said, 'So ... this road is closed for a reason.'

'Why?'

'Um ... well ... I think we're on a military training road. Hence the "Do Not Pass" sign we saw earlier.'

'Well, what the fuck do we do?'

And I cannot believe these words actually came out of my mouth. I said, 'Just blend in.'

Blend in! Because two homos driving a dirty, rented, metallic blue two-door Ford Focus, both in singlets and Le Specs sunnies were going to convince the army that we were meant to be there. We rolled past the tanks in silence (we decided it was best to turn Taylor down temporarily) and stared straight ahead.

Oddly, not a single tank stopped us. We rolled straight on through, found a turn-off to the highway and jumped back on there. Irritatingly, the highway was flowing perfectly at this point, and seemed to have been doing so for some time.

As we pulled in to a service station to fill up with petrol and clean off our mud-caked car, Jeffery got down on one knee. I thought, *Odd time to propose but okay, I'll go with it.*

But he wasn't looking at me, he was looking at the car. He said, 'Yep. I don't think we'll be getting our bond back.'

All the way to Jeffery's gig we laughed about the situation, the lesbians, and the Maserati probably still stuck on the Nevada/California border.

🎤

A week or so after we'd gotten back from Vegas, I was down at the shops around the corner from Jeffery's house buying ingredients for dinner. Jeffery had had some bad news about a gig he had been really hoping to score, so I'd decided to cook him dinner. Having said that, I'm a control freak, so in any relationship I will usually cook dinner regardless of the situation. Except when I'm in the African jungle and Julie Goodwin is around – I made an exception for that. I'm not an idiot.

I love supermarkets in America – they're so grand and full of things that a supermarket wouldn't dream of selling in Australia, like cheesecakes the size of your head or catering packs of croissants that would feed a small country. Or cilantro, which is American-speak for coriander. Cilantro! Sounds like the pool boy in a Brazilian murder mystery. Brazilian as in the country – not the waxing technique. Although that is also a mystery to me.

Usually my manager Andrew would only call me if I was on wifi but if it was urgent he'd make an international call to my US number. I was halfway down the ice-cream aisle, marvelling at the sheer variety of flavours, when he called me.

'Hi. ITV Studios just called. They want you to be a contestant on the first season of Channel Ten's *I'm a Celebrity . . . Get Me Out Of Here!* They reckon you could win it. What do you think? You're not guaranteed in as yet but I need to tell them if you're keen or not.'

Without realising what I was saying, I said, 'Sure. Why not?'

Although it was the first Australian season, I already knew a bit about the show because of my British cousins and friends. In the UK, the show is in its billionth season and is truly their most popular show. People absolutely lose their shit for it. I also knew it involved torturing celebrities for the public's enjoyment. I am not ashamed to say, however, that the thought of suddenly being called a 'celebrity' clouded any concerns I had about the torture aspect. As you'll later read, it took twenty-four hours of life in the jungle for that to rapidly be reversed.

I walked home with the shopping and almost felt guilty telling Jeffery my exciting career update when he had just had bad news about his.

He laughed and in a very American way said, 'So . . . you have to . . . eat bugs and shit?'

I explained that there was more to it than that but yep, pretty much!

He said, 'So I won't be able to talk to you for six weeks?'

'I won't be allowed to talk to anyone but the other celebrities.'

'That sucks. I'll miss you.'

A few weeks later, when Jeffery drove me to the airport to return to Australia, it was a similar car ride to the one we'd had in Melbourne months earlier. Jeffery and I sat in a sad silence, knowing our incredible summer together was coming to an end and we were unsure when we'd see each other again. Jeffery had written me a note that he'd slipped in the front of one of his books, which he'd instructed me to read once I was on the plane.

As I sat on the flight home to Australia I felt so many emotions: thrilled and already nostalgic for the incredible time we'd had together, so in love with him (confirmed by the sweet note he'd left me) and yet completely unsure of what the future held – apart from 'the bugs and shit', which were now looming (or should I say 'buzzing') on the horizon.

10

I'M A CELEBRITY
. . . HAVEN'T
YOU HEARD?

Back home, I busied myself for two months of *I'm a Celebrity . . .* preparations, which included many different interviews, doctors' assessments and psych assessments. In early November I was told, 'Good news – you're not dying. And the better news is you're not *too* crazy.' (But I was just crazy enough, apparently.) 'You got the gig. You're going to Africa.'

I was stoked. I knew this was by far the biggest career opportunity of my life at that time. And Channel Ten were already pouring tons of money into the promos, which were running around the clock and on every billboard and bus shelter, with people speculating who the celebrities would be. It was all very cloak and dagger. I had signed a contract to keep the secret to myself and a select few loved ones. I can't keep a secret to save my life . . . just ask any of my now ex-best friends – I'd be a terrible spy. Give me two white wines and I'd give you the nuclear codes. Or a hand job. So the whole top-secret thing was incredibly difficult for me.

On the day we shot different 'in-studio' elements, from the opening credits to our still shots, to the infamous 'pressing the blue Channel Ten logo' button, we were chaperoned through the rooms of a huge Sydney studio. It was weird knowing my future celebrity campmates were in the other rooms. I tried to look for sneaky clues and listen out for voices and quickly peek around corners when nobody was looking, but the production crew were hardcore and wouldn't let us out of their sight.

A week or so – and about sixteen vaccination shots later (I'm immortal now, just FYI) – I was walking through Sydney Airport in a discreet hat and sunnies, as per the network's instructions, off to Africa. I was originally planning on getting a hat the size of a rural satellite dish like the one Andie McDowell wears to the first wedding in *Four Weddings and a Funeral* because that's my idea of discreet, but in the end I just went with a baseball cap. By then the excitement had also turned to a little bit of fear. I was starting to have nightmares about what I might have to do or experience – or eat, for that matter. And whether the Australian viewing public would like me or not, and if they'd vote me out straight away.

All this was vastly outweighed by my determination. I kept reminding myself that I was funny, and that I had a strong management team looking after me, great friends running my social media and a handsome boyfriend in

America who, thanks to the healthy pay cheque from this show, I would get to see more often.

Oh, and as I always forget to mention . . . the chance to make some money for my charity!

That sounded genuine, right? Selfless and giving, remember?

&

Without doubt the weirdest, most surreal and physically exhausting day of my life was the day I was thrown into the African jungle with nine other celebrities and nothing more than the clothes on my back. That's not actually correct (I also had some spare undies, socks and a framed picture of Harry Styles as my 'luxury item'), but when am I ever going to be in a situation again when I can say that again?

Before going into the jungle I truly had no idea who the other celebrities were – although, like all of us, I'd made some educated guesses based on newspaper articles. There were some wilder guesses too – Pamela Anderson, Kevin Rudd and Melissa Joan Hart (Sabrina the Teenage Witch) were all mentioned. Ugh, imagine having to eat okra and loin of wildebeest with those three? I'll pass. But I knew that Barry Hall was going to be there because the driver who picked me up at the airport in South Africa told me. He didn't realise he wasn't allowed to, of course. Because, fair enough, the Johannesburg locals weren't quite across the logistics of an Australian reality television series. The driver simply said, 'I picked up this footballer earlier . . .'

'Oh yes, what was his name?'

'Barry Hall.'

And I thought, *Oh, shit!* I really believed there was no way in hell I was ever going to be getting chummy with a footballer, maybe because of my previous run-in with the Sydney Swans. I think that's what the producers thought as well, because early on, Barry and I were very much pitted against each other – which of course I completely understand: it makes for great TV. I'm someone who absolutely judges a book by its cover (by the way, just quietly – how good is mine?). I'll happily judge you before I've even spoken to you. And all I knew about Barry Hall was that he was famous for punching people on the football field. Team that with my previous experience of footballers – which is guys I went to high school with and my short-lived career playing for the Applecross Hawks in Grade 4 – I predicted a bromance was not on the cards for us.

I entered the jungle on a Friday morning, having already been placed in lockdown in a luxurious African lodge for five days. I remember thinking at the time how glamorous and decadent the whole thing was, not realising that the producers were letting us have a last taste of being spoiled and indulged before dumping us in the harsh reality of camp. I was woken up at 3 am by my chaperone to go into hair and make-up. It was such a strange feeling, getting dolled up for TV so early – I felt like Karl Stefanovic getting ready for *The Today Show*! I put on an outfit I had spent weeks choosing, wondering if Barry Hall had done the same. We were told we had to wear a cocktail party outfit which 'could get ruined'. I decided on a powder blue jacket, a white open-necked shirt, khaki shorts and a pair of tan shoes, which I'd had for quite a while and which, more importantly, I was therefore completely comfortable with getting destroyed.

At 4 am the lodge ranger took me to the local air field in one of those open-top *Jurassic Park* vehicles. (I just re-read that sentence back to myself. How gay is it? I believe the straights call them Jeeps.) I dare you to go to Africa and *not* make a *Jurassic Park* joke. It's very hard. I'm talking classic *Jurassic Park*, not that new-age *Jurassic World* shit with Bryce Dallas Howard running away from a T-Rex in Witchery pumps. That first day I was fully expecting a velociraptor to appear at any moment with Sam Neill in tow. Either that or a Channel Ten producer running over to apologise, saying they'd made a mistake and that they'd actually meant to book Josh Thomas.

Being a fan of the British version of the show, I assumed we'd be parachuting into the jungle, as that's how they always do it. And as someone who has no desire to para-chute ever, I was strangely zen about it. In fact, I just resigned myself to most things on the show, things I would *never* dream of doing. It's amazing what you can get out of me with a pay cheque and a camera (strictly on prime-time I mean – not on onlydudes.com).

I could see other open-top vehicles arriving at the air field but they were just far enough away that I couldn't make out who was in them. Plus the chaperones were holding enormous black umbrellas over our heads. I started to hear what could only be choppers landing behind me, and I turned to see people getting into the choppers one by one. Then it was time for me to get into my chopper. I said goodbye to my chaperone and off I went. I thought, *Oh my god. This is it. This is* truly *it!*

And man, was it spectacular. It was like 'Circle of Life' – I could literally hear Elton John singing. I was Simba and the chopper pilot was Rafiki (and like Rafiki – he knew the way).

Going up in that chopper, I still couldn't quite believe that they thought that having me, Joel Creasey, on the very first series of *I'm A Celebrity . . . Get Me Out Of Here! Australia* was what they needed. This was a multi-multi-million-dollar production! Of course I was flattered and thrilled and excited, but oh, so nervous.

A cameraman was sitting in the chopper with me, so I was trying to control my nerves, very aware that this was probably the first Australia would see of us and would already be picking their favourites. As I said, I judge immediately; when watching a competition show I pick my favourite straight away and back them until they are eliminated pretty early on (I'm a terrible judge of character). So I knew I had to look good.

I also wanted to look funny. Not physically, of course. But I wanted to present myself as a great comedian. I wanted to look strong, too. Obviously it would have been amazing to win the money for my charity, but let's cut the shit – I wasn't going on the show to win, I was going on to raise my profile. I was there to prove that I am really funny. And most importantly . . . that you should definitely purchase tickets to the stand-up tour I was coincidentally launching off the back of the series.

All ten choppers started lining up in the air, and it was surreal. The launch episode is one of the few I've had the guts to watch and the helicopters flying over Africa looked beautiful. I caught a glimpse of a woman in a white dress waving to me (she turned out to be Miss Australia Laura Dundovic), but I couldn't see anybody else.

After soaring over the beautiful savannahs of South Africa for a while, we began to land, one by one, on an air field that felt smaller than the last one. My chopper had to hover because there were actual lions by the drop zone. Another friendly reminder that this was not the Blue Mountains but fucking Africa.

As I exited my chopper, I was blindfolded. Not in the fun way. I wasn't even allowed to see what was around me – all I knew was I would be meeting the other celebrities at a cocktail party. Either that or ASIO were getting more flamboyant.

Blindfolded, I was shepherded through a series of tents and given a final primp and preen by hair and make-up – I'm telling you, helicopters are *not* good for your deliberately casual quiff. Then a producer approached me and said,

'Right. This is the last time you will be able to speak to anyone off camera. This is the last time you will be off air. Walk towards the gate. Good luck. You're my favourite comedian, by the way.' Clearly not from Colac.

It was the most surreal feeling. The real weight of what I was about to do suddenly started hitting me. Unlike in the chopper, where I couldn't stop thinking how lucky I was, now I was terrified. A 'what the fuck are you doing?'–type terror. This certainly wasn't like stepping onto stage at a stand-up gig, where I'm one hundred per cent in control. But I had signed up for the show without hesitation when asked, so I trusted my gut. Like so many brief romances, I decided to just go, 'Fuck it!', and head in.

Through the gate I walked, into the garden of one of the most beautiful houses I had ever seen. The *Grand Designs* team would cream their pants over this place. Turns out it was called the Manor House, and was owned by a guy who was the unofficial local mayor, and it was also where the hosts Chris Brown and Julia Morris were staying. Standing on the grass to the left was an African choir of about forty beautiful women singing some sort of African chant, which I'm sure Beyoncé will be sampling on an upcoming album. Chrissie Swan later ended up christening these ladies the Human Doorbell, because they started singing every time a celebrity walked past.

At this point I was feeling, well, nothing actually. Once I'm in performance mode I know I have to shut everything else off and just perform. There was a red carpet with a waiter holding a cocktail. I grabbed the glass before realising it was a mocktail and immediately put it down, most likely with a look of disgust. Mocktails are the devil's piss as far as I'm concerned. You're not drinking alcohol? That's fine. Have a Sprite.

I walked down the red carpet and onto the deck where an infinity pool looked out over the sprawling African jungle. It was spectacular. There were martini glasses of devil's piss laid out everywhere, platters of exotic fruit (me included), vases of flowers, deck chairs . . . And standing there in front of me were two other celebrities. One was Marcia Brady. Yes, *the* Marcia Brady AKA Maureen McCormick from *The Brady Bunch* (who was already in tears for some reason) and my now best friend Chrissie Swan.

Chrissie screamed. We knew each other. Not well, but we'd always gotten on in the past. We said something like, 'Can you believe we're doing this?' Chrissie then introduced me to the crying Marcia Brady. We had a brief conversation and two seconds later we heard the Human Doorbell starting to chant. And turned around to see Merv Hughes.

I introduced myself. Chrissie introduced Merv. Marcia Brady said something bizarre and then Leisel Jones entered, followed by Laura Dundovic, Tyson Mayr, Lauren Brant, Barry Hall (eye roll from me) and Andrew Daddo.

And that was it – that was the ten of us. We finished being introduced to each other, and the hosts Chris and Julia arrived, pointed towards the jungle and said, 'Welcome to your new home.' We were kitted out in our jungle gear, popped into another chopper and off we went. The game had begun. *May the odds be EVER in your favour,* was all I could think.

People always ask the same questions:

Was it dangerous? Yes, it fucking was. We had a huge safety briefing in the couple of hours between the cocktail party and being tossed into the jungle. Some local rangers walked us through what we'd need to do if we saw different types of snakes, spiders and animals. I am absolutely petrified of snakes. I'd actually planned on having some hypnotherapy before heading to Africa but missed the appointment due to a hangover. Standard. By day five in the jungle I started to wish I'd been too hungover to make my flight to South Africa at all.

At the safety briefing they also talked to us about the baboons. What I didn't realise is that baboons are fucking arseholes. Total fucking arseholes. No one told me that. You don't learn that in school. The ranger said, 'Whatever you do, don't look the baboons in the eyes.' Sounds like some celebs I could name! 'They're extremely territorial and they'll see that as a turf war challenge – particularly from women. So, ladies, *do not* look the baboons in the eyes because they're actually quite sexist.' Which made me wonder how many shaved-down baboons are currently on the Liberal Party's front bench.

197

Within thirty seconds of the ranger telling us not to look the baboons in the eyes, Maureen McCormick had located a baboon and stared it down. I thought, *Um . . . were you listening just then?* As a result, Maureen single-handedly made our lives a living hell for the following six weeks, as these baboons sat in the trees all day long around our campsite, pelting shit at us (actual shit – not, like, random knick-knacks). All because, like so many before them, they were trying to kill Marcia Brady. That is a completely insane reality. Every time a lump of monkey shit would hit my shoulder, piffed from a branch above me, I would death stare Maureen, who just seemed blissfully unaware of what she'd done.

Were you actually in Africa? Yes, see answer to question one. Very fucking dangerous.

Did you masturbate? You can't begin to realise how many times I've been asked this question. I guess I'd ask people too. Because you're on camera 24/7 *Big Brother* style, it was impossible. Your only options would have been in front of the cameras with the entire control room watching, or in the long drop, which was far too disgusting and smelly to even imagine cranking one out in there. I don't think any of the other celebrities did either. There was just nothing there to arouse you. Although strangely, my Harry Styles picture did go missing on occasion.

Something I've never admitted before, however, is having a wet dream one night. I felt like I was fourteen again. It was about Week Five of the show and it happened in my sleeping bag (thank God. I wonder if you can have a wet dream sleep-walking? That footage would have made *The Daily Mail* fo shiz). The next morning I had to sneak out of bed and race down to the river to fix myself up.

'Just taking an early morning shower!' I yelled at Marcia Brady as I raced past her.

But the first day was truly the weirdest day of my life. After the safety briefing we were flown over some mountain ranges and had to dive out of the chopper into a crocodile-infested river. Everybody starts work that way, yeah? Then we had to pull ourselves across the river on a raft. Determined not to be pegged early on as the 'weak gay', I made sure I was at the front of the raft and didn't stop pulling. I had rope burns up my arm for the following six weeks; I looked like Jean Valjean in the opening scene of *Les Misérables*, and frankly didn't hate it. Then we trekked for hours through the jungle until we finally made it to the campsite. We didn't get in until very late that night, and of course everyone was vying to be Camp Leader, but more importantly, for 'screen time'. Dinner had to be cooked over the campfire, and Andrew Daddo, Chrissie Swan and I sat back when all hell broke loose as the other seven celebrities tried to take the role of head chef. I swear I watched three celebrities cutting the same string bean. It was absolutely nuts.

I was fine and 'on' for the first few days but by about day three or day four I started to crack. That was about the time the comedown kicked in. The excitement was starting to wear off and the reality that this was where I was going be living for potentially the next six weeks was starting to sink in. We were outside. We couldn't contact our friends and family. We were detoxing from sugar, coffee, wheat, dairy, social media – life in general. There was no clock so we had no idea what the time was. The few occasions we would see producers at Tucker Trials they would even have their watches covered with tape. We had no idea where in Africa we were, and once you're in the camp, all the cameras are automated like in *Big Brother* so you don't even see the camera crew. We only ever saw the other celebrities. You feel so vulnerable and so isolated. And that's why the show makes such *great* TV.

One of the main features of camp life was the Tok Toki, which was like a diary room. It was a little hut on the edge of camp and inside was a two-way mirror, behind which was a camera. In front of it was a little speaker through which you could talk to the producers, who, it turns out, were about two kilometres away at the technical base (with a crew of almost 500 if you can believe). You couldn't go into the Tok Toki and ask them to check your emails, or anything about the outside world, you could only really go in there and answer the producers' questions – and they would then use our answers to chop up and narrate the show. Often they'd probe you on a certain matter or try to get an opinion out of you on any drama that may have happened in camp, but for the most part the producers were pretty fair. At no point did they change things or twist what happened in camp.

Chrissie and I loved the Tok Toki because we could go in there and have a laugh and show off and just have fun, without someone else shooting you a look for being too noisy. It meant a brief and often welcome reprieve from the other celebrities.

As well as the Tok Toki, there was a 'Voice of God' speaker in camp, which the producers used to talk to us. They didn't use it often – it was mostly to direct us when to sit on the logs if Chris and Julia were coming into camp, or if there was an animal close by we shouldn't be going near, or to call someone up to the Tok Toki – or to tell Maureen to stop tormenting the fucking baboons.

The first official 'live' day of the show, I was nominated for the first Tucker Trial. Tucker Trials were voted for by the Australian viewing public, so I figured whoever was voted in to do a Tucker Trial first up must have been the one the viewers liked the least. It was essentially who they wanted to punish the most. So . . . you know . . . hearing my name read out felt good! I was lumped with the Circle of Strife challenge, where I had to put my hand into five different holes (admittedly not much of a stretch for me), not knowing what was inside them. Turns out it was fun things like scorpions, rats, snakes . . .

I knew I couldn't fuck up the first challenge and just got on and did it, trying to laugh my way through it. Luckily I completed the challenge and brought home ten stars for the camp, the highest amount you could win. Stars equalled meals for the camp. This made the others very happy and ensured I didn't get nominated for a Tucker Trial for quite a while after that.

By about day five, the first Wednesday of the show, Chrissie and I were done. We were tired and cranky and had no idea if the show was rating nor if there was any point to the whole exercise. She was missing her kids and I was missing my family, but really missing Jeffery; the last time I had spoken to him, he was stuck in a blizzard in New York. Chrissie and I looked at each other and said, 'Let's walk. We don't need this shit. Why are we degrading ourselves like this?'

There's a very funny (in hindsight) clip of Chrissie and I sitting in the Tok Toki begging producers to let us leave with tears streaming down our faces, looking absolutely manic. The producers convinced us not to leave and told us to give it a few hours' thought. Chrissie and I walked out of the Tok Toki and were caught on camera (we were such idiots, there was nowhere to hide) whispering to each other: 'They know we can't leave. You and I *are* the show.' What arrogant arseholes! But it still makes me laugh.

The producers also booked us for appointments with the psychologist, Kate, who was the only person outside of the camp we were allowed to speak to. We had individual appointments with Kate but of course she was only allowed to listen and couldn't provide any information about the outside world. She didn't smuggle in any chocolate either, like we'd hoped.

Chrissie and I decided to sleep on it that night, and the next day woke up and discussed it again and we still wanted to go, but a little bit less than the day before. And the next day was a little bit less again, and so on, until we eventually just surrendered to the whole experience. I don't think I actually would have left, and I don't think Chrissie would have either. Plus my skin was looking amazing thanks to our jungle diet.

I learned to deal without most things in camp. I learned to love being away from social media and my phone. Look, I'm Gen Y, I have my phone in my hand all the time. As I'm typing this, it's sitting beside me with Snapchat open (not many dick pics today, disappointing). But it was nice not to be constantly checking Facebook and Twitter and Instagram (when I say that, I mean checking how many followers I have on each, obviously). Whenever I appear on TV, I'm constantly checking social media to see what people think of me. I'm a performer – I'm insecure and constantly need to be validated. But with this show, I had no means of doing that. I also knew my team on the outside, my manager and my best friends, were really looking after me. I think Thomas was particularly relishing his new responsibility – and pointing any particularly cute fans in the direction of his own, private, social media accounts.

One thing we never learned to live without, however, was coffee. We would spend a good few hours of the day talking about coffee: how we drank it, how many we'd drink a day, our favourite cafés, our least favourite coffee shops. Our whole world was coffee obsessed. Eventually Chrissie and I ended up going up to the Tok Toki and offering to donate five thousand dollars to a local Save the Rhinos charity for one jar of Moccona. That would've averaged around a hundred dollars a cup. We also thought it was a great storyline for the show and would've high-lighted just how desperate we were. The producers, who seemed to be following a 'we do not negotiate with terror-ists' policy, didn't go for it. Chrissie and I were shattered and spent the rest of the time teasing them that they would be single-handedly responsible for the demise of the rhino species. Selfish.

And, fuck, we were hungry. We were *really* hungry. Everyone was losing weight rapidly. We were only eating eight hundred calories a day, which equals one chicken salad – something you might have as an entrée before eating a main meal and dessert. At brunch. The food and hunger situation led to a lot of tension, and meal times were where all the blow-ups happened. Including me exploding at the (divine) Merv Hughes. It had been a particularly tense few days when Merv thought it appropriate to start wielding the machete and yelling at everybody. I ended up saying, 'Merv, I speak with complete confidence on behalf of camp when I say shut the fuck up.' Not surprisingly, I was voted into a Tucker Trial the day after that aired.

Here's how our days worked in camp. We'd get up super early, at around 6 am (remember we had zero concept of actual time). The sun would rise, so we would have no choice but to get up too. Someone would light the fire. I started going down to the river while that was happening, not to meditate – I've never been able to meditate – but just to compartmentalise what was going on and where I was, and to remind myself that I was on a TV show, because you do truly start to believe that this is your reality and you live here now. On particularly crazy days you also started to believe that all these Tucker Trials and challenges they set for you were the Australian viewing public and the producers punishing you. At one particularly low point I convinced myself Australia hated me and I should relocate to Paris. Who did I think I was? Melissa George?

I also went down to the river during the daily lighting-of-the-fire to distract everyone from the fact I had no fucking clue how to light a fire myself.

After that was breakfast, which was always porridge, so it didn't take long to cook, eat and wash up. And when I say porridge, I mean literally just oats and water – no brown sugar or banana or rhubarb coulis; it was beige snot. After breakfast we'd start to hear some noises from Chris and Julia's set, which was about three hundred metres above us, hidden among the trees. At around 10.30 am, Chris and Julia would come into camp to tell us who had been nominated for the next Tucker Trial or, on Sundays, who was being eliminated. Sundays were always our favourite day of the week because it meant that one of us was going home. We'd all pack our few belongings in anticipation it would be us. Of course, the day I was eventually eliminated,

I hadn't packed my bags. But I truly could not have given two shits by that point.

If you weren't going into a Tucker Trial, that was it for the rest of your day. You'd cook a little bit of rice and beans (which, unlike porridge, took fucking forever to boil) for your lunch in the heat of the roasting African sun. Then all afternoon you'd have nothing to do but wait for the Tucker Trial celebrity to return. And when there is nothing to look at but the same trees and each other, when there is nothing to write on, nothing to read, not even a car driving past or the sound of construction, nothing new to preoccupy your mind, you do start to go stir-crazy and the hours draaaaaaaag on. Some of those afternoons felt like eternities.

At first we would make up games to entertain ourselves. We made a chess board and painted rocks (with paint comprised of fire ash and water). Miss Australia Laura Dundovic would host personal training classes; I took part in maybe two. Andrew Daddo started Craft Club, whittling away at branches and trees. And when Julie Goodwin arrived she got into knitting using two sticks (made in Craft Club) and some twine from a bag we had.

Chrissie and I weren't into any of these things. We are crafty, just mentally, not practically. She and I preferred to sit down by the river and laugh. We nicknamed ourselves the River Monsters as, while the other celebrities would lie in the sun, tanning their incredible washboard abs, we'd sit in the shade upstream fully clothed. We discussed every topic known to man.

I'm a Celebrity . . . Haven't You Heard?

The first intruders to come into camp to break up the monotony were the couple from *The Bachelor*, Tim Robards and Anna Heinrich, who came in on the Sunday after the elimination of the first contestant, Leiesl Jones. When I got back home after being voted off, I discovered that when the Australian public heard that there was going to be a celebrity couple going into camp, a rumour started that it was going to be Keith Urban and Nicole Kidman. Can you IMAGINE? Watching Nicole and Keith with Marcia Brady certainly would have put some entertainment back into our days. Tim and Anna were lovely, but they were a couple, and we were all missing our loved ones, so we were a bit jealous of them. We were all a little bummed Leisel had left so early too. Frankly, we were all secretly happy when Tim was eliminated the following weekend, leaving his girlfriend behind on her own (in tears). It also meant we got to know her much better.

Things did get even more interesting at the end of week two, when Julie Goodwin entered the jungle as an intruder. I was beside myself – Julie was my favourite contestant from *Masterchef* and my best friend Ashleigh and I obsessed over her in every episode from that first season. We would actually attempt to cook a lot of her dishes, and I loved that with every dish Julie was cooking, it always felt like what she ended up making was a chocolate cake. The judges would come in and say, 'Okay, contestants, it's time to present us with a seafood platter!' And Julie Goodwin would go, 'Nah! I'm making a chockie cake!' And it worked, because of course she ended up winning the show. I don't want any of that quail egg shit they're pumping out in the current seasons. I just want Julie Goodwin's home cooking. I also loved that no matter what Julie was cooking, she always looked a little bit crazy, covered in flour with a spatula or other random utensil stuck in her hair. Even in the jungle when we were eating porridge and rice and beans, somehow Julie still had a little smudge of flour in her hair. As I lay in bed the night of Julie's arrival in the jungle, I thought of Ashleigh and how she would be laughing so hard knowing Julie was now trapped with me.

Chrissie also delighted in Julie's arrival, and she and I would invite Julie down to the river with us, where we'd quiz her for hours. We'd say, 'Potato salad . . . Go!' and we'd make her rattle off the ingredients and method as quickly as possible.

The other intruder to arrive with Julie was Freddie Flintoff, the English cricket captain who ended up winning the show. He was a nice guy, and he had been on the English version of the TV show, *A League of Their Own*. He still does the show over there with James Corden. Freddie even had me on as a guest once the show was finished. What bothered me when he came in was the producers trying to bait me when I went up to the Tok Toki to be interviewed about his and Julie's arrival. They'd say, 'So you probably don't know who Freddie Flintoff is . . .' which I found irritating and a bit presumptuous, because I knew exactly who Freddie Flintoff was. But I was relieved they didn't ask me anything about his cricket career or statistics – I'd have had nothing.

I loved Freddie, but his arrival did make my position in the camp a lot trickier, as Freddie was essentially a comedian too – just a lot less polarising than I am.

My favourite stories from the show of course feature Maureen McCormick. She was so kooky, but she's gorgeous and, my God, she is a delight, one of the most delicious humans I've ever had the pleasure of meeting or having baboon faeces thrown at me with. Chrissie and I still talk about her regularly, wondering what she's up to, what she's saying and which dangerous animal she's befriended. Without doubt, the craziest sentence I have ever heard in my life came out of Maureen's mouth. It was the final week of the show, and it was down to six of us: Chrissie, Freddie, Barry, Anna, Maureen and me. It was afternoon and we were all sleeping, willing the hours to pass by more quickly. By this point we were counting the hours till the finale and home time. The line of scratches on the log/homemade calendar by the fire that we'd been marking the days into was getting longer and longer and we were so excited. But we truly did not have a single fucking thing left to say to one another. We had exhausted every possible topic.

This particular afternoon Maureen walked back into camp – where she'd been, no one had any idea. Sometimes she would disappear for hours on end and we assumed she'd been eaten by a lion, and then she'd suddenly appear. Lauren Brant used to think she was getting special celebrity treatment off camera. But I genuinely think she would just wander off, lost in her own world.

So Maureen walked back into camp and said to no one in particular, 'Hey guys, you know baby hyenas, right?'

I had been lying down pretending to be asleep but I realised this might be worth getting up for. What *was* TV icon Maureen McCormick's position on baby hyenas? What was her hot take on them, having been surrounded by them for six weeks in the African jungle?

So, intrigued, I got up and said 'Yes, Maureen . . .'

And I'm so glad I did, because that's when she repeated herself but added, 'Do they grow into hyenas?'

I was speechless for the first time in my life. 'What . . . Sorry – what?' I couldn't believe it. What a bizarre question.

Luckily for me I didn't actually have to say anything because at that point Barry Hall, who really hadn't said anything for the entire six weeks, finally snapped and spat, 'Well, they don't turn into fucking giraffes, Marcia!'

If I hadn't already fallen madly in love with Barry Hall by that point, I certainly did then.

My favourite story from *I'm A Celebrity* . . . never made it to air, but it too involved Maureen McCormick – and Julie Goodwin. Two of my favourite people on the planet. I can't imagine any time when these two are in the same situation and it wouldn't be hilarious.

I'm a Celebrity . . . Haven't You Heard?

Every so often the producers would give us secret missions to spice up camp life and the show itself. They weren't always major things that would change camp in any way but they would be to win a reward like some chocolate or an ice cream. You know, those things you probably just have in your fridge. Those things you don't normally spend all day trying to win. A few weeks after she'd arrived, Julie Goodwin was called up to the Tok Toki around mid-afternoon. The speaker box said, 'Julie Goodwin, please come up to the Tok Toki,' and immediately, Julie was stressed, it was like she was suddenly in a *Masterchef* pressure test. Julie, let me just say, is the single most lovely, gorgeous human I ever met, but she is also one of those people who seems to stress no matter what. Bear in mind we were called up to the Tok Toki on a daily basis, so this wasn't out of the ordinary either. But still, it was enough to tip Julie over the edge.

Julie went flying up to the Tok Toki, a cloud of flour in her wake, despite the fact she hadn't been near a kitchen in four weeks. When she got up there, the producers told her that they had a secret mission for her. They asked her not to tell the rest of us about it, but they wanted Julie to be back in the Tok Toki at the crack of dawn the following morning to find out the specifics of the secret mission.

Julie agreed to the mission and said, 'Yes, of course, no problem, I can do that, but how will I know when it's the crack of dawn?'

211

It was a good question because of course, although we did normally wake up when the sun came up, sometimes if you were lucky, you might sleep in an hour or so. There were no alarm clocks (if you didn't count the baboons sometimes throwing shit at you to wake you up), so there was no possible way of telling the time. The producers realised that this was a problem. They couldn't just do an announcement over the speaker either as it would wake the entire camp and thus reveal the secret mission. So eventually the producers said to Julie, 'Get Maureen to wake you up.'

Something you must know is that it seemed that Maureen never slept the entire time we were in camp. I don't know how she's even alive – she must be a vampire. Every time we would look at her, she was wide awake. Actually, I tell a lie – she would always manage to nod off ten minutes before dinner was served. She had the most inconvenient timing. But otherwise: no sleeping for Marcia Brady. Even in the middle of the night, if you even slightly opened your eyes, Maureen would instantly be there, asking 'How are you going? What are you doing? Do you want to chat? How are you sleeping?'

So in the Tok Toki, Julie Goodwin said, 'Excellent idea, good plan, I'll get Maureen to wake me up,' and headed back down into camp. She walked past us very cagily but trying desperately to appear nonchalant, and Chrissie, Freddie and I immediately turned to each other and said, 'Well, Julie's definitely been given a secret mission!'

Julie went and found Maureen, pulled her aside and said, 'Maureen, I need your help. Can you please wake me up first thing tomorrow at the crack of dawn?'

Now if you had asked that same question of any other celebrity in the camp, they would have immediately asked, 'Why? Why do you have to get up first thing tomorrow morning? Have you got a meeting? There is nothing to do here, we are stuck in the middle of the African jungle and there is nowhere to go and nothing to do. *Why do you have to get up?*' But of course, that's not Maureen McCormick's way. Maureen's immediate response was, 'Sure. Does it matter if it's still dark?'

I personally would have seen that as a problem, I think most would. But Julie Goodwin, being particularly stressed and not wanting to stuff up her secret mission, panicked and said, 'No, no, just wake me up as early as you can,' which Maureen agreed to.

We usually went to bed at what must have been 8 or 9 pm, but to us that felt like midnight. It was dark, we were constantly tired and hungry and there was nothing else to do. Eventually it came time for Maureen to wake Julie. We were all oblivious to this story, by the way, until Julie recounted it to us the next day.

Maureen walked over to Julie's bed, leaned right down over her ear and hissed loudly, *'First warning!'* which of course is not the gentlest way to wake an already stressed person. Julie immediately and violently flung herself out

213

of bed, a mushroom cloud of flour and a couple of spatulas flying into the air.

In the darkness Julie went racing – *bolting* – up to the Tok Toki. She slammed open the Tok Toki door, sat down and completely flustered said, 'Right! I'm here for the secret mission!'

The overnight producer Kelly said, confused, 'Julie – what are you doing here?'

Julie repeated, 'I'm here for the secret mission! Sorry, am I late? Have I ruined it? I'm so sorry – I've stuffed up the secret mission! I asked Maureen to wake me up, but she mustn't have woken up early enough!'

Producer Kelly said, 'Julie, you can go back to bed . . . for a while.'

And Julie said, 'I'm so sorry – I just thought it was time, I'm so sorry . . . I'll go back to bed.' And got up to leave. But just as she exited, she turned around and said, 'Hang on – how long have I been asleep for?'

And Kelly said, 'Julie, you've been asleep for ninety minutes.'

That means Marcia Brady woke Julie up at *9.30 pm*! Ninety minutes after she went to bed! Imagine starting your day at 9.30 pm! The crazy thing was that Maureen hadn't even slept yet. She obviously thought that ninety minutes was an entire night, and an appropriate time to wake Julie up.

When we were told the next day, we laughed like hyenas (baby *and* adult). Which was impressive, because there were hyenas everywhere. That was until a Marcia Brady–induced baboon shit missile hit us. And we promptly shut up again.

Life in the jungle was simple. There were no commitments and no responsibilities, we were just told what to do. There was no worrying about social media or what people thought of you. There was no worrying about what we looked like. The first week of the show I tried to make myself presentable, but by week six I had this awful, shaggy, Jesus-like beard and I weighed about as much as an Olsen twin's finger. My hips and ribs were so prominent I actually had trouble sleeping on my front from about week four onwards. I was starting to get embarrassed about the way I looked.

But I had completely surrendered to my surroundings and I loved it. I could sleep all day, laugh with Chrissie Swan whenever I wanted and, when I was feeling down, I could swim in a fresh water lagoon complete with waterfall (apparently no crocodiles) while monkeys played in the trees overhead. I felt like Mowgli in the fucking *Jungle Book*. Similar tan, too.

So to be eliminated just a few days before the finale – to suddenly be pulled away from all of that – was incredibly surreal. When I was in there, all I could think about was getting back to the outside world and how this experience had given me a greater appreciation of my life. We would regularly comment on how we'd never again take things like coffee or eating a nice breakfast for granted. Though to be honest, I think we all forgot saying that thirty seconds after elimination.

Anna Heinrich and I left the show in a double eviction. She came sixth and I came fifth. (I only know this because I double checked with the producers.)

I was thrust back into my normal existence, and I was me again, on top of the fact that I was also a celebrity who had just been eliminated from a reality show. The first season of a reality show where even people who weren't watching knew what was going on. I think the whole Marcia Brady factor helped: 'Oh my God, I saw a show on TV last where Marcia Brady had to swim in elephant shit to win food for Andrew Daddo!'

Suddenly I was back in control. I could get a coffee whenever I wanted, I could have food whenever I wanted and I never had to use a long drop ever again. But I was pretty bummed to leave in a double eviction – the constant TV producer in my head knew I wouldn't have as much screen time in the upcoming interviews.

We had the length of one ad break to say goodbye to our campmates and race up to the treehouse set that Chris and Julia broadcast from. I hugged a crying Maureen, said goodbye to Freddie, hugged Barry and then almost burst into tears saying goodbye to Chrissie. Which was absurd – I'd see her in a week. But she had become my rock and my lifeline. As I left, I whispered in her ear, 'You have to win this. For us.'

Then producers were talking to us, hugging us, apologising for treating us like shit for six weeks. I had producers saying, 'I'm sorry I couldn't talk to you when you asked me for the time in week three . . . I really wanted to tell you, you were my favourite and I love you, but I couldn't.' One producer even gave me a fresh bottle of water, which felt so strange after they had deprived us for so long.

Up in the treehouse I was interviewed by Chris and Julia, given a glass of champagne and some M&Ms (apparently I was the only celebrity to drink the champagne, which I like to think is my biggest achievement of being on the show). They showed me a package of my time in the jungle and I couldn't believe what the jungle and the show itself looked like. All I could think was, *Oh my God, is that what I look like? Who is that dirty, skinny, bearded man?* They showed a really sweet clip of Barry Hall talking about me, and then some live footage of Barry looking really down and upset about me having left, and I almost cried on national television over this guy I had really not expected to get along with at all – this big, tough footballer I had fallen completely, madly in love with, and who was just one of the nicest guys I'd ever met.

Straight after we were eliminated, Anna and I were taken to the crew base, which was really close to the celebrity camp, but of course we had no idea about that. Crew members came running over to us for photos, congratulating us, slapping us on the back. It felt amazing.

I asked if I could borrow a phone and I made a thirty-second call to my manager, Andrew, asking, 'Do I still have a career?'

He responded, 'Yes. I am *so* proud of you.' I think I started to cry.

While the show was being broadcast live in Australia at 8.30 pm, it was only about 11.30 am in Africa and Anna and I still had a full day ahead of us. First up we were required to have a psych and medical briefing and that's when I realised just how much weight I had lost. Kate the psychologist talked us through a few things and prepared us to be released into the outside world where our profiles had grown immeasurably and the public now had opinions about us, some good and some bad. (I'd pissed off quite a few Merv Hughes fans, as it turns out.)

People often ask me what my first meal was after coming out of the jungle. Of course I had a burger and fries and Anna had the same thing. The meal was incredible.

Then our crazy media schedule began. I started with interviews with some of the big magazines back in Australia, like *New Idea* and *OK!*, as their reporters had all been waiting up to see who was eliminated.

Then Australia went to bed so I had a few hours off. I was taken to a luxury mansion where I could shower (which felt *crazy good!*) and look at myself naked in a mirror for the first time, which was really confronting. I immediately shaved my beard off and made sure my penis still worked. Then I began photo shoots for the Australian magazines.

That took a couple of hours but I had time to sneak in a phone call or two. I FaceTimed my mum, and I tried to reach Jeffery but I couldn't get hold of him because of the time difference with America. Also African wifi isn't great, and these were such important phone calls to make I didn't want them to stuff up.

After dinner, at about 10 pm, I was taken back to the crew base to start press interviews. By then Australia was waking up, and Anna and I sat there and did fifty back-to-back breakfast radio interviews. A lot of the questions were very similar like 'How did you find your time in the jungle?' Many of my questions were about Chrissie and Barry, and a few were about my argument with Merv, which I found quite funny, because although Merv and I had squabbled, by the time Merv had been eliminated a few days earlier, we were the best of friends. And still are.

And then, suddenly, it was done. I was out. I was a celebrity and I was out of there. I was put on a plane back to Australia, seated next to Julie Goodwin, who had been eliminated the day before. Fuck, we got drunk.

We landed in Sydney and there were paparazzi everywhere, people wanting photos, people saying, 'My child loved you on the show!' and 'My daughter cried when you were eliminated!' It was all so odd. I'll also never forget the flight attendant at the business lounge in Sydney saying with a huge smile, 'Welcome home. Can I make you a coffee? I know how much you missed it.' What a fucking legend.

When I landed back in Melbourne, Jeff, one of my managers, picked me up. He had hamper after hamper after hamper and bottles of French champagne in the back of his car. I was welcomed home by Thomas and we sat on my balcony for hours, laughing and chatting about the show.

Flash forward to the next night and I was at my favourite nightclub, Poof Doof. Yes, that is the real name of a gay club in Melbourne. How brilliant is it? Gays are so good at taking words and just owning them. I feel like gays have done what rappers did with the N word . . . except we added glitter and Lady Gaga. I've also been to gay clubs in Europe called the Cockpit and the Male Box.

So there I was drinking and partying all night long, and had an utterly insane moment at about three in the morning when I realised Chrissie Swan was still stuck in the middle of the African jungle and, only forty-eight hours before, I had been there too. But now here I was back in Melbourne, living my life, drinking a vodka soda and flirting with boys. It was the weirdest, most bizarre experience.

I had a whirlwind year off the back of *I'm a Celebrity* . . . perhaps irresponsibly so. I took every TV show that was offered and appeared everywhere. I ended up burning myself out.

At the end of 2015 I was asked to go back to Africa as a host of the *I'm a Celebrity . . . Get Me Out of Here! Australia* after-show called *I'm a Celebrity . . . Get Me Out of Here NOW!* I said no twice but I was eventually persuaded, and frankly, sold a different show and concept to what I ended up getting in Africa. I was told repeatedly, Your show is the sister show to the prime-time show. We are *family*.'

We broadcasted live from the African jungle on Channel Eleven immediately following the main show finishing on Channel Ten. The highlight was getting to go back to Africa and live in the lap of luxury. We stayed in a beautiful house complete with four butlers an hour away from the celebrity campsite and the show set. I got to meet some amazing people and experience Africa in a way not many do. Before this I had hosted shows like *The Project* and morning TV, but never the same show night after night after night. I got a baptism-of-fire introduction to live nightly television, and it's fair to say I got fucking burned.

The lowlight was the show itself. Whereas the main show has a huge crew (which is absolutely required), we put together our one-hour-a-day show with an official crew of six. We would wake at 4 am to drive to work and would go live to air around 11 am. I was the anchor and host of the show but I also took on writing duties, penning all the jokes and openers and closers. To make matters harder, crew from the main show seemed to shun us. If we were a family, to them we were apparently their dirty step-cousins, even though we were all working for the same company and had the same goal. I remember asking an executive producer from the main show one day for some advice and he shrugged and said, 'It's not my show, mate.' So much for 'family'.

In an attempt to make the show work, I took on more responsibilities, filming segments in the afternoon to play in the next day's show in the hope that injecting some of my humour would help. One afternoon I found myself back in a Tucker Trial – something I'd sworn I would never do again. Who willingly puts themselves through that? But an executive producer from the network I really liked and respected asked me to do it. And I was paranoid about my perception within the industry, knowing that the show was a ratings bust, so I agreed. Suddenly I found myself chained in a tank in a Houdini-type situation while water rose around me and crocodiles and snakes slipped all over me as I tried to unchain myself.

As I said, we got slammed in the ratings and reviews. Torn to pieces.

I got incredibly depressed in Africa the second time around. I hated waking up every day and going into work knowing that nobody was watching and everybody on set knew it. I had very little room to move in the live show and ended up just feeling like a talking head. I wasn't myself. I was embarrassed and my ego was bruised.

After work each day I would eat takeaway in bed in this stunning house in Africa looking over the savannah. I would shut my blinds and medicate (definitely not meditate) myself to sleep, then wake to my 4 am alarm and want to throw up.

I was also counselling people on set who knew the show wasn't going well. I would look down at the celebrities roughing it in the jungle and feel incredibly jealous. I would've taken raw eyeballs, baboon shit and a dirty old camp bed over this experience any day. I counted down the days till I could get home and literally ran to the plane at Johannesburg Airport on that final day.

I'm A Celebrity . . . Now was, without doubt, the worst professional experience of my life. And I felt incredibly guilty complaining about the job, because I *had* a job. In television. In Africa. Staying in a beautiful house and experiencing a magical country that so many people never get to in their lifetimes. I'm just not very good at failing.

I was mad for a long time after *I'm a Celebrity . . . Now*. Mad I'd taken the job and mad at what had transpired. But oddly, it was Maureen McCormick who made it all right. I was in America shortly after the show finished and arranged to catch up with her, as I always do when in LA. We were sitting in a restaurant in Venice Beach, glasses of wine the size of our heads in hand. And she said, 'You know what? I've been in this industry my entire life. And I've made so many mistakes. But shit happens. And the sooner you learn that shit happens, the sooner another opportunity will come your way.'

I had no way to respond. No advice I could return. Except to finally – and kindly – confirm for her that baby hyenas do, in fact, grow into hyenas.

Gosh, I love that woman.

11

A PROPER COMEDIAN

Performing at the Melbourne International Comedy Festival Gala will always be one of my greatest career achievements.

For those not familiar with the gala, it's a televised comedy special on once a year and includes the top twenty or so Australian and international comedians performing at that year's Melbourne Comedy Festival and for that reason is always guaranteed to be a great show. Not to mention all the comedians are trying to entice you to buy a ticket to their live show – so they're throwing their 'gold' material at you. That's an industry term for best material. Obviously, my material, like my hair, is platinum.

The Gala traditionally aired on Network Ten but has recently moved to the ABC. When I was growing up, we used to sit down as a family and watch the gala together. I probably started watching at twelve years old and I felt so grown up. My parents were always big fans of comedy, so I think they just viewed it as an important part of their children's education. Either that or they were drunk and thought we were watching *Round the Twist*.

I always used to watch the Gala, or any stand-up for that matter, for the ladies. I've always been more a fan of female comedians. Is it sexist to say I find women funnier than men? Because I do. I'm not sure what it is, but I guess I've always been attracted to the story-telling style of stand-up as opposed to the other forms like one-liner comics, or prop comics or whimsical acts. I'm a story-telling comedian myself. And I think this style lends itself better to women. No idea why. The only comedy shows I've ever bought a ticket to were performed by women, I've only ever had female comedians as my support acts and it's in my contracts that, if I'm on a line-up show within Australia, there must be at least one woman on the bill. I say 'within Australia' because I don't quite have the power to make those sorts of demands overseas – yet. I'm comin' for you, New Zealand! And it's not because I'm trying to make some sort of political stand, just more that it gives me something I want to watch while standing in the wings waiting for my turn.

As a child I used to sit and wait for all the women performing at the Gala: Judith Lucy, Denise Scott, Kitty Flanagan and my all-time favourite, Fiona O'Loughlin. When I was really young I was allowed to stay up until Fiona had been on. By the time I was fourteen I was allowed to watch the whole thing.

I never particularly imagined myself on the Gala stage. At that point in life I was taking my performance far more seriously and was determined to be an actor. In fact, I remember being completely in awe of these comedians in a 'how the hell do they do that?' way. Which is a question I get every day now as a professional comedian: 'I don't know how you get up there and do that!' But now I truly can't imagine *not* doing it. I don't really get nervous, it's more an anticipation – I'll look forward to a big show for days. That's just me, though. I know some hugely successful comedians who get incredibly nervous before a show and relish harnessing that nervous energy and using it for their performance. Not me. I'm not pacing backstage, or jumping on the spot or doing air karate – I'm usually on Instagram checking out how many people in the audience have tagged me in their selfies – and if they're cute enough to ask them backstage.

I made my first appearance in the Gala in 2013, having bugged my manager, Andrew, the previous few years to get me on. There are actually two galas that go to air these days. There's the Melbourne International Comedy Festival Gala, which is the one that's been on for years and where all the comedians donate their time because it raises money for Oxfam. I guess this is the more prestigious of the two because of its history. Not to mention any time you work for Oxfam you totally feel like Angelina Jolie *sans* the creepy necklace with the blood on it. (Gosh that's some vintage Ange for you, remember that shit?) I am Team Angelina, if you were wondering. Love Jen but Ange forever. Guess it's all over now though isn't it? (I'm obviously still not coping with the split.)

The other show, which has been running for almost ten years now, is the All-Star Gala, which is filmed a week later. With the size of the Melbourne International Comedy Festival, there are too many headline comedians to fit in one show and they had to create another. The line-ups are always equally as good, there's just perhaps a little more jostling among comedians to appear on the Oxfam Gala purely because it airs earlier during the festival and therefore allows for more exposure and more potential ticket sales. If you don't think established, successful comedians are money hungry . . . you're wrong.

My first booking in 2013 was on the All-Star Gala, and I called every single person in my contacts list crying. I was finally in one of the Melbourne International Comedy Festival Galas and I wasn't even twenty-three yet. To me this meant I was a proper comedian. I was one of *Australia's comedians*. So fuck, I'd better deliver a good set!

The galas have been filmed in theatres all over Melbourne, most regularly at the Palais Theatre. The Palais is the largest theatre in Victoria and it is gorgeous. It's opposite Luna Park in St Kilda and, much like the prostitutes who work the local corners, is constantly surrounded by scaffolding as the facade is crumbling from the salt air. Inside is stunning and so large you feel like you're in an arena. Once again . . . much like the prostitutes . . .

March of 2013 was my fourth Melbourne International Comedy Festival – that year I was presenting my new show, *Drama Captain,* and it was my first time setting foot on stage at the Palais Theatre, though I'd sat in the audience many times, once on a date to see a hipster band called *Boy and Bear* whom I lied to my date about and said I loved. Honestly didn't know a single lyric.

I dressed myself for the Gala as I didn't have the money or forethought at that point to hire a stylist. This is also before I had any decent taste of my own, so I went to David Jones and bought the most expensive shirt on offer. It was a black shirt with heavy gold stencilling. I teamed it with navy Nudie jeans (cropped) and black leather lace-ups. Gross – one of those looks that ages worse every single day. I actually have a hard time watching certain gigs back if I don't like what I was wearing. This was one of those gigs.

Having said I don't get nervous before a gig, there are exceptions. And televised galas are gigs that I believe all comedians get nervous before. Because sure, there are three thousand people sitting in the audience, but then add the million people watching at home. And that's not all. When you are finally on a televised comedy gala you are – perhaps for the first time – being perceived as part of the upper echelon of stand-up comedians, so you can't help but shit yourself a tiny bit. Not only do you have to deliver your set well enough to prove your worth, but you could be on after a comedian who has been doing this for thirty years and is a comedy icon. Perhaps the most terrifying part is that everyone in the industry pays close attention to the festival galas. Backstage at these events is really quite daunting, because every manager is there, watching keenly. I guess in a way we're athletes and they're the bookies looking to see who's 'in form' this season. And let's be honest, schadenfreude feels pretty great when somebody else fucks up.

I was on third after the interval, following comedy legend Rich Hall, who went on to win Best Show at the festival a few weeks later. No pressure whatsoever. And of course I had Andrew watching backstage. I also wanted to impress him, the man who'd taken a punt on me a few years back and finally secured me a shot at the comedy big leagues. I remember standing in the wings waiting to go on, the backstage buzzing like a NASA launch site with crew and camera operators, sound guys and producers everywhere. A runner had handed me a bottle of water to sip before I went on but every time I had a drink I would choke and I ended up having to stop and just concentrate on pacing my breathing and remembering my fucking material.

Tom Gleeson was hosting the 2013 gala and he was doing a spectacular job. In fact, everyone had been nailing it, so I didn't want to be the first one to fuck it up. Then suddenly Rich Hall had finished, Tom had announced me, I'd gone out, done my three-minute spot (that's right: you literally only get one hundred and eighty seconds to prove yourself, although I suppose that's more than I've given some dates I've been on) and I was off. It was all over. It was such a blur. I remember the audience laughing, at one point even clapping – and that was it. I also remember thinking, *Gosh this theatre is even more gorgeous from the stage* and *This outfit I have chosen is TIMELESS. I will never regret this decision.*

I'll never forget Andrew thumping me on the back with his huge hand in the way only he could and saying, 'You fucking killed it, mate. Well done.' I was really proud.

My parents and Ashleigh were in the audience that night. Apparently all three of them teared up while I was on stage. I know this because Ashleigh told me after my twenty-eighth glass of champagne at the after-party, after I asked her for the thirty-second time to tell me about it again.

The following year I was booked for the Oxfam Gala. I was thrilled to be chosen for this gala as it was the one I had always admired growing up. My parents once again attended and by this point I was working with a stylist, who put me in a cropped blue suit. I can actually bear to watch this performance. I was up against it though, as I was closing the show. Normally going last is a huge compliment, but at a gala it's not a great spot to be in: galas are notoriously long shows because hardly any of the comedians stick to their allocated three minutes. Me included. We often refer to these shows as a 'glamorous hostage situation' for the audience. But Eddie Perfect was the host that year and he did such a marvellous job of keeping the show cracking along. I had my best gala performance to date.

And no gala would be complete without a debrief with Ashleigh, my parents and twenty-eight champagnes after. This year with an added Thomas.

In October of 2014, before I went into the jungle on *I'm a Celebrity* . . . I had been told I would be hosting the Oxfam Gala the following year. I was of course elated and honoured. The offer put me in a very elite group of people who had hosted the show, ranging from Magda Szubanski to Dave Hughes. I remember calling my parents, knowing it would really mean something to them as well. They immediately booked flights.

It was quite tricky to prepare for, however, as the gala was taped in mid-March and I was leaving for Africa in January. And before that people were on Christmas and New Year holidays. Let me tell you, there is no other group of people as good at stretching their summer holidays quite like the entertainment industry. So that meant the preparation we could do in November and December was minimal as by that point we weren't even sure which comedians would be appearing on the line-up. We came up with a concept to do something with my mum as a co-host and that was really all the information that had been locked down before I was tossed into the jungle and cut off from the outside world. I just had to trust Andrew would know how to answer any production-related question that came up.

I was voted out of the jungle on Wednesday, the 11th of March (it was a dark day, you probably remember), and landed back in Australia late on Friday. The gala was on the following Tuesday. Being voted out before the finale was a blessing in disguise because it at least gave me *some* time to prepare for the show. But we had a strategy in place in case I'd won the show: I would have landed in Australia twenty hours before show time; I was going to be taken straight to a hotel across the road from the Palais (instead of my apartment a whole twenty minutes up the road) and we were going to rehearse through the night. Even with the extra few days, we ended up rehearsing through the night before the gala. Sleep was certainly not an option.

The concept that had been devised in my absence was the show would begin with me 'running late' to the gala courtesy of my African adventure (conveniently both shows were on the same network). The big screens in the theatre would show pre-recorded FaceTime conversations between me and my mum, who had arrived in time for the show, and was live on stage. The cute idea was that because I was running late my mum would cover for me until I arrived with a dance routine by her Zumba class. (I used to regularly tease my mum and her Zumba obsession in my stand-up shows.) The screens would then rise, revealing thirty dancers in lycra, and Jenny would lead a dance routine. Mid-dance I would come running into the theatre with Mum pulling me into the routine with her, finishing with confetti cannons, lasers, etc.

From there I would do a quick change on stage into a suit and begin the show.

A Proper Comedian

This concept never really sat well with me. It wasn't the idea I had quite envisioned for the show, but by the time I was out of the jungle and back in the real world it was too late to change it. Plus everyone had been working so hard on my behalf that I didn't want to step on any toes.

To choreograph such an opening number in only seventy-two hours was a huge undertaking. And there was so much room for error on the night. Not to mention I'd just arrived home from the first season of a highly rated reality show, with media following me everywhere. I was getting countless interview requests, which I wasn't saying no to either because I was about to embark on a massive national tour.

It's only writing this now that I fully realise and appreciate what a trouper and a legend my mum was. She landed in Melbourne on Sunday evening to be greeted by her emaciated (but finally clean-shaven) African warrior son. She was immediately sent off to dance rehearsals while I went to interview after interview after interview. My schedule didn't allow for me to come in for dance rehearsals until the night before the gala. My mum's fake Zumba class was comprised of very fit twenty-year-old dancers, and it was quite funny walking in to see my 59-year-old (and to her credit, also very fit) mother trying to learn all the steps and keep up with them.

Not to mention she was already nervous about the following evening. During our staged FaceTime calls she was going to be the only person on stage in front of three thousand people. *Three thousand people!* Not only that, she was going to be the first person to even be seen on stage at the 2015 Melbourne International Comedy Festival Gala. To be honest, I don't think anybody ever asked my mum if she was cool with it. Nobody said, 'Hey, do you even want to do this?' She was essentially just pressured into it by the producers. I, of course, had wanted to include my mum in the show, but I'd never envisioned sticking her out on that stage on her own to open the entire fucking thing. But in true Jenny Creasey fashion, she went along with it. To help out her son.

The day of the Gala was insane. Not only did I have the opening dance to wrap my head around, I then had to actually host the show itself: perform stand-up and welcome people on stage. The dance was just one three-minute component of a three-hour show. I also had twenty interviews to get through, beginning with breakfast radio at 6 am, plus several photo shoots for different publications.

If you can believe it, we were still rehearsing the dance fifteen minutes before the show was due to start. Doors were supposed to be opened forty-five minutes prior. I don't think we ever ran it once smoothly before we did the dance itself, live in front of three thousand people – and then the rest of Australia.

Luckily that day my writing partner, Janelle, had arrived in town to take some of the pressure off. She had helped write the script for the night while I was busy eating ostrich eyeballs and chatting to Marcia Brady in the African jungle.

A Proper Comedian

On big gigs I'll always try to bring Janelle with me as she is such a calming presence and, as a brilliant performer herself, understands what you do and don't need pre-gig. Sometimes you want to talk, sometimes you just want to sit and stare at the ceiling. Plus Janelle is always great for a gag if you need one. I swear I've thrown the words 'paper clip', 'eggplant' and 'judicial law' at her before and she's come back a split second later with a joke.

For such an iconic theatre, the backstage area at the Palais isn't particularly glamorous and dressing room space is limited, with most comedians sharing a dressing room with four or five others. What was cool this night, however, is that they had given my mum her own dressing room with a bunch of flowers waiting in it.

About fifteen minutes after the show was officially due to start they called places and my mum was led to the stage and I was taken down into the bowels of the theatre to the chroma-key they had constructed: a video booth and a green screen to relay back my 'taxi trip' to the Palais to the screens in the theatre.

The curtain lifted and there was my mum, Jenny Creasey from Applecross, in her Zumba gear, standing alone on stage at the Palais Theatre in front of three thousand savvy comedy fans at the most prestigious comedy gig in Australia. I can't even imagine how nervous she was. Not only was she worried about her own performance but she even had said to me pre-show, 'I just don't want to stuff it up for you.'

She delivered her lines perfectly, of course. What else would I have expected from a former West End actress? I was actually having more trouble myself, I think, as it was hard to time my lines with the audience reaction from fifteen metres below the stage in the chroma-key. After my last phone call with Mum, the screen rose and all the dancers came out (something I'd imagine a lot of them had done before) and started the routine with her. Then I had thirty seconds to run through the bowels of the Palais Theatre into the orchestra pit where a ladder led up to the stage. I absolutely bolted there, flanked by half-a-dozen producers and stage managers, ripping bits of clothing off me and attaching microphones and ear pieces. I made it to the ladder just in time, raced up it and onto the stage, where I received a huge round of applause. It was very exciting to be setting foot on stage for the first time post-Africa. Mum and I completed the dance routine, finishing with us both being lifted into the air by dancers and confetti cannons exploding overhead. You know . . . subtle.

The crowd applauded, my mum and the dancers exited the stage and five stage hands raced on to do a 'staged' quick change into my suit. Then I had my next hurdle to overcome – the fucking show itself. I opened with some stand-up, completely out of breath, and welcomed to the stage the first comedian, Dave Hughes.

For a large part of the show I stood in the wings with Janelle, working on the fly to produce different introductions for comedians and adapt to the show as it went on. At one point a producer came running up to me and handed me a script to learn about Oxfam that was half a page long to deliver on stage five minutes later. Being the whole point of the show, Oxfam isn't something you can really stuff up or joke about, so let's just say that segment wasn't exactly smooth.

At another point during the second half the producers decided the show needed a bit of padding between acts so I yelled at a runner to 'Find Fiona O'Loughlin as quick as you can!' Moments later Fiona and I were on stage doing a bit where Fiona made a donation to Oxfam if she could pash me on stage. We had a very over-the-top pash, rolling around on the stage, and it was very funny.

I could not have been more relieved when the Gala was over. The most stressful gig of my life was done (though my first night in the Eurovision commentary booth in Ukraine may have usurped this – stay tuned). Once again, I debriefed with my parents and Ashleigh and Thomas over champagne. I hadn't been completely happy with my performance as I was very conscious it hadn't been nearly as slick as Eddie Perfect's the year before – everything had felt extremely rushed. I was just hopeful it could be tightened and polished up in the edits before it went to air.

After the Gala my schedule was packed all week. Plus, on the Monday of the Gala airing I had something like forty interviews lined up in the hope of attracting viewers and great ratings. We were going up against *My Kitchen Rules* on

Channel Seven and *The Block* on Channel Nine so I knew we had a tough fight on our hands.

On Sunday night, the night before the gala was to air, I went to bed at 9 pm as I was due up at 4.30 am to begin my press run. Mum was still in town, as she had been helping me get through all the administrative things that had built up while I was away as well as helping me get my head together. Optus had very kindly cut my phone and internet connection off while I was out of the country. Clearly my Optus account manager was not an *I'm A Celebrity . . .* fan. Mum was leaving Melbourne around midday to fly back to Perth, where she was throwing a soiree at home to watch the Gala on TV with Dad and some friends. She was opening the fucking Gala! I know she thought that was pretty cool. I did too.

I'd been asleep for two hours when I woke up around midnight to go to the bathroom. I quickly checked my phone and saw a missed call from the head producer of the show and a message saying, 'Call me please. No matter the time of day or night.'

I called immediately of course and the sound of his voice when he answered was so solemn, I knew immediately what was up.

'I don't know how to say this, Joel. I am so sorry. I really am so, so sorry. This is truly one of the most awful things I've ever had to do. Your mum has been cut from the Gala.'

I felt sick. I couldn't even stand. I collapsed onto my bed.

I simply said, 'Okay,' and immediately hung up. Then I raced to the bathroom to throw up.

I sat in bed, shaking and crying. Fast asleep in the other room was my mum, a woman I would do absolutely anything for – if anybody ever hurt her I would hunt them down and exact the wrath of ten thousand Michelle Bridges – and she was thinking she was flying home to watch herself, Jenny Creasey, on the Melbourne International Comedy Festival Gala! It was to be her glamorous return to showbiz after all these years!

The rage built up inside of me and I grabbed my phone. I'm not proud of myself, but I called Andrew and started yelling as loud as I could without waking my mum. Andrew had also been asleep and wasn't aware what was going on. But I was furious, hissing down the phone, telling him to pass on every threat under the sun to whoever was responsible for this. I ended with: 'I haven't signed a contract for this yet so let them know they can cut me from the fucking broadcast too. They won't even have a fucking show!'

Andrew, to his credit, hung up and called the network and the festival. There was a back and forth for a few hours, including me firing off abusive texts with tears streaming down my face. The answer we received was that the network wanted the show to 'begin with stand-up' – something they could have told us when the dance routine idea was green-lit by them weeks and weeks earlier.

I also felt I'd been tricked into everything. And I couldn't believe they were only making the decision at

1 am the morning the Gala was due to air; I didn't believe for a second they didn't know earlier. I knew why they'd done it, though. If I had been told on Sunday, Andrew and I could have pulled out of the jam-packed press schedule the following day in protest. But instead I was up at 4.30 am to begin a press tour for a show I knew wasn't my proudest work. A show my mother had just been cut from.

For years I had entertained the idea of hosting the Melbourne International Comedy Festival Gala, the show that inspired me to begin stand-up. The show that I had to beg my parents to let me sit up all night and watch. The show that was an annual tradition in the Creasey household. For years I had imagined how I would do it when it was my turn to host, and all the tricks I'd pull out. Now my pizzazz had been removed and all the TV audience would see was me hosting the Gala like any other show. No unique opener or exciting way to begin, no way to put my own stamp on the whole production. Not even a fucking confetti cannon.

I also knew I had to do one of the most revolting, heartbreaking things I would ever have to do: tell my beautiful mother she'd been cut from the show.

I got up at 4.30 am and jumped into the car with a Channel Ten publicist I'd worked with before. I thought about getting haughty with her, then realised being an arsehole to her wasn't going to help – she had nothing to do with it. So off we went from interview to interview, promoting the show. I was on autopilot, completely numb.

Interviewers had been instructed to not ask about my mother being in the show as was written in the original press release. Luckily most places wanted to talk about Africa anyway.

I got home at midday just in time to see my mother before she left for the airport. I had been dreading this moment all day. I was already in tears in the foyer of my building and by the time I was in my apartment in front of my mother I was in full sobbing, Clare Danes-crying-in-*Homeland* mode.

I walked straight in and said, 'Mum, I am so sorry. I don't know how else to say this or what happened. But you've been cut from the Gala. You won't be on TV tonight.'

And Mum responded with the worst thing I've ever heard. Even typing this makes my stomach churn, it's the moment I have always tried to block out. My gorgeous mother, who had been forced into doing this performance by multiple producers and network executives, something that would frighten the most famous comedians in the world, looked up at me and, in a quiet voice, said, 'Oh. That's okay. I'm sorry, Joel. Was it my fault?'

And I've told her so many times that it wasn't her fault. Because it wasn't.

I totally understand why the network cut the dance routine. And trust me, that Joel Creasey in bed crying and yelling down the phone the night before the Gala would've punched me for saying that. But the 8.30 pm timeslot on a Monday is competitive. Going up against two juggernaut shows on competing networks, you really don't want to give the audience time to switch between the 7.30 program ending and the 8.30 program starting.

What really makes me cringe, though, is the way the show had to be edited. With my mum and the dance routine being cut, the onstage costume change didn't make sense too, so it also had to be cut. Therefore the first thing you see on the 2015 Melbourne International Comedy Festival Gala is me walking out on stage sweaty, out of breath, shirt untucked and tie skewiff. The audience at home didn't know I'd just done a dance routine, they must've just thought I was a messy slob who gets exhausted walking the distance from the wings to centre stage.

That night I did a live appearance on *The Project* to promote the Gala airing an hour later – smiling, cracking jokes and selling the shit out of it. Once that wrapped, I stormed out of the building and had dinner and margaritas with my friend Alex and turned my phone off till the next morning. I was too terrified to check social media.

I never spoke about that Gala again. I still haven't watched that show back. I never want to see it.

12

TOTES HEARTBROKEN

I'm not going to lie to you – this chapter was really hard for me to write. Mostly because I titled it using the abbreviation 'Totes'. But as any comedian will tell you, there's no other job in the world where your sole objective is to make people laugh. And that task is almost impossible to face when all you want to do is cry. There isn't much that's funny about a newly broken heart. Though eventually there is . . . when your promoter asks you if you have a new stand-up show for them to tour and you say, 'Holy fuck, yes! Do I have some fresh material for you!'

Prior to heading into the jungle, at the end of 2014 I made a quick trip to LA to cash in on a voucher Jeffery and I received after complaining about bad service at a hotel (we had become *those* kind of gays). During the trip we had a ridiculous argument about something so insignificant I can't even remember what it was (it wasn't hotel related, I know that much). We'd also started to float the idea of an open relationship, given how far away we lived from each other.

I'm not completely against open relationships. I think they can work and can often help a relationship. I also believe that gay men, especially, are extremely good at separating sex and emotion. And I knew that I was in love, so anyone else I was to have sex with was purely for that reason. But I also felt some slight cracks starting to form in my relationship with Jeffery due to the sheer physical distance between us, so of course I was willing to do whatever (or whoever – zing!) I could. This option felt like it might ease some tension (sexual *and* emotional).

Although the suggestion of sleeping with other people had been made one night after a few drinks, we were still tip-toeing around the subject. Or at least I was. I left LA without having actually uttered the words 'open relationship'. And upon my return to Australia, our nightly loved-up FaceTime chats and constant communication carried on unchanged. So I assumed (and hoped) that all was smooth sailing.

For those reading this thinking *What the fuck is an open relationship?* I'm going to take a punt and say you're straight. Or ugly. According to the *Concise Encyclopaedia Britannica of Gay* (I'm sure it was Margaret Court who reviewed it on Goodreads) an open relationship is essentially a relation-ship where you are allowed to sleep with other people. Common rules are that you can't sleep with a friend, you can't sleep with the same person more than once (so as not to form an attachment) and the other person cannot sleep over after you've got it on. You are allowed to kiss, though. It's not like Julia Roberts playing a prozzie.

All of these rules were what Jeffery and I were following, essentially, without having confirmed the arrangement with each other. Well, I thought.

At the end of the year, I found myself in London performing my show at the Soho Theatre, a run that was to be followed by a trip to Berlin and Prague with my parents and older sister, Holly. Jeffery had introduced me to his friend Giles the last time I was in LA. Giles is 'terribly British' and we instantly got on as two foreigners in LA who didn't quite understand who the casting executives or show runners were that Jeffery and his friends talked about. We also look scarily similar and discovered we were born on the same date – hello, Lindsay Lohan in *The Parent Trap*! Jeffery had asked a few times whether I was going to catch up with Giles in London. I told him, 'Yeah, probably,' and he seemed uncomfortable with the idea. Full disclosure: I enjoyed seeing Jeffery like this; it seemed to pique his interest in me again. But I also knew it was incredibly unhealthy to toy with him emotionally.

Giles is a brilliant actor and was doing a show at Shakespeare's Globe when I was in London so I went along to see it. (Side note: the show was brilliant, but ol' William didn't design his theatre for those of us with back troubles, forsooth.)

After the show, Giles and I went drinking at a private club called the Groucho Club where he's a member. The closest thing to a private members' club I'd even been to was the Applecross Tennis Club, so this was next level. I remember seeing paparazzi going insane taking photos of a celebrity (who turned out to be Kate Moss) arriving at the club. I was instantly pumped. Inside, the club was a maze of rooms with fireplaces and over-the-top Christmas decorations. It was full of celebrities and important-looking people but never felt crowded. We ordered cocktails unique to the club called 'Twinkles'. As a result of the Twinkles, we ended up getting blind drunk and having sex in my apartment. (I hope I'm not moving too fast for you.)

It's a difficult situation to describe. Jeffery and I were still a loved-up couple in constant communication, but we had discussed sleeping with other guys, so I figured I might as well test the waters with Giles.

I woke the morning after my night with Giles to a text from Jeffery asking, 'Did you sleep with him?'

I agonised over my response, I couldn't work out whether to lie or tell the truth. I ended up replying just, 'Yes.'

Jeffery replied with something along the lines of 'Hot'. But I knew immediately he wasn't happy. I also knew he had been using the open relationship card too, so he couldn't really be upset. I didn't think he was angry, I thought maybe he felt he was missing out. Or perhaps Jeffery knew the connection Giles and I had as he'd seen it in person. In fact, it's only writing it here do I realise I was the first to break the cardinal rules of the open relationship, both 'Do not sleep with a friend' and 'Do not let them stay the night'.

A few days later, Jeffery said he wanted to come to Europe. I was thrilled, but couldn't help assuming it was a result of Giles and me sleeping together. As great as Giles was, I knew I was head-over-heels in love with Jeffery so, before he could second guess the trip, I organised his flights and a week later, two days after Christmas, Jeffery was in London.

We had a really fun few days and then headed off to Berlin with my parents. (Now, it must sound like my parents just turn up unexpectedly wherever I am in the world – and they do. They really need to get some hobbies and stop spending my inheritance.) Jeffery left us before we went to Prague. I kissed him goodbye, knowing I was off to Africa and wouldn't be with him again for months.

After coming out of the jungle, things with Jeffery had completely changed. He had sent me an email every day I was in the jungle for me to read once I was eliminated, but when I spoke to him, he seemed distant. He was reluctant to visit me in Australia, and when I kept asking why, he said he was too busy or couldn't afford it. Meanwhile there was a lot of public interest from magazines and publications about our relationship. When asked, I would answer enthusiastically about Jeffery, but almost felt like I was lying.

'When is he coming to Australia?' I was asked several times a day.

'Soon!' I would reply, not even believing my own bullshit.

My extensive work commitments meant it was literally impossible for me to leave Australia for those first few months post jungle. Jeffery and I discussed our relationship again, reminding each other of how in love we were while also formally agreeing to the open status of our relationship. But I was so busy I didn't really have time to be hooking up with other guys, plus my profile was now so high I had to be careful. In fact, having a boyfriend overseas was really convenient for me during these flat-out work months.

Unable to convince Jeffery to travel to me, I managed to race over to LA once again for a four-day trip. It was a pointless amount of time and I just felt rushed. It also meant that I would land back in Australia to make my debut performance on *Have You Been Paying Attention?* with a fried and jetlagged brain. (It wasn't my best performance. Turns out I had *not* been paying attention.)

I was due to head to LA in July once again, as I had the previous year. This time I was going so I could attend the premiere of a movie Jeffery had written and starred in. Then I was going to Montreal for Just For Laughs, as I'd been invited back. After that I was going straight back to LA to finally spend a proper few months with Jeffery. Oh, and also hopefully become an instant American TV star by treading the boards on the comedy club circuit and 'taking' auditions.

In the weeks leading up to me arriving in LA, Jeffery had seemed in a particularly good place, mentioning repeatedly how excited he was for me to be coming and even saying things like, 'We should get married so you can get a green card and move here.' It felt as if our relationship was stabilising. I had also vowed not to rely so heavily on Jeffery this time. I was going to try to make some of my own friends in LA and finally face my fears and drive the fucking car. In fact, I was going to hire my own car so as not to be such a burden.

The shit hit the fan pretty much immediately on my arrival in LA.

To summarise a rather long and painful story, I discovered on my second day there that Jeffery had met someone else. I held off on bringing it up with him as I hadn't wanted to ruin his film premiere – and I also totally wanted to go to a Hollywood film premiere. I went along and sat beside him, so proud of his film, genuinely stoked for him (and waiting to see how big my name was in the thank-you credits), but I was also embarrassed, as I knew I wasn't wanted there. It took every fibre of my being to smile and act normally. Later on, he was so busy with his film colleagues and friends that it felt as though everyone had forgotten I was there. At one point I went to the bathroom and sat in a toilet cubicle, flicking through Facebook and texting friends back in Australia. Think Lindsay Lohan in *Mean Girls* on her first day at high school.

The next morning, I couldn't hold it in any more and exploded. I told him I knew he'd met someone else. I spoke quite confidently, thinking that surely whatever he and this new guy had couldn't outweigh the admittedly difficult but special relationship we had created.

To his credit he did say, in no uncertain words, that he didn't want to be with me any more.

I felt as though my world was imploding. All I could hear was that white noise when your TV can't find a station (at least, that's what I think it is – obviously I am far too young and fabulous to have lived in anything other than the digital age). We yelled at each other while I frantically (and very dramatically) packed my bags, throwing my clothes across the room in the most over-the-top fashion I could muster. At the same time I texted my outrageously organised friend Bradley and asked him to find me a hotel.

Bradley is the kind of guy who is near a computer and ready to help no matter the time of day. He responded immediately: 'I've booked you into the Viceroy Hotel in Santa Monica, they're waiting for you. Go, go, go!'

An hour after the fight had broken out I was in an Uber, single, embarrassed and completely numb.

Now, I don't know what the fuck Bradley had told the Viceroy but there were staff waiting for me to arrive. They took my bags out of the car and escorted me straight in. I was in tears and looked like an idiot, but I do remember thinking, *Gosh, the service here is good, I must remember that for TripAdvisor!* Turns out the service was good because Bradley had booked me a $2000-a-night suite – all they had left. As far as I was concerned, for that price the hotel should've supplied someone to fucking cry for me. At that price they should've supplied a new boyfriend!

I went up to my room and fell in a heap on the bed. I checked my phone and discovered it had died and I started to freak out. I discovered that, in my rush to make a dramatic statement as I swept out of Jeffery's house, I had forgotten to pack a charger. I had to find one! Surely by now Jeffery had realised his awful mistake and would be desperately trying to contact me! I mean, come on – who would want to dump *me*? (Apart from every boyfriend I have ever had.)

It seems the more expensive the hotel room, the fewer amenities are provided. I asked for a charger at reception but all they could offer me was deconstructed oxygen and attitude, so I headed off to search the surrounding Santa Monica area. I was so out of it, though, I got completely lost and ended up at the famous Muscle Beach, where women who make Arnold Schwarzenegger look like he has muscular dystrophy lift weights the size of small cars above their head. I must've seemed like a complete lunatic, crying and staring at these women. In fact, I know I did. An Australian tourist spotted me and contacted the newspapers. But the recognition did put a temporary spring in my step.

After walking around for hours I found a phone charger and went back to the hotel. I plugged my phone in and checked it every two seconds to see if it was back on. Ten minutes later it finally came back to life. The white Apple logo that appears when you turn an iPhone on seemed to linger for an eternity. And then the home screen appeared. Nothing. Not a single message. I shut the blinds and started to fall apart again. The occasional phone call came through from my friends Bradley and Em, checking in to see how I was going. I was a mess.

Later that night I texted Jeffery, begging him to come and see me. Even as I typed it I knew how pathetic it was. I hated myself even more. But I couldn't stop myself. He said no.

Your loss, arsehole, I thought. *This is a $2000-a-night mattress.*

Then I lay in bed, writhing in agony. I couldn't believe that merely months ago I'd been in the African jungle with all of Australia watching me, feeling so tough and empowered. Now I was completely alone and utterly heartbroken. I truly could not believe the physical agony. I couldn't believe that I, a strong, independent, sassy-as-fuck man, had allowed somebody to inflict such pain on me.

Word had spread through my squad and they put together an around-the-clock international watch with calls coming in to check on me and send me things if I needed them. I am so lucky to have the friends I have, they really do rally around and fiercely protect me when I need them. Several offered to fly over (okay, that was just my mum and dad – you know them, they'll go anywhere for the frequent flyer points). And someone had called Andrew to let him know what had happened, as this event changed my next few months' work plans dramatically. Plus both of our potential incomes.

Andrew was amazing, springing into action and making other arrangements for me. It was decided that although I was due in Montreal in four days' time, it was probably best not to arrive there earlier, as we didn't want me having a breakdown in front of really important people from the industry or from Channel Ten, who were televising the gala.

The next day I returned to Jeffery's to pick up the rest of my stuff (including that fucking charger) and in some weird fucking twist, we decided it was best that I stay the next two nights at his place before I left for Montreal. Perhaps in the back of my mind I thought I had a bonus two days to win him back. I'm not sure what I thought I was going to do. Slip into some lacy Nigella Lawson nightgown and seduce him in the night?

I left the Viceroy the following morning after having what was probably a $300 omelette from room service (which I barely touched). But when I got to Jeffery's, he had ducked out to work, so one of his friends very kindly took me on a trip to Orange County. He had to do some consulting work and I lay on the beach (it was nice to have some new scenery to cry in) and got completely sunburnt on my back as I couldn't reach it to apply sunscreen. That only led to more tears as it reminded me I was alone again. 'I don't have anybody to apply my sunscreen any more!' I wailed. It did, however, cross my mind that I could conveniently blame any potential future skin cancer on Jeffery, so that was a comfort.

After returning from Orange County (and discovering that I never want to go to Orange County ever again), Jeffery was at home. I put on a brave face and marched past him, showered and went out with a girlfriend who happened to be in town – and completely wrote myself off. I returned later that night to discover Jeffery asleep on the couch and sadly walked past him to bed on my own.

The next day, Saturday, was one of the weirdest days of my life. And it went so fast. It was overcast and storming; the only other time I'd seen LA like that was the day many years earlier when I landed for Ashleigh's brother's funeral. Jeffery and I spent the morning crying, lying in bed, hugging and fighting, and then repeating that sequence over and over. We eventually came to our senses and decided to have a 'nice afternoon together'. What a ridiculous fucking idea. So we went and bought some burritos (as you do when you're in the US) and watched YouTube clips of our favourite musical theatre actresses (as you do when you're homos). Every now and then we would break out into a fight before apologising and laughing maniacally. It was all so weird. Mid-afternoon, I discovered I had my flight times wrong and instead of flying out the following afternoon, I was actually departing much earlier at 7 am. The knowledge that I had lost almost half a day with Jeffery sent me spiralling again. I was really clutching at straws at this point.

All day I felt like a total dickhead. I kept thinking, *I bet Jeffery wishes his other guy was here. He probably can't wait to get me out of his house!* At one point, as snot and tears ran down my face, I said, 'Should we have sex?'

The suggestion was met with a pretty lacklustre reaction and I thought, *Well, I gave it a crack.* I'm not sure what I was thinking, perhaps that I'd bust out some new amazing sex trick I'd been keeping up my sleeve all this time and he'd go, 'My God, I'm an idiot! What was I thinking?'

(By the way, as a rule I don't normally have sex while wearing sleeves. I normally do it completely naked and preferably without tears or snot. Hot, right?)

Eventually we fell asleep in each other's arms and the next morning, Jeffery drove me to the airport. Here's where I get even lamer. As I said, I live my life as if it were a movie, so during the night I woke up and snuck out of bed (again channelling Nigella Lawson). I knew I needed to write Jeffery a letter and that was my only chance. I went to the kitchen, sat down cross-legged on the floor, tapped the letter out on my laptop and then wrote it on paper. I think I then sprayed some of my fucking aftershave on it (my level of romance is Marty Maraschino – 'like the cherry' – in *Grease*) and shoved it into my backpack.

When Jeffery dropped me at the airport the following morning I stepped out of the car, face covered in tears and snot once again, handed him the letter and said goodbye.

That was the last time I ever saw Jeffery.

I'll stop talking about him specifically at this point because I've bashed him enough on stage (my stand-up show the year after was spec-fucking-tacular) and I will always have enormous respect for him. He is one of the most talented, creative and hilarious men I have ever met, hence why I fell so hard in the first place. But from here on in my time overseas became my story of healing. Yes, I used the word 'healing'. Move over, *Eat, Pray, Love*.

I will end by saying that Jeffery is now engaged to the same man he left me for. I was knocked out of the semi-final by the eventual Grand Slam champion. So you know what? Fucking good on him. I actually think that's pretty cool that they're engaged. And that man is a very lucky guy. As I write this, though, gay marriage still isn't legal in Australia, so technically I don't even have to recognise Jeffery's engagement.

As I've mentioned before, I do want to get gay married one day. Or as I call it, married. It's so bizarre that Australia has not made this possible yet. It seems so odd for such a progressive country. And rather shameful on the inter-national stage. I remember tweeting recently, 'America, you're really embarrassing yourself', after yet another one of Trump's fuck-ups. And an American replied, 'Um, you guys don't even have gay marriage yet.' *Touché*, sir. *Touché*.

Having said that, the day gay marriage is legalised I will lose a lot of stand-up material. Every cloud has a silver lining, I guess.

I spent a strange week in Montreal. Most of the time I was completely numb. I checked my phone constantly. Eventually Andrew confiscated my phone and ran my social media, knowing I had to concentrate on the job at hand. The festival wrapped with me at a gay strip club with Alan Cumming. We sat in the corner drinking and laughing at the rather tragic strippers and it was then that I reminded myself the world wasn't ending and that I was actually pretty fucking lucky. Those thoughts were fleeting, however, and I returned to my hotel that night and cried myself to sleep again.

After Just For Laughs in Montreal I was due to fly back to LA for a few months. Andrew and I discussed the options and decided that this was not a good idea. We decided I should go to New York instead, then duck across to Edinburgh for my season at the Edinburgh Fringe and *then* fly to LA. At which point I would hopefully be less likely to stand in front of my now ex-boyfriend's house in tears, crying, with a boombox on my shoulder while he and his new man, y'know . . . moved on with their life.

For many comedians, the Edinburgh Fringe is considered the pinnacle of international performance. But my experience at the Edinburgh Fringe Festival was excruciating. I performed the final two weeks of the festival in a small, one-hundred-seat venue in the main hub. I was so distracted by my broken heart I gave the show no thought. I was performing a best-of so it wasn't the material that needed the work, more the promotional,

257

getting-a-fucking-audience-along side of things. To be fair, I never met my producer from the festival and I think my show got lost among the throng.

I stepped on stage each night to perform in front of tens of people. It was a serious ego check for me, having just come off a sold-out run of theatres in Australia and even New York. Each night after the show I would drink too much at the artists' bar, stumble home, eat a Tesco's curry, sleep all day and wake up to do it all over again. You know – living the dream! My usually pretty strict exercise regime went out the window (no one was asking for a topless photo shoot at that time, thank God) and I truly hated life. My immediate family flew to Edinburgh (spending my inheritance again!) along with several of my relatives and I had very little interest in seeing any of them. I just sort of ghosted through town, lost in my own thoughts, unsure what to do next. I left zero impact on Edinburgh and vowed to never return.

Then I landed in New York. I was writing this book at the time, so I figured I could go to New York and become Carrie Bradshaw for a few months. That didn't happen – I definitely had more of a Samantha approach to my time in the Big Apple. Long story short: I fucked my way through New York, sleeping with the hottest men I could find to give me some sort of validation. Although during the day I wandered around feeling palpably empty and alone.

My birthday rolled around. I spent the first half of the day genuinely expecting Jeffery to come marching up to my Airbnb to sweep me off my feet. Then I spent the second half of the day expecting a phone call or, at the very least, an email. But nothing came through and I ended up heading out (in the Airbnb owner's clothes who was conveniently the same size as me) and writing myself off at a karaoke bar singing Kelly Clarkson's 'Since U Been Gone'.

The next day I stopped checking my phone for Jeffery's number. And I haven't since. (I also didn't want to pay for international data roaming. So that helped.)

I returned to Australia at the end of that trip so happy to be home. The last few times had been bittersweet but this time I nearly launched myself over the counter and pashed the customs officer as he said, 'Welcome home, Mr Creasey.' I could finally be in my own apartment with all my friends around me and process what had happened without the distractions of work or being a tourist or being completely alone.

When I go through a break up, I go back to my other love, my work, and make that a priority, filling my days with as much of it as I can. I'm so lucky to have an audience who supports me and sends me the most wonderful messages. It's those people I turn my concentration to and perform for. Performing has always helped me through any situation, no matter how utterly shittastic that situation has been.

What I've taken away from falling in love and having my heart broken is that I do love love. Truly. But dating in Australia is weird. In the gay world, most people know who I am and I can never quite work out what their intentions are. I can't do Grindr because people report the page, thinking it's a fake profile, and it gets removed. Or they screenshot it and post it to their social media saying, 'Oh my God, crazy! I just saw Joel Creasey on Grindr!' But why is that crazy? I am a twenty-something-year-old gay man.

That said, I have done Grindr in the past. I have sent dick pics in the past. I'm a Gen Y gay man. Why wouldn't I? A website recently threatened to release them. I lost sleep over it for a week and eventually shrugged my shoulders and thought *Who cares*? It really reflected more on the creepy people making the threats. Plus I learned that it's best to send your dick pics to individuals and not websites.

I love the way love makes me feel and I love the person I am when I am in love. And although I wouldn't wish the agony of heartbreak upon my greatest enemy (jokes! I would . . . Russell Crowe), I cannot wait to fall in love all over again. And who knows what may happen next time?

Because that person I was post Mardi Gras in 2014 was the best version of myself there has ever been.

Excited, nervous, determined – and in love.

13

WOMEN WHO
INSPIRE ME

A s I've mentioned repeatedly, my parents were in *The Empire Strikes Back*, so our entire family grew up watching the Star Wars movies. I was obsessed and knew the names of every planet, character and ship, as did my best friend Ashleigh. We devoured it all. But whereas most little boys always wanted to be Han Solo or Luke Skywalker, I would always play Princess Leia – the backbone of the Rebel Alliance. Without Leia, the Rebels would never have defeated the Empire. I love the idea that Leia had the plans of the Death Star on a floppy disk – a floppy disk! No joke, floppy disks were *almost* even before my time! But floppy wasn't ever really the right adjective, was it? Beanies are floppy. A rabbit's ears are floppy. I've known a few floppy dicks, though. I was offended at first but just put it down to alcohol.

It was in Montreal in 2016 that I had the privilege of working with Carrie Fisher – Princess Leia herself – when

I was performing on one of the big televised galas and she was the host. But on these huge galas you don't usually see the other comedians; you are so consumed with your own performance that you normally sit in your dressing room, keeping to yourself and only talking with your team of managers and agents. When it comes time for your performance, a producer takes you to the wings, you walk on, do your show, and go straight back to the dressing room to debrief and ask 'How the fuck did I do?' So although Carrie was on stage as I was, I never actually saw her.

I was due to interview her after the show, as I was once again hosting the coverage of the festival for Channel Ten. I'd interviewed all the big international stars that year but we hadn't quite managed to lock in Carrie. Her agent said she was tired, but after she'd seen my set and heard about my family link to Star Wars, she agreed to the interview.

It was 11 pm when she walked into the room. I was shaking and extremely nervous. The only other time this had happened was with Joan Rivers . . . and possibly Cosima De Vito from the first season of *Australian Idol* when I was younger.

I said, 'Good evening, General Organa,' a very nerdy reference to her position in the just released Star Wars film, *The Force Awakens.*

She rolled her eyes and said with a smile, 'Now, I hope your parents aren't related like Luke and Leia turned out to be.'

I laughed too hard and then we began the interview. She was magnificent, funny and dry. Everything you'd dream she'd be.

Then things got weird. After the interview, Carrie stood and gave me a hug. I was stoked. And then the hug dragged on . . . and on . . . and on. She wouldn't let go. We ended up sitting and she hugged me some more. Every now and then she would whisper something in my ear and then go back to hugging. I was trying to make conversation and couldn't quite believe what was happening. The camera crew and producers from Channel Ten were equally amused but had to pretend that nothing weird was happening, so they just sort of loitered while trying to make themselves look busy.

I said to Carrie, 'I loved your book so much. Are you going to write another one?'

And she whispered in my ear, 'Well, if I do, Harrison won't be happy.'

'Harrison Ford?'

'Yes.'

'Why?'

'Well, you know, we were sleeping together for years.'

Honestly, I almost exploded. I could not believe it. I had just been told by Carrie Fisher herself – daughter of Debbie Reynolds, Hollywood icon – that she was banging Harrison Ford while they filmed *Star Wars: A New Hope*, one of the most legendary films of all time.

After that, Carrie finished her hug (we were clocking in at over ten minutes by then) and left, with her dog in tow.

I had to sit down and take a breather to process what had happened while all the camera crew said, 'What did she say? What did she say?'

Carrie died a few months later and I was distraught. She was my princess, my leader of the Rebel Alliance.

It was also revealed just before she died that she'd had an affair with Harrison Ford. But I'll never forget how special it was that I got to hear it direct from her mouth.

🎤

I love women. I adore them. My favourite comedians, actors, singers, artists and people are all mostly women. If women ran the world it would be a much better place. Don't get me wrong, I love men too. I have also loved a lot of men. Intimately. And I do genuinely love being a gay man. But I have always felt a special connection to women.

I don't think that has anything to do with my being gay, though. At all. It has to do with the fact that I was surrounded by women in my household. My mum, my grandma, my sisters, our dog. Amazing women. And my dad is the greatest champion of women. The admiration and love he has for his wife and daughters has truly been passed on to me. I am stoked to have been given that gift. The way my dad looks at my mum gives me hope for love. And I know I'm lucky to be able to say that. Of my friends, my parents are one of the few couples still together.

But here's where my love for women goes – I need them in all areas of my life. For example, I probably won't get into a TV series if there isn't a strong female lead. I stopped watching *The Walking Dead* after season three when most of the ladies were killed off. I don't like musicals unless there's a female lead who gets a fabulous, spine-tingling power ballad. And when I go to the tennis, I would usually rather see a Williams than a Federer or Nadal. As I've mentioned before, in stand-up, I always tour with a female support act and I have it in my contracts (where possible) that there has to be a woman on the bill if I am performing in a line-up. Not because I'm trying to look cool by making some equality stand, more so to give me someone I enjoy watching.

It's safe to say the most important member of the Creasey family has always been a little lady named Bella. Perfectly white and the runt of the litter, Bella has more sass than Nicki Minaj and has always been a hit with the males down at the park. Yes, Bella is a dog – she's our gorgeous West Highland terrier. That's not how I would describe one of my sisters. Can you *imagine*? They're nowhere near as good looking!

So smokin' is Bella that she was the dog on the City Farmers ads (a pet and livestock chain in Western Australia). She would model all the dog coats and look beyond gorgeous in her traditional black and red tartan jacket. She ended up getting a little too old for it, and then she put on a bit of weight. So now she's a retired plus-size model. Bella is one of my favourite reasons to return home to Perth, where she still rules the roost. When we first got Bella we decided to put a few rules in place, ie, no sleeping on the couch, on anybody's bed, etc. They went out the window after about two days and it feels weird to think we ever even tried. Bella now gets to sleep wherever and, frankly, *do* whatever the fuck she wants. She's only the size of a small handbag but on my last trip back home I ended up moving to the couch after she planted herself in the middle of my bed. I wouldn't dare move her for fear of being berated by Dad: 'Don't touch Bella! Let her sleep.' I had a breakfast radio interview in the morning and a show the following night, but sure, Bella should sleep . . . she'd only been doing it all day.

My sisters Holly and Alice are beautiful people and complete moles at the same time. I've always admired Holly as I think you inherently do with your older sister. Holly is the type of person who just gets on with business and doesn't fuck around. Alice and I are much more dramatic and over the top, but Holly will have quietly broken up with a partner, say, and gotten on with life without bothering anyone. Meanwhile Alice and I will rant and rave, go after them on social media, write a chapter or two on them in a memoir . . .

Holly lives in London and has a successful job in advertising. She is much more of an academic too. She is extremely disciplined and has excellent self-control, something that Alice and I also don't really possess. I used to love sitting in the audience of school performance nights or productions to watch Holly on stage. It definitely helped plant the early seeds of performance in me. Holly and I have always gotten on effortlessly, thanks to her putting in more effort than me, truth be told. She also covered for me in the early days when I needed money or when I had fucked up and couldn't let Mum and Dad know. Holly isn't the type of person to ever demand anything of life, or believe she is owed anything, which has been an incredibly grounding lesson for me during my time working in entertainment, where it is too easy to get lost in yourself.

Alice is far more similar to me. She is fiery, erratic and extremely funny, which explains why we often bump heads. Alice is tough as nails and doesn't take shit from anyone. Like me, she loves to bite back no matter the person or the position they hold. I often wonder if she has gotten that directly from me, and sometimes grimace when I see her doing it, thinking, *Fuck, I'm definitely to blame for that one*, as she snaps someone in half. If you've ever trolled me on Facebook you may have received a trolling back – that's Alice; very protective of her older brother and my first line of defence. When I was on *I'm a Celebrity* . . . and my social media was under siege from haters, Alice spent her days clapping back at them. Basically, what I'm saying is: Fuck with me and feel the wrath of Alice.

Alice has a real grasp of comedy and the complexities of timing and delivery. She is also extremely satisfying to make laugh, having a guttural cackle you can hear from blocks away. Alice also lives in London, but like me she has stayed more in the arts and is a hair and make-up artist working in TV and fashion.

When Alice was eight she was diagnosed with Type 1 Juvenile Diabetes. I remember she was in extreme pain for about a year, which would manifest itself in different ways and come on in bursts. I feel so guilty now, but I would often roll my eyes, thinking she was doing it purely for attention. I'd even mentally critique her performance: *I would've gone for tears first and* then *thrown myself on the floor.* It wasn't until she was taken to hospital one day that the doctors diagnosed her. I was in Grade 7 at the time and came home from school and couldn't find my parents – they were at the hospital, where Alice needed to stay for a week. My mum never left her side, sleeping in the chair beside her bed every night. Our whole family had to go from knowing literally nothing about diabetes to suddenly being very aware of food we had in the house and the effects it could have on a Type 1 diabetic.

Alice's diagnosis meant she had to be given injections of insulin four times a day in her leg or stomach and would constantly be finger-pricking herself to check her blood sugar levels, not to mention monitoring her food. That is so much for an eight-year-old to handle and I often forget what an amazing woman Alice is to have dealt with this shit all her life.

In the early days, while her body was trying to adjust, I remember three occasions when Alice went into a diabetic seizure during the night. I woke up in my bed the first time, terrified, wondering what the moaning and screaming coming from the end of the hall was, thinking somebody had been murdered. But it was my poor mother trying to revive her daughter while we raced to call the paramedics. Every time they responded quickly.

Mum was also tasked with giving Alice her injections of insulin, which I can't imagine having to do – your daughter crying from the pain of the injection, but knowing that you have to do it to make her better. I know my parents have blamed themselves for and beaten themselves up over Alice's diabetes, as parents do with any ailment their child gets.

(Note to self: Blame next hangover on Mum and Dad.)

These days Alice has a pump that automatically regulates her insulin. The advances made in technology in a mere fifteen years are amazing. And Alice truly does handle her diabetes with grace and dignity. I cannot recall the last time she used it as ammunition. I mean, I fucking would – constantly. 'What's that? Your restaurant is fully booked and you can't seat me? *I have diabetes, you arsehole!'*

My mother Jenny has always been one of my heroes. I've always found her hilarious, not to mention the most beautiful creature on planet earth. She has effortless style and a huge wit. She is irritatingly nice and it truly is a wonder that she produced a son who talks shit about people for a living – I've never heard her utter a bad word about another person. My mum is a friend I love having around and we speak on the phone every day.

Look, if I started listing friends who inspire me, I would fall into the trap of not mentioning someone and end up with them getting shitty with me. There are references to all the women who have shaped and influenced my life littered throughout this book.

However, one woman who has had a huge part to play in my life in recent years is my business partner, Janelle Koenig. I call her my 'business partner' because it seems the title that best fits what she is. She is technically my writing partner; she and I write all my 'jokes' together, although it's a bit hard to call them jokes as I don't actually tell jokes. What I do before the start of a new tour is bring Janelle the stories I have gathered in the past year, and we shape and order them into a show. But Janelle is also involved in every other aspect of my life. She is my business partner in the sense that every business decision is run past her and she is pretty much across my schedule at all times of the day. Just this morning I shot her a message as I'm hosting an event for a vodka brand. I said, 'Need jokes on vodka.' When I next checked my phone, there was a list of gags waiting.

Janelle is a comedian herself, having had a successful career in stand-up in Melbourne in the 90s and early 00s. She was really the second wave of stand-up comedians in Australia, coming through around the same time as people like Greg Fleet and Wil Anderson. I'm in about the sixth or seventh wave. One night when I was fourteen, I was sick and Mum let me stay up late with her on the couch.

She was watching the Comedy Channel on Foxtel and *Stand Up Australia* was on. I felt so adult being allowed to sit up with Mum and watch the show, especially when the material was so blue. I remember seeing a foul-mouthed Asian-Australian comedian who seriously made me laugh.

Years later, after I had moved to Melbourne, I was back in Perth performing some stand-up at Rosie O'Grady's pub and I stood up the back of the room while that very same comedian was on stage. I approached Janelle after the show and told her the story of seeing her on TV and we became friends immediately. Janelle had moved to Perth because her partner works in the mines and she had just had a daughter. With the extra time on her hands, Janelle offered to 'have a look over your new show for you' if I liked. It was my third tour, *Naked*, and I said, 'Yeah, why not?' having not previously collaborated with anyone on material. We have been inseparable since, and have just launched my eighth tour, our fifth one together.

Janelle knows everything about me and could divulge some rather scandalous secrets. My management refer to her as my 'comfort blanket' and know that, for high-pressure gigs, it's best to include Janelle in my contract, as I work better when she's around, even if it's just knowing she's in the wings, keeping an eye on me. My career truly would not be where it is without Janelle. She and I have grand plans for world domination.

Sometimes Janelle's on the road as my support act, but she also still performs her own stand-up and hosts radio in Perth. If you ever get a chance to see her full solo show, do. You'll see why I feel like I'm stoked to have this secret/not-so-secret weapon in my corner.

Naturally, she has also proofread this book for me. So hey, Sugar Tits. Cheers for the vodka gags.

🎤

She might not be exactly real, but Xena the Warrior Princess was another great inspiration. I loved Xena. As I've mentioned about seventy-eight thousand times, I love women, especially powerful women. I think women should run the world and men should just shut up and kiss me. I think a lot of young gay men my age really identified with Xena: a sassy underdog who looks great in leather. Gabrielle I always found a bit annoying, though. I mean, how did she survive six seasons fighting warlords, dragons, gods, etc, in sandals and a hessian crop top? One of the first men I ever thought about while masturbating was Ares, the god of war (I always had high standards in my fantasy life at any rate). Well, the actor who played Ares in the *Xena* series, not just some illustration in an old textbook. Bit creepy, given the actor playing Ares was in his forties and I was fourteen.

I still watch *Xena* if it's on telly and I own all six seasons on DVD. *The Project* on Channel Ten asked me to interview Lucy Lawless two years ago (that's Xena for those losers out there) and I was beside myself. It was to be a live cross from Supanova at the Flemington showgrounds. Supanova is one of those big comic-con events where people dress in costumes from TV shows I've never seen and go along and trade comic books and compare stories about being virgins and chess champions. A generalisation, yes, but surprisingly accurate, I think you'll find.

All these nerds were of course in hot pursuit of Xena, who was the big name at Supanova that year. Well, her and the chick who was 'Amazon' in Channel Seven's reincarnation of *Gladiators*. Here's a confession: I always wanted to be a Gladiator. I thought they were so cool. I'm friends with Tiffiny Hall from *The Biggest Loser,* who was one of the Gladiators on the reincarnation series. I obstinately refuse to refer to her by anything other than her Gladiator name, Angel.

When I rocked up to Supanova to interview Lucy Lawless and saw how huge the event was, I walked around thinking selflessly (as per usual), *Suck it, nerds, Xena's mine.*

I did the interview and Lucy Lawless could not have been cooler, nicer or in better shape. Seriously, she could still do a back flip over eighteen of Hades' henchmen and throw her chakram at a devil all the while yelling, 'Ayayayayaya!' – in her sleep. Her chakram, by the way, was a little metal Frisbee thing she'd throw at bad guys. I always found it weird how she could throw it through the air – it would chop off the heads of ten soldiers and then come flying back to her where she would catch it perfectly, without slicing her hand off. I pointed this out to Mum one day when I was watching *Xena* and she said, 'Oh well, I guess she's perfected the technique.'

In our interview, Lucy Lawless was weirdly sexual – in a fun way. I remember accidentally brushing her boob while gesticulating a little too wildly. Instead of letting it slide, I said, live on air, 'Oh my God, I just touched Xena's boob!'

And she said, 'Do it again, I liked it,' with a laugh.

I thought about doing it. Why not? How often do you get to touch Xena's boobs? I mean, I don't particularly like boobs but I guess if I'm going to like any boobs it'll be Xena's. Then I remembered the whole 'live on air' thing. I was also worried the nerds standing behind me with rock hard boners might explode in a tsunami of jizz and prescription glasses.

After the interview, Lucy Lawless gladly posed for photos with me and then with all the fans waiting to see her. I watched for a while and was so impressed with how she had a personal interaction with each fan. They all wanted to know about Xena, and she never did the whole Hollywood actress thing I've seen so many times of 'Oh, let's not talk about that, let's focus on my other projects'. Like when I recently asked Reese Witherspoon about *Legally Blonde* in an interview. Not. Impressed. I sometimes think about Lucy Lawless at Supanova whenever I'm doing a signing after a show and, on the rare occasion when I might be tired or upset or wanting to go to bed, I think, *What would Xena do?* And proceed to pull out my chakram.

It doesn't cut my hand on return, either. I've perfected the technique too.

But then again, I think that in most situations at most times of the day.

Without doubt, my stand-up inspiration is the greatest comedian of all time, Joan Rivers. I know that's a big claim but I will fight anyone who disputes it. She was a pioneer for female comedians (as much as she hated being called that) and a pioneer for comedians like me who perform pop culture stand-up. Her career spanned longer than anyone else's. And in terms of firepower, I am yet to see a comedian who could match her rapid-fire delivery of scintillating jokes, or 'zingers', as we call them in the industry.

I first discovered Joan Rivers when I was fourteen. I had just got a laptop and had wifi in my room and one night stumbled across a clip of hers on YouTube. I obviously sort of knew who she was but I was a young teenager – I was only just coming to terms with what a boner was. Once I saw one clip of Joan Rivers, I needed more. And more. And more. I fell deep into a YouTube black hole, staying up all night to devour every piece of stand-up and every talk show appearance.

Joan made jokes about the frivolous world of pop culture, celebrity and fashion. And she made no apologies for being obsessed with that world. She was utterly fearless and didn't care what anybody thought. I felt safe knowing that there was someone like her in the world. Not to mention she was a champion of not only gays but anyone who was just a little different or unusual. For a young boy who was at the time coming to terms with his sexuality (and boners), Joan was a great inspiration, as she pulled no punches and nobody was allowed to tell her who or what she should be.

It was watching Joan Rivers stand-up maybe a year later that I suddenly went from thinking 'I love this person' to 'I am this person' and 'I want to be this person'. That was when I started mulling over the idea of giving stand-up comedy a crack.

Eight years later, I was Joan Rivers' opening act.

It was October 2013 and I was preparing to go on my first holiday. I had just finished filming *A League of Their Own* and had had a successful stand-up tour and saved enough money to fly to New York and put myself up in a nice hotel for ten days. My dear friend Kris, a fellow performer, had told me to get in touch with his mates Chip and Ron, who run a little cabaret bar called the Laurie Beechman Theatre in midtown New York, where Joan Rivers would regularly trial material, to see if she had any shows I could attend.

I'm so fucking glad I sent that email. I mean, I could've just looked the dates up on the internet. But I sent the email and a day later got a reply saying, 'Joan's seen your stand-up. Would you like to open for her when you're in town?'

I read and reread and reread the email because I was convinced I had temporarily forgotten how to read. I couldn't believe it.

I immediately said yes and started to freak out – was I good enough to open for this woman? What if she thinks I'm shit? Don't they say never meet your idols?

I called Andrew, who was going to be in New York too, and we excitedly made plans. I then shouted, *'I'm opening for Joan fucking Rivers!'* from the rooftops and plastered it across every form of social media I could find. I almost re-joined Myspace just to get another avenue for boasting. Time and time again I've heard stories of Joan Rivers' generosity and warmth, and this was just one of those times. All it took was one sentence spoken to another person: 'He should open for me.' Little did she know it would change a young Australian performer's life.

Joan loved stand-up so much that if she happened to be in New York (where she lived), she would perform on a Monday night at the Laurie Beechman Theatre and then donate the money to charity – even at eighty-one years old. 'I shouldn't get paid for this, I'm testing out material on you,' she would claim. She was such a consummate professional that she would give you ninety minutes of solid Joan Rivers gold. Money didn't matter to her, laughs were the currency she craved.

I was terribly nervous the first night I opened for Joan. I sat across the road at our hotel bar with another of my managers, Julie, and had a couple of wines to calm my nerves before Andrew joined us to head to the theatre. I stood backstage, terrified. Joan hadn't arrived yet, so I wasn't sure if she was even going to see me perform. Although I was nervous to have her watch me, I was more upset that I wasn't going to get the opportunity to show her what I could do.

My time on stage was such a blur that I can't remember how it went but I remember there were laughs. Then I walked off stage, and straight into Joan Rivers.

'That was fucking hilarious,' she said.

I almost simultaneously burst into tears and projectile vomited.

She took my hand and had a conversation with me about stand-up comedy. At no point did she talk to me like a senior talking to a junior nor was she remotely patronising. She just spoke to me as a peer and even asked for some advice on a bit she was going to try out that night. Then she went on stage to perform the most amazing stand-up comedy I had ever seen. It was simple, not overthought, not depressing or political like so much stand-up is these days, just downright fucking funny. It was the closest I've come to having a religious experience.

Coming home to Australia with the Joan Rivers tick of approval meant so much for my career and I could never thank her enough for it.

The last time I opened for Joan Rivers was the night before she went into a coma and, sadly, passed away.

It was 2014 and I was again in New York. By this point I was fine with opening for Joan. I felt far more relaxed, and just like I was working with a friend. She had also come to like me so much that she had loosened the 'no swearing' rule she normally asks of her support acts. This isn't an uncommon rule for support acts – often the headline comic wants to be the first person to swear to get the full effect. At the time I was performing my New York Fringe Festival run in town with my friend, Thomas. I would do the show earlier in the evening and then race across town to open for Joan. The final night I opened for her was my birthday. My parents had flown in (of course they fucking had) to celebrate with me but also to see their son open for a legend.

That morning I awoke to discover that despite relatively small crowds my Fringe show had received a five-star review in *Time Out New York*. I was so stoked. Hopefully this meant some people would buy a fucking ticket. That afternoon I did my show with Thomas to a quarter-full audience and then taxied up town to the Laurie Beechman Theatre. I walked out on stage, did my performance, introduced Joan Rivers and walked off stage and tried to sneak back into the crowd to sit and watch the show with my parents and Thomas.

But before I could make it back to the table, I heard Joan say, 'Joel Creasey, get the fuck back here.'

I froze. This had never happened before. What was going on? But importantly, what the fuck had I done? I trepidatiously walked back to the stage. She met me at the edge, took my hand and guided me to the microphone stand.

279

She kept hold of my hand and, with her free hand, pulled a piece of paper out of her bra.

It was the review of my show from *Time Out New York*. She read the entire review to the audience and then said in her gorgeous Joan Rivers growl, 'I am so proud of this guy. He is so fucking funny. Isn't he fucking funny?' And the audience cheered. Then she said, 'He's got three more shows at the fringe festival. You want me to start the show? Pull your phones out now and book tickets to see him.'

The audience laughed and she said, 'I'm not kidding. Pull your fucking phones out now and book tickets. I'm not starting the show.'

I ended up selling out the rest of my fringe festival run.

Once Joan had drained the room of their patronage for me, she said, 'And it's your birthday, isn't it?'

I couldn't believe she knew. I said, 'Yes.'

'And your parents have flown across from Australia, yes?'

I just nodded.

'Where are they?'

The lights came up on the audience and Terry and Jenny Creasey, ever the showponies (and probably with two bottles of wine in them by this point) waved enthusiastically. Joan Rivers then said the words I will be quoting on my posters from now until the end of time: 'Joel Creasey – he is a fucking star.' She told my parents how excellent she thought I was, and how lucky they were to have a son who was so funny.

I couldn't believe it – the ultimate validation from my hero. It is much harder to come out to your parents about wanting to be a stand-up comedian than to tell them you're gay.

The next day Joan went into a coma and passed away. I was heartbroken. I kept telling people, 'I saw her last night. She'll be fine. This is the media making it sound worse than it is.'

Then I flew to LA and she was still in the coma. I was on the treadmill at the gym (that's what you do if you're a gay in LA) and saw the news flash up on the TV that she had died. I was crushed. I fell apart. It felt like there were no problems in the world we couldn't face head on while Joan was alive.

My then boyfriend Jefferey knew I'd be upset and was outside the gym, waiting to pick me up. We went home and watched the news about what had happened on loop while my phone rang off the hook with Australian media outlets wanting a comment.

That night in West Hollywood and all around the world, gay bars hosted Joan Rivers–themed drag nights. That made me smile. Joan would've fucking loved it.

I have come to the realisation that I've got to stop working with my heroes. Joan Rivers, Carrie Fisher ... Meryl Streep better be careful.

I've decided to start using my powers for good, though. So I've recently become a *huge* Donald Trump fan!

14

MY EURO 'VISION' FOR THE FUTURE

O nly recently somebody said to me, 'I grew up watching you on TV.' I was taken aback at first and then shocked to discover he was nineteen and that it was really quite possible. Although I'm still often overwhelmed with nerves, anxiety and the occasional desire to throw in the towel and say 'FUCK IT! THIS IS ALL TOO HARD! I'M GOING BACK TO McCAFE!', after almost ten years as a full-time professional stand-up comedian, I have finally started to feel more confident in my place in the industry.

I love Andrew and always will; he was my manager for seven years and had literally been there with me for every high and through every devastating low, yet towards the start of 2016 I inherently felt it was time for me to move on and began to investigate other management situations. I know without doubt that I wouldn't be where I am today without Andrew and can't thank him enough for all the work he did for me. He went everywhere with me and I loved having him around, both as a colleague and best friend. Very few people know me like Andrew does, and I knew he was going to be shocked and hurt by my decision to leave, which made the task all the more painful.

By 2016, life with Andrew had possibly become too easy. In a way, I'd stopped trying – to the point that I'd contemplate catching up with mates but actually found it easier just to hang with Andrew. I knew I needed to change things up . . . purely for my own sake. I was getting complacent, which I didn't like.

I found Melissa, my new manager, after having been a fan of her achievements for a long time – and also by remembering that I had liked her dress at the Logies. (Fashion choices are always an important factor when making a life-changing decision – I told you I'm judgemental.) I was also incredibly intimidated by her, which I liked too. But I was perplexed as to how I was going to leave Andrew. I felt like a traitor and a monster, and had no idea how to convey that this decision had absolutely nothing to do with him personally or professionally – it was just something I had to do for me.

In September 2016 I met with Andrew and his business partner, Jeff. The meeting lasted five minutes – I told them I was leaving, burst into tears and walked out. I felt as if I was breaking up with a boyfriend. I suddenly realised how hard it must've been for all the guys who have ever dumped me. Shit, being the dumpee is *so* much easier!

And Andrew never said a word. I know he must have been infuriated, disappointed and very hurt. Like Sandra Bullock in her Oscar winning role, I had completely blind-sided him. Yet I had to go with my gut. Even though my gut still churns every time I think of how that meeting went.

I also swapped hairdressers that year. I could tell that story too but I feel like my editor is going to say no, so I'll just leave it at that.

Although 2016 was a rough year, it ended on a high, when I was awarded *GQ* Comedian of the Year. I've never won an award as a comedian. Ever. Nor do I particularly want to – I don't think they're necessary. It's strange to think that awards can even be given to comedians, as comedy in itself is so subjective. But I must admit I was thrilled, and I really needed it, mentally. I took my dad to the awards ceremony, because he is my Man of the Year every year, and I felt so proud to show him off. Dad has never asked me to conform to the idea of your (or his!) 'average' man. He has never once winced when I've been camp, loud or brash. To be fair, he does often sport a pearl necklace on a black leather strip, so it may be a case of pot-kettle-black. He always brings all his mates along to my stand-up shows, where I regale the audience with some pretty hard-core stories about life and sex. Gay or straight, listening to your child's sex stories must never be pleasant. Particularly given the sex stories I tell are normally about the times the sex isn't pleasant.

Dad was hilarious walking the *GQ* red carpet. He'd sussed out who the alcohol sponsor was on our way in and kept mentioning them – they must've been thrilled with the extra publicity. During the ceremony, Dad sat beside Angela Bishop, behind Iggy Azalea and in front of Ken Done. It was a more bizarre collection of individuals than the guys who went beyond the wall in *Game of Thrones* Season 7, Ep 5. It was a seriously fucking cool night that ended with an after-party in Matt Preston's hotel room that lasted until 5 am.

I ended 2016 by getting into bed at 10 pm on New Year's Eve. I had decided I wanted to begin 2017 fresh and *sans* hangover and a stranger in my bed.

It must've worked, because 2017 got off to a seriously great start when I received a pretty exciting phone call. It was February and I was standing in the kitchen of my mate Matt Gilbertson's house. I was performing at the Adelaide Fringe Festival and preparing to launch my eighth stand-up tour, *Poser*, that very night. I was feeling the pressure, as I was now with new management and I wanted to give them a great show to tour.

Melissa called, very excited, and asked if I would be interested in being the host of the Australian Eurovision broadcast, as the previous hosts were moving on. I immediately replied in the affirmative, of course! Asking a gay man if he wants to go to Eurovision? That's like asking a vegan if they want to bring down the mood of a barbecue. The answer is going to be yes every time.

Eurovision had always tickled me due to the sheer camp factor of it all. Country versus country in the biggest song competition in the world. Who can belt it out higher? Who can cram more key changes into one song? Who can stage the most ridiculous, hip-thrusting choreography? Which country can sport the most costume fabric that should avoid naked flame? I've been a huge fan of Eurovision for many years and have hosted Eurovision parties at gay bars around Melbourne. One of my dearest friends, Max, even works as a Conchita Wurst impersonator. To be fair – it's not *that* challenging to dress in drag when you don't even have to shave your beard off (sorry Max).

So I signed on as host, alongside Myf Warhurst. I am a long-time fan of Myf's, having grown up watching her on *Spicks and Specks*. And now that we've worked together, you'd be hard pressed to find a bigger fan than me . . . Except for maybe that one at the top of the flue in the fizzy lifting drink room in *Willy Wonka and the Chocolate Factory*. That's a pretty fucking huge fan.

There was heavy speculation around who Australia's new Eurovision hosts would be and we had a tough time keeping the secret, all the while knowing hundreds of other people in the industry were also after the jobs.

In early April, Myf and I were unveiled as the Australian hosts of Eurovision 2017. The public reaction was really amazing and it was truly such an exciting day – I celebrated by drinking a bottle of French Champagne at the Adele concert, during which Adele pointed at me and told me

I looked like a dancer. I'm not sure whether it was because I was genuinely dancing well or she was just being borderline homophobic but either way I loved it. I was quite surprised by the Eurovision reaction, to be perfectly honest. Not because of a lack of faith in what I could do, but because the previous hosts had been so incredibly popular, and they essentially introduced Eurovision to much of Australia.

By May, Myf and I were both off to Kyiv (I know – I'm still as surprised by the spelling as I'm sure you are) in the Ukraine, along with an Australian delegation of about twenty people, including Australia's Eurovision entrant, Isaiah Firebrace. It's a good name for a pop star, don't you think? Isaiah was seventeen years old and had just won *X-Factor.*

The Ukraine wasn't at the top of my list of places in the world to see – in fact I don't think it was on the list at all. There are very few places in the world you can go where there's a serious language barrier, but Kyiv is one of them. It took me a few days to adjust to the city – and ordering food. My first experience at a local café didn't go too smoothly. I thought I was ordering a packet of chips and a can of Coke and I ended up with a cheese sandwich and a glass of milk.

It was exciting walking around the city, though. It had been transformed for Eurovision as if the Olympics were in town. Essentially it was the gay Olympics. Eurovision flags hung from flag posts everywhere and there were posters in all the shop windows. Outdoor stages for live performances from contestants appeared in every major square. Just like the sound a vibrator makes, the city was abuzz.

As the hosts for Australia, our main job was to provide live commentary from our very own 'Aussie' booth in the arena during the semi-finals and the grand final, just like football commentators (I assume that's how it works for them, I really wouldn't know). But our job also consisted of backstage interviews with artists from forty-three different countries, shooting footage around the streets of Kyiv and press commitments with Australian media back home. This was no quick *Getaway* segment – this was intense work.

Tuesday evening was our first night in the commentary booth, broadcasting live to Australia. The show would begin in Kyiv each night at 10 pm, so the Western European countries would see it at around 8 pm and Australian audiences would get the show at 5 am on SBS, which many diehard fans wake up to watch. During this broadcast they would get to hear Myf and me but not see us. Then, for those not so eager for the early start, the Australian broadcast would be repeated at the more palatable time of 7.30 pm, with our commentary but also including all the pre-recorded packages we'd been filming.

As Eurovision neared, the feedback online around Myf and me hosting began to turn outrageously aggressive for absolutely no reason ... Myf and I hadn't even gone to air yet! Suddenly people seemed to think we had 'stolen the jobs' of the previous hosts, which was simply not true.

My Euro 'Vision' for the Future

To further rock our confidence, an Australian reporter who was in town opened his interview with Myf and me by asking sensitively, 'So Australia hates you – thoughts?'

So it's safe to say that, as we stepped into our commentary booth that first night, we were nervous – although we hadn't admitted it to each other. However, we were also both extremely confident in what we could do, given our great chemistry: we'd fallen in love immediately during our screen test. We'd both done our homework and were extremely prepared, and we made a pact to each other to just relax and have a bit of fun, which was essentially our job: to be a fun, informed presence to guide Australia through the show. And I mean, come on, you can't find a higher authority on music in Australia than Myf Warhurst, although Jenny Creasey would challenge that statement after a few wines.

The first night, we arrived at the Eurovision Arena in Kyiv at around 6 pm. Security was insane and delegations required a police escort into the arena. I felt like Schapelle Corby arriving home in Brisbane. On top of that, metal checks and bomb checks and multiple levels of accreditation were required to get you backstage. The outside of the arena was lined with members of the Ukrainian army facing the road, each about three metres apart and holding a machine gun. Because nothing says 'international unity' like a weapon of mass murder. Due to the weather, they were in these long, wet-weather camouflage coats. They looked like Dementors guarding Hogwarts.

Once you got there, however, backstage itself was quite relaxed. All the artists and delegations mingled together. In true Ukrainian style, there was one little café set up backstage with room-temperature beer and a couple of sad-looking sandwiches. I'm told previous host countries provided slightly more extensive catering, but Ukraine really just did the bare minimum. Myf and I loved sitting back there each day watching these artists who were now globally famous line up and pay for a packet of chips and a can of 7Up (although what they'd get was a cheese sandwich and a glass of milk).

Myf and I had been backstage several times already as we'd been filming interviews with all the artists. There were some seriously brilliant and bizarre acts. My personal favourites were Slavko from Montenegro, who looked like Hugo Weaving crossed with a *Game of Thrones* Dothraki at Mardi Gras. He had a ponytail that went to the back of his knees, which he would whip around like a helicopter while singing his pop-dance number. Another act I loved was Jacques from Croatia – a larger man who sang an Andrea Bocelli/Celine Dion style duet . . . with himself. He wore a suit that was casual on one side and formal on the other. It was a bit of a trip.

On the night of the first semi-final, while most of the delegation went with Isaiah to prep for his performance, a small group of us, including Myf and me, prepared for the commentary portion of the broadcast. At 9.15 pm we headed to our commentary booth. There was something like fifty booths located high up on either side of the stage overlooking the arena. Australia's was between Denmark's and Austria's, whose commentators had been doing the job for years and looked Myf and me up and down with the kind of conceited 'Hmm, we've not seen you before' glare usually reserved for gay saunas and my mum's Zumba class. Graham Norton, who commentates Eurovision for the UK, was in a commentary booth nearby too.

When we arrived at our booth we were surprised to see technical crew there, along with a few Australian producers attempting to get a connection to Australia. Although we could speak to the technical crew in Australia through our headsets, for some reason they couldn't get us to air.

After about twenty minutes, panic started to set in thanks to the live broadcast rapidly approaching. People started to move faster and faster. Myf, with many years of radio and technical experience under her belt, sat in the booth and tried to communicate between the Australian and Ukrainian technical teams – she reminded me of a spy specialising in secret international liaisons. Given that she presses all the buttons for her radio show back in Australia, she also had some insight into the board in our booth. But she too was confused – pressing the button that would get our voices to go out live in Australia just wasn't doing that. Nor were *any* of the buttons.

I helped by pacing outside the booth and chewing anxiously at my nails. Every now and then I'd pop my head in and helpfully inquire 'Anything? No? Okay,' and then start on the nails on the other hand.

At 9.55 pm there was still no solution – and we could see people starting to take places on the main stage of the arena, with the director talking to the audience, informing them the show was about to commence.

At 9.58 pm, with no other option, Myf and I took our seats and just decided to see what would happen. Our notes that we'd spent weeks preparing had been knocked all over the floor as people had grabbed at cords and leads for the past half an hour. Crammed in behind us were several people still trying to fix the problem. As the countdown to showtime began on the stage, people in our booth started to raise their voices frantically, because we still didn't have a solution.

Seconds before we went to air in Australia, as Myf and I made one last ditch attempt by frantically prodding at buttons, Australia said they could hear us on the correct broadcast channel. But they could only hear us if we held down the mute button on our board in the commentary booth – and kept holding it down whenever we wanted to talk. Sorry . . . what?

Completely perplexed and realising our whole booth had been patched wrong, we had no other option but to follow their instructions as the show was beginning and we were now live on Australian TV with our toughest critics, the diehard Eurovision fans who had been bashing us online for several days now, listening.

Extremely stressed and panicked, Myf and I pressed the mute button and began to speak. The conversation we'd had about being 'totally relaxed and just having fun' was now completely wiped from our memories. We plastered smiles on our faces, looked at each other and I began: 'Good morning, Australia, but good evening, Myf! Ladies and gentlemen welcome to Eurovision 2017 live from Ukrai–'

Suddenly through our headphones Myf and I heard, 'AUSTRALIA! THIS IS UKRAINIAN TECHNICAL SUPPORT! TURN YOUR BOOTH ON! TURN YOUR BOOTH ON! YOU ARE NOT TURNED ON!'

Myf and I were simultaneously shocked, confused and angry ... our booth *was* on! Hadn't we just solved this problem? Hadn't we had a cavalcade of people from Ukrainian technical support in and out of our booth over the last hour? As much as we'd love to have responded, 'Our booth is fucking on!', we were on air in Australia and thus were unable to say this (although our faces may have).

The screaming continued down our headphones as we tried to push on.

'I'm very excited, Myf, there are so many amazing acts performing toni–'

Then another voice came on the line, the voice from technical support back in Australia who had told us to hold the mute button down.

'Guys! Hold the button down! You're not holding the button down. Why aren't you holding the button down?'

Myf and I continued talking while holding the button down as we'd been doing all along. I wanted to say *'If I hold this button down any further I am going to push it straight through the fucking desk and into Sweden's commentary booth below!'*

With two separate voices screaming into our headphones, Myf and I were taking turns mouthing, 'What the fuck is happening?' to the producers behind us.

'All right, Myf, here is act one for Eurovision 2017 . . . It's Lindita from Albania!'

Finally the act for Albania walked on stage and Myf and I were fine to stop talking, turn the board off and talk off-mic. We threw our headphones off, swung around to our producers and said, 'Oh my God, what the fuck is happening?' We were both starting to shake.

Technical support team members were running in and out of the booth, grabbing at leads. Myf and I were talking down the microphones to both Australia and Ukraine, trying to explain the problem. But all too soon Albania had finished and Myf and I were back on air.

We began talking again.

'Well, Myf, that was Albania. What did you think of her perfor–'

'AUSTRALIA TURN YOUR BOOTH ON! AUSTRALIA TURN YOUR BOOTH ON!' we heard, followed by, 'AUSTRALIA! PRESS THE BUTTON DOWN!'

This kept happening for the next hour of the broadcast. We were commentating when we could, and simultaneously being yelled at. For the three minutes of each performance we would race around the booth pulling at leads and shouting. At one point I was pressed up against the wall, standing on one foot while someone grabbed at a lead under the desk, all the while pretending to have a conversation and hoping Myf was saying at least something similar. The last thing we had a chance to do was actually *watch* the acts, which made commentating on them a little tricky. But frankly that was the least of our worries. At one point, perplexed as to what to do, I just started shoving Ukainian brand cola bottle lollies in my mouth. I either needed the sugar hit or was trying to kill myself by asphyxiation – it was all a blur and I can't remember.

Apparently, the broadcast back in Australia kept dropping in and out – sometimes they were hearing us, other times they weren't. Sometimes they were hearing Myf. Sometimes they were hearing me. They must've thought we were having conversations with ourselves. The crazy part was that the quickest way for us to find out if people could hear us was by tweeting, 'Are we on air, Australia? Can you hear us?'

Which of course meant opening the hellmouth of Twitter and seeing people say, 'Wow, Joel and Myf are doing a shit job', or 'Oh, look Joel and Myf are off air . . . they were so shit SBS have fired them already.'

At one point, to lighten the mood, I tweeted, 'Gosh, this is so stresful in here, guys! I am desperate for a drink.' I wrote it so fast I didn't spell check and immediately someone replied 'Umm . . . there's two "S"s in "stressful".'

I read this, turned to everyone in the booth and yelled, *'I fucking hate humans!'*

People watching at home were completely unaware that we were in a hot little box in Ukraine, people yelling at us, people grabbing at cords, unable to hear each other, all the weeks of preparation and notes totally out the window – it was seriously a nightmare. All the jokes I'd planned, gone. It was one of those horror days at work. And it devastated us, because we so badly wanted to do a great job.

The broadcast finished at around 1 am, after which we filmed a cross to Karl Stefanovic and Lisa Wilkinson on *The Today Show*, where the line dropped in and out once again. Completely shattered, being smashed online, shaking and at times in tears, Myf and I sat silently beside each other in the delegation bus back to the hotel. Some producers (all of whom were lovely) kindly asked if we wanted to have a drink, which we declined, going instead to Myf's hotel room where we decompressed with a beer and a Xanax.

Then I went back to my hotel room and collapsed into bed as my phone was flooded with messages along the lines of: 'Thanks for ruining Eurovision, arsehole!' (Which I thought was a bit harsh coming from my grandma.)

The great part about that first night is that Myf and I realised the next day (over a dirty burger at the local fast food joint 'Star Burger' around the corner) was it literally *could not* get worse than that. Nothing more could actually go wrong, our show could really only go up from here.

During the second semi-final, our commentary booth was watched like a hawk. We could've had the Crown

Jewels in there and they would've been perfectly safe. And by the grand final, we were flying and the sentiment online had begun to change as we won them back.

It's funny, but when something goes wrong during a TV or radio broadcast, people assume it's all the fault of the hosts, because you're the face of the program. People genuinely thought it was Myf and me who had patched our commentary booth wrong. We are only people who talk for a living. I don't know what plug goes in where. Just ask the first (and last) girl I slept with. She'll tell you.

Our disastrous first night in the commentary booth aside, Eurovision was some of the best fun I've ever had. I was delighted to return to Australia where people would stop me on the streets to discuss their favourite acts or Slavko's ponytail. And I was thrilled to make a friend for life in Myf.

🎤

After Eurovision, my publisher called me and told me that I really needed to finish my book, as it was now a year overdue. I responded by saying, 'Well, if I'd delivered it on time, you'd never have had that exciting Eurovision story, would you?'

They didn't reply, so I figured I'd better just shut up and get on with it. And that's where I leave you.

I'm not an author, I'm not an intellectual, I'm not an actor or singer or philosopher, I'm just a boy from Perth who loves to show off and tell jokes. So I'm really not sure how to wrap up a book. I tweeted JK Rowling and asked for advice but she never responded. She's a bit busy trolling Donald Trump to be honest.

So I thought I'd end with ten interesting facts about me that I haven't covered in the book. It was either that or an acrostic poem. But I thought that might be pushing it.

1. I did, at one stage in my life, have my boat licence. I love boats and we had one for many years growing up. Getting my licence meant I could drive the family boat that we used to go to Rottnest Island off the coast of Western Australia for summer holidays on. Our longest and most beloved boat was called *Anacapri* – a 44-foot Randall that we'd renovated. My dad managed to run it aground on a sandbank on our first trip . . . only metres away from the yacht club. I believe the story is now legend and Dad's mates still tease him about it.

2. I am rather obsessed with the actress Jessica Chastain. I think she is one of the most beautiful people on the planet and check her Instagram every second day just to stare at photos of her. Is that weird? It's a bit weird, isn't it?

3. When I was twelve years old I owned my own business. I decided I wanted to be a DJ and got a loan from Mum and Dad to buy the equipment. I used to

My Euro 'Vision' for the Future

DJ family friends' functions under my official DJ and business name 'Joel Jivin'. I started to get bookings for school discos and when I 'retired' at age fourteen, I had quite an impressive system. Dad used to drop me off at the discos and help me set up. At times I was getting a couple of hundred bucks a gig! There wasn't that much to it – I just played the *So Fresh 2002* album and said no to anyone who requested anything else.

4. I wear a bracelet or a ring of some description on my left hand when I'm on stage. I'm not sure why, but I can't go on without it now. On the rare occasion where I've forgotten to wear one, I quickly grab anything I can find backstage – an elastic band, a piece of string – and whack it on.

5. I'm allergic to mango. How exotic and pathetic at the same time. I discovered this rather awkwardly when I was eighteen years old and flirting with a boy around a hotel pool. We ordered mango daiquiris (in case there was any confusion over our sexuality), which they made with fresh mangos, and I started to blow up in all the wrong places. It's safe to say the date didn't end with us getting it on. I am quite embarrassed to tell people about my mango allergy because I realise how silly it is and often think I'd rather have the reaction to the mango than the reaction I get when I tell people. The most perplexing part is I don't know how

I got through eighteen years of life without trying a mango! I blame Jenny.

6. I am quite the aviation geek. I love planes and always have. At one point I even entertained the idea of being a pilot. I still do, really. I could be Australia's answer to John Travolta, but with my original face. If you point to an aircraft I can probably name what make and model it is. Given that I fly so often, I actually love going to the airport and instead of sitting in the lounge, I'll sit by the departure gate and watch the airlines (particularly the international ones) come in and out. I also . . . um . . . oh God . . . I also collect plane figurines. There! I said it.

7. I've mentioned earlier in the book that I love drag and drag queens. I should just clarify I will never do drag myself. I'm afraid I'll love it too much and will never get out of drag. My drag name would be Sara Tonin. She would never show up for work on a Sunday and be a total nightmare of a person on a Wednesday.

8. I once vomited in a bin in Times Square on the way home from a one-night stand. I was also missing a shoe, and a bunch of tourists asked me to take their photo before they realised what a wreck I was and quickly hurried away. Is it bad that I'm proud of this story?

9. People who say, 'I'll give it one hundred and ten per cent' annoy me. You can't have more than one hundred per cent. If you just give it one hundred per cent, I'll be thrilled. If you give me one hundred and ten per cent you're giving me something I didn't ask for. Also, people who scuff their feet – please pick up your feet. It'll ruin your shoes and it just looks silly.

10. I once smacked Barry Humphries on the bottom on stage and it was one of the proudest achievements of my life. I've also pashed Magda Szubanski on stage, held hands with Joan Rivers and been slapped by three separate Real Housewives.

So there you go. That's it. I'm not sure what else to tell you. All I can say is thank you for reading this. Thank you for (hopefully) enjoying this. Thank you for supporting me. Thank you for letting me LIVE MY BEST LIFE (okay, I'm getting a bit Dr Phil now) and thank you for helping me on my quest for fame, fortune and world domination.

I need to stop writing now because I'm rambling.

Really. I must stop.

Now.

Ever your humble(ish) court jester,

Joel x

THIRSTY

ACKNOWLEDGEMENTS

Many thanks to my whip-cracker and partner-in-crime Janelle Koenig. My gorgeous family, Mum, Dad, Holly, Alice, Nan, Pop and Bella. My management team Melissa Le Gear, Mark Klemens and the smokin' hot team at Profile Talent. Bec Sutherland, Katie Minchin and the babes at Live Nation Australasia. Mr Andrew Taylor, Heather Tyas and Jeff Green. My life partners and the best friends a narcissist could wish for, Ashleigh Bell and Thomas Jaspers, not to mention the divine Kyle Minall, Brad Donovan, Max Corstophan, Chrissie Swan, Bradley John, Em Rusciano, Jack Stratton-Smith, Lynette McGivern, Carlos Mangubat, Marita McCausland, Bec Williams, Laura Ruddle, Di Rolle, Fiona O'Loughlin, Matt Gilbertson and Karl Chandler. My personal trainer Andy Brand, and the only man who will ever touch my hair, Stavros Tavrou, and the team at Rakis. My airbrusher Shannon Dean (I'm actually 67), Matt Wood, and my

US manager Jodi Lieberman. The people who always make sure I'm kept out of scandal, Kelly Black and Karen Griffin – thanks, or please let me have just one? Haven't decided. Susan Provan, Bridget Bantick, Gideon James and the wonderful people at the Melbourne International Comedy Festival. Andy Mac and Nicole Dixon at Rocket Science and Ted Robinson at Good News Week Productions. Thanks also to Brad and Fiona Stannard, John and Jane McAllister at the Comedy Lounge in Perth, and Greg Brindle and David Steadman.

To every single person who has bought this book or ever bought a ticket to see me live, stopped me on the street and told me I'm funny, asked for a photo or even given me a big wave . . . thank you a million times over. To Jeffery and every man who has broken my heart . . . cheers for the material. To my gorgeous publishers who made this happen, Roberta Ivers, Fiona Henderson, Dan Ruffino, Anabel Pandiella at Simon & Schuster and editor Kylie Mason – thank you! And thank you to Celine Dion for guiding me through the darkest of days with your bizarre talk-show appearances, outrageous fashion statements and flawless vocal performances.